SCHOOL
MOMS

SCHOOL MOMS

PARENT ACTIVISM,
PARTISAN POLITICS,
and the
BATTLE *for*
PUBLIC EDUCATION

LAURA PAPPANO

BEACON PRESS, BOSTON

BEACON PRESS
Boston, Massachusetts
www.beacon.org

Beacon Press books
are published under the auspices of
the Unitarian Universalist Association of Congregations.

27 26 25 24   8 7 6 5 4 3 2 1

This book is printed on acid-free paper that meets the uncoated paper
ANSI/NISO specifications for permanence as revised in 1992.

Text design and composition by Kim Arney

Library of Congress Cataloguing-in-Publication Data is available for this title.
Paperback ISBN: 978-0-8070-1646-6
E-book ISBN: 978-0-8070-1267-3
Audiobook: 978-0-8070-1482-0

*This book is dedicated to public school students
who show up every day trying to learn and to grow,
and to the parents, teachers, librarians, principals,
and school leaders working to ensure they can.*

CONTENTS

WHY PUBLIC SCHOOLS MATTER

I DID NOT PLAN OR EVEN WANT TO WRITE THIS BOOK. Rather, I *had to*. Public schools matter to our democracy and to our future. And they are under attack from people who don't really know or care very much about what schools do or how they work.

The first thing to reflect on is this: Public schools gather everyone. All are invited. There is no test you need to pass, no amount of money or influence or fame you must possess to be allowed in. Do you know how rare that is in America today?

This has made public schools the place where people from all backgrounds and circumstances have come together to learn. It is where parents have volunteered and, regardless of their political bent, have worked alongside other parents for a common purpose.

The twentieth-century education reformer John Dewey recognized that public schooling was—yes—about gaining skills and knowledge that would benefit individuals. But that it also helped prepare youth for a communal role. As one scholar put it, Dewey insisted that the "training of democratic citizens would not come from abstract study of government or political obligations but must be rooted in the social relations and experience of the school itself."[1]

In other words, the *experience* of school—not just the curriculum or the facts learned—is the thing. That is now under threat from the far right. And that is why I wrote this book. I have a personal and professional stake in public schools: I am a former PTA mom. I am a volunteer mentor to public school students in grades three to eight. I am an education journalist who has spent over thirty years writing about K–12 and higher education. I am also the product of K–12 public schools, and even in high school served as a student representative to the New Milford, Connecticut, Board of Education. The meetings then were dull compared to what we see now. Coming to them as I did after sports practice and my after-school job working in a darkened *New Milford Times* building filing tear sheets so the newspaper could bill its advertisers, I often fell asleep to the comforting drone of adult voices sorting through the mundane business of running the public schools.

Growing up as I did with parents who were practically kids themselves—they were seventeen when I was born—for me school presented itself as a beautiful, steadying force, especially after my father left our family when I was thirteen. Life could be unpredictable—I had been enrolled in four different school systems by sixth grade. But I could count on teachers, classmates, and the regular hours spent at tan Formica–topped school desks.

Each school I attended had its vibe, of course. In one we baked bread to learn math and wrote reports on history field trips in real black ink with fountain pens. In another we read the textbook and answered questions at the end of the chapter. But they all had the comforting and familiar rituals that marked a day—homeroom to recess and dismissal—and the year with its marking periods and vacations and much-anticipated field day in late spring.

You got to know kids and became friends, sometimes for dumb reasons like that they said something nice about your lunchbox or you let them borrow a pencil. I met Fidelia because I was new and she was friendly. Hanging out at her house, I got to discover a vivacious Colombian family and her grandmother's killer *arepas*, delicious fried cornmeal cakes. Jill lived the middle-class ideal: her family's home was always clean and well-stocked with snacks, the laundry done daily and folded. And unlike my mom, who worked multiple jobs and left us long lists of chores, her mom had snacks ready that we did not have to clean up after.

In high school I learned that the nerdy guys were hilarious and, as my kids would put it, "a good hang." I suspect their politics were different from mine, but I didn't know or need to find out. It just didn't matter. What mattered was that they were willing to put on hand-sewn clown costumes to help me out with my Clowns Around business, or just sit in somebody's basement rec room and listen to the Rolling Stones and talk for hours.

I remember being with these same guys in advance placement English, and even though things at home were rough with my dad not paying child support and my mom angry about it and all of us broke, I thought about how happy I was. It was largely because school *worked*.

School was the place where, as a kid, I could decide things for myself, including who my friends were, what I cared about, and how hard I was willing to work to succeed. I also learned other things. I would run for class president and lose after one of those guy friends who was also running spread a false rumor that I wanted to get rid of music in the cafeteria at lunch (who would actually do that?). It was a lesson in the power of misinformation. He also lost.

This is to say that a lot goes on in school that is not about lesson plans and curriculum. School is about relationships. It is about people trying to improve themselves and connect with others and, through those connections, build a rich community. I personally find the questions and problems of education riveting. This is why I have spent decades trying to make sense of how schools achieve their goals (or don't) and the roles they play in our lives.

As a journalist I have covered a breadth of issues, and over time I have visited hundreds of classrooms. I have watched teachers teach and students learn and interact. I have studied their faces as they worked on problems and observed their body language. I have heard the throwaway banter that erupted between official lessons. I have paid attention to policy as well as to what is on the classroom walls and to the atmosphere of a school when you walk down the hallway.

There has been a lot to write about. I have covered lawsuits over school funding, battles over the teaching of sex education, the rise of standards and testing, the insane competition for elite college admissions, the marketing campaigns of state higher-education campuses that once simply sought to serve those in their region or state, and the soaring cost of higher education. I have reported on equity and access, mental health struggles and financial aid, LGBTQ+ students on Christian campuses, the proliferation of educational technology, the quest of low-income first-generation students to "belong" in elite spaces, on the college-or-bust mentality, and the challenge to it.

I have tracked reform movements such as No Child Left Behind, Race to the Top, and the school turnaround movement; undertaken research to parse the ways children learn to read, bilingual education, parent-school communication, and the value of computational thinking; analyzed data;

and more. Schools don't always get it right. Innovative ideas may fall short of expectations, and some teachers and leaders are simply not up to the task.

But I did not write this book to critique personnel or pedagogical approaches. I wrote it because I saw schools—which I have engaged in and written about—being misunderstood and attacked for things that, in some cases, they do not even do (no one is trying to change the gender of your child!). I am not precious or misty-eyed about school. I understand the shortcomings and the trendy ideas that end up broken on the floor, failed notions that were supposed to transform learning.

These types of issues are not what is being debated now. The debate that is occurring across the country is not actually about education and schooling. The current tug-of-war is not rooted in a passion for the success of all children. It is not about the skills and knowledge students need to become contributing adults and citizens. Neither is it about differing beliefs in how we raise our own children and instill in them the moral and social values that make them good people and make us proud parents.

Rather, this debate is about the hijacking of public education by a far-right Christian movement. It is about the quest to do away with the community-rooted education enterprise and the foundational American belief in the worth of every single child.

It is true that public education has long been the site of tension and disagreement. We have debated what should be taught, how it should be funded, and who should be in control of which aspects of public education. During World War I it became clear that we had a national interest in educating our youth. Data at the time found that 25 percent of the 2.7 million men who had been rejected for the draft were illiterate.[2] This spurred a call to create a federal Department of Education, but the idea faced opposition. Many did not want the federal government intruding into what was considered a local matter. Congress did not approve the creation of the new department until 1979. Before it became a federal agency, however, federal education offices existed and mostly collected data, something which the Department of Education, importantly, now still does. Over time, the federal government also exerted some influence through targeted funding (which it still does), like amping up science education after the Soviet Union's launch of Sputnik in 1957.[3]

A landmark Supreme Court decision, *Brown v. Board of Education of Topeka, Kansas*, made clear a national commitment to educate all children,

together, in the same schools. Still, some states and districts avoided integrat-
ing schools for years. Even today, public schools in many American school
districts remain stubbornly segregated. But in 1965, on the heels of the Civil
Rights Act of 1964, President Lyndon B. Johnson, as part of the War on
Poverty, signed the Elementary and Secondary Education Act. This provided
oversight and funding, including Title I grants, federal money directed to
high-poverty schools and targeted to help low-income students, and grants
for special education, among other spending streams that continue today.

Johnson made clear that ensuring access to quality public schooling
for every child was a national-level concern. In his address to Congress on
February 28, 1967, he described his education agenda: "to provide equality of
educational opportunity to all Americans—to give every child education of
the highest quality, no matter how poor his family, how great his handicap,
what color his skin, or where he lives."[4]

The act has been reauthorized, revised, and reframed as different admin-
istrations and politicians have left their mark on it. For instance, the No
Child Left Behind Act (2001) brought mandatory standardized testing and
accountability; the Every Student Succeeds Act (2015) allowed states more
flexibility in meeting standards. We have not achieved Johnson's vision—far
from it—but we have accepted a collective interest in every child's access
to education.

Yet while federal dollars and oversight are important, public schooling
remains primarily a state and local responsibility. Just 8 percent of K–12 public
school funding comes from the federal government; 92 percent is from state
and local sources (actual percentages vary greatly by state and local district).[5]

Given the strong state and local involvement in public education, some
state lawmakers and local school boards have seized on this authority and
made education a high profile partisan issue. They have brought the political
divisions of the early 2020s into schools and classrooms. At the same time,
under the Biden administration, the Department of Education has interpreted
Title IX of the Education Amendments of 1972, which prohibits discrimination on the basis of sex, to include protections against discrimination on
the basis of sexual orientation and gender identity. That offers a safeguard
for transgender students. But it has not stopped far-right politicians at the
state and district levels from pursuing anti-LGBTQ+ laws and policies. This
has increased the workload of the Department of Education's Office of Civil
Rights (OCR), which investigates discrimination complaints, including

from districts that have passed or supported harsh policies.[6] In a July 2022 report, the OCR said it expected to receive 28,457 complaints for FY2022, the highest on record, and 70 percent more than in FY2016, which at 16,720 had been the highest on record. The OCR expected a 22 percent increase in complaints between FY2021 and FY2022.[7]

These numbers substantiate what has become apparent: public schools are coming under fire. As a nation we may be committed to principles of access and equity, but some, carrying the flag of "parents' rights," are demanding control over which books can be on library shelves, what teachers can say aloud in class, which restrooms transgender students may use, and even whether a teacher may use a child's preferred name or pronoun in school. With so much conflict, it can feel as though public education itself is up for renegotiation. And that is the goal. The far right, by peppering public schools with attacks, seeks to sow doubt in the fundamental value of public education. Why, they ask, do we need public schools at all? Why not do as Arizona did in 2022, which is create Empowerment Scholarship Accounts, a type of education savings account (ESA). The Arizona plan puts taxpayer money into an account or on a debit card for parents to spend on education expenses in lieu of sending children to public school. (In 2023, more than 30 legislatures took up bills to create ESAs or expand voucher programs, which provide coupons parents can use to pay for private schools.)[8] It has triggered a furious conflict over the "privatization" of public education.

In some ways, this debate is unsurprising. Public schools carry the weight of our cultural differences. Even though, for more than a century, they have been nonpartisan gathering places and a center of civic life in America, they have spurred debate. Often, friction has been over disappointing test scores, funding formulas (do school systems rely too much on property taxes?), or disagreements over how math or history should be taught. In combing through old magazines, I was struck by how often we have raised alarms about our "troubled" public schools. A headline in the March 1947 issue of *Ladies' Home Journal* warns, "Our Schools Are in Danger." A story in the February 1971 issue of *Parents' Magazine* could have been written at almost any time in the previous century. Titled "Schools in Trouble," it promised a "hard-hitting analysis of the failures of public education."

But what is happening now is not a debate over the institution's short-comings. Rather, this is a move by the far right to use public schools to gain political power. The campaign by extremists ignores the messy job of educating every single child, regardless of background, circumstance, or academic ability. Instead it seizes on the convenient fact that schools touch everyone. When you control schools, you control society.

This is why I am compelled to speak up, and to do it in the only way I know how, which is by asking questions, listening to those in a position to know things, then sharing stories and insights—by reporting. To research this book I spent four days at the first Moms for Liberty Joyful Warriors National Summit in Tampa, Florida. I traveled to Texas, Tennessee, Pennsylvania, and New Hampshire. I spent hours and hours watching videos of school board meetings. I visited two Harvard libraries to pore over old articles and piles of retrieved documents to understand where and how what we are experiencing echoes the past.

But most critically, in my travels and over Zoom I have met with people on the front line, in their homes, in coffee shops, in libraries, in hotel lobbies, in pizza shops. I visited a third-grade classroom, met up with a teacher in a supermarket and with school board candidates outside polling sites on a sweltering summer day. In one case I discovered that someone I was trying to interview was attending the same college athletic reunion event I was; we met in the dining room over tea the next morning.

What I appreciated about all the people I spent time with—whether or not they are quoted in this book—was their willingness, even eagerness, to share what they were experiencing. We have crossed a line, and people who have worked in and around education can feel it. Just as I was compelled to write this book, I heard from many that they were compelled to speak up. I am grateful that they have done so.

As a mother who has raised children in both suburban and urban settings and has volunteered in public schools in both, I am struck by the relentless energy and determination of today's parents. I salute these "school moms"—a term that I intend as wholly complimentary and includes all highly active school parents—bring serious professional skills, hours of labor, and care to the tasks they take on. They have always been around, breezing down school hallways or sitting at a checkout desk in the library to help out. But in this new environment, their tasks have shifted. Parent involvement is no longer only about organizing the back-to-school picnic and the teacher appreciation breakfast or keeping track of orders for the wrapping paper fundraiser. Now it also includes tracking school board agendas, organizing meeting turnouts, reviewing proposed state legislation, creating Facebook pages where parents first spread the word about conflict in the schools and building—and then turn those Facebook groups into bona fide organizations with their own websites and missions. Parents have become expert in digging through campaign finance filings and other public records. They sift through news reports, connect the dots to local issues, and share. Parent involvement at this level is no longer casual. Recently a north Texas mom texted me to share an article about fallout from the book policy recently adopted by a local far-right-dominated school board requiring the district to review all book donations: the Rotary Club was rebuffed as it prepared to donate a copy of the *Webster's Dictionary for Students* to each third-grader, as it had done for over a decade. (The new edition contained twenty-two new words.)[9]

School moms, in other words, are fighting for public education in their communities. This book is about that battle—and why it matters.

CHAPTER 1

WHAT THE "WAR MOMS" WANT

THEY CALL THEMSELVES JOYFUL WARRIORS, but there was a kind of righteous anger in the air at the Marriott in Tampa, Florida, as Moms for Liberty held their first national summit in July 2022.

Despite the suffocating heat and humidity plus daily afternoon thunderstorms, it was a busy time in the city. The Marriott is adjacent to the Tampa Convention Center, which was hosting Metrocon, billed as "Florida's Largest Anime Gathering." The sidewalks and lobby were alive with people in elaborate costumes that involved wigs, stockings, glitter, Colonial garb, sleek suits, horns, and more. And the JW Marriott across the carpeted pedestrian bridge from the hotel was hosting the Florida Democratic Party. If ever there was a collision of cultures, this was it.

Conflicting allegiances were visible everywhere. Outside the hotel was a large protest in support of abortion rights; a smaller one targeted Moms for Liberty. A local Moms for Liberty chapter mocked both protests on Twitter. Inside, at check-in, the woman at the reception desk gave me an upgrade to a high floor and water view, confiding, "I'm with you guys. I'm upgrading you all!" She shared her hope that Donald Trump would appear on the Moms for Liberty rostrum (no chance, as Governor Ron DeSantis was the first speaker). When I found myself in an elevator with three anime convention goers, they interpreted my "Moms for Liberty" lanyard as a giant "Keep Away" sign, not realizing that I was also in effect in costume. I registered under my name for the conference and dressed to fit in, wearing a white top, blue slacks, and a red blazer with an American flag pin pinched into the lapel. The encounter highlighted to me how we Americans have become suspicious of one another. Not without cause.

Each morning of the conference, I passed through the metal detector erected on level 2, which offered passage into a white, far-right Christian world—a kind of alternate reality. As I listened to keynote speeches and strategy session after strategy session, I saw speakers lay a foundation of a distorted groupthink. Then, like an ideological conveyor belt, the speakers carried the moms to ever crazier places, stirring fears that their children were being brainwashed and indoctrinated into Marxist ideology and that they were being groomed by teachers to want to transition from one gender to another. By the time I left the final strategy session, on Social Emotional Learning, time was running over and my co-attendees, lined up at the mic to ask questions, were ready to revolt. And that was exactly the point of the convention: to stir up emotions.

THE COVID OPPORTUNITY

Moms for Liberty was conceived out of anger and frustration (originally about school mask mandates). The cofounder, Tina Descovich, hit on the idea for the group shortly after she lost her Brevard County school board seat to Jennifer Jenkins in August 2020. A few months later, in December, Descovich, along with Tiffany Justice, who had served on the Indian River County school board, officially incorporated Moms for Liberty as a nonprofit in Florida. They officially launched the organization in early 2021.[1]

In a *Washington Post* editorial in November 2021, Descovich and Justice celebrated that "after years on the back burner, education is suddenly the issue changing our political landscape." They pushed back at suggestions that the images of angry "school board moms" who appeared across the country on news broadcasts and social media posts, were merely a frustrated fringe. Yes, they did show up to protest "masking policies, critical race theory, sexually explicit materials," they said. But what people were seeing, Descovich and Justice asserted, was a window onto a larger issue.

"Our movement is about something much more profound. Frustrated by an education system that has long put powerful interests above the well-being of students, parents are finally reclaiming our natural right to direct the education, upbringing and care of our children," they wrote. Masking was the flashpoint that let like-minded parents find one another and organize. While more than three years on, the mask issue seems trivial, it is important to acknowledge the timing. Descovich had gone anti-mask at the very moment when the state of Florida was overwhelmed with extremely high numbers of Covid-19 cases: on tracking maps, the state appeared as berry-red. This was also before a vaccine was available.[2]

There are still moms on both sides in Brevard County who are angry over how the issue unfolded. One important thing to remember about Florida—something Governor Ron DeSantis likes to talk about—is that his education department in July 2020 declared that schools would be returning to in-person learning. He now boasts, as he did at the conference, that "while they were infringing freedoms, we were lifting people up. We made sure that every single kid in this state had the right to go to school in person five days a week."[3]

The DeSantis brand, as he makes clear when speaking and as has been pointed out in profiles, is that he "doesn't give an F" what anybody thinks. That's probably not entirely true, but he capitalized on that trait at a time of scientific uncertainty. After all, this was a moment when CDC guidelines changed so often that the agency's recommendations became a theme of jokes, like one in a December 28, 2021, tweet: "The CDC said just wear jeans and a cute top."

Early in the pandemic DeSantis offered what many craved but was scientifically unavailable at the time: certainty. Yet his policies became rigid, politically symbolic—and likely resulted in deaths in Florida. According to the Florida Education Association's Safe Schools Report for the 2020–2021 academic year, forty-six active educators died from Covid-19 between the state education commissioner's reopening order on July 6 and the end of the school year. (There were questions about the validity of state Covid-19 data around this time; an analyst was fired after claiming her superiors were hiding cases and deaths).[4] An early national study that looked at county-level data between April and December 2020 found deaths from Covid-19 "rapidly increasing after 3 to 5 wk of opening schools for counties that adopt in-person/hybrid teaching methods with no mask mandates." The study also found that wearing masks, prohibiting sports, and adopting online instruction were consistent with reduced cases after school openings.[5]

I was aware of this report. But as I sat in an air-conditioned conference room in the Melbourne (Florida) Public Library in July 2022 with two moms, one a school board candidate with "Jesus" in cursive tattooed on the inside of her left wrist, who was a Christian but no longer a Republican, and the other a parent of an LGBTQ+ student with an elderly mother living nearby, they spoke about that period of time with the detail of those reliving a trauma.[6]

I had not realized how ready I was to push past Covid times. I recall the worries of those months: We skipped Thanksgiving, and each family member took one or more tests before gathering at Christmas. When we visited extended family in New Haven, instead of a pancake breakfast, a run, and traditional dinner, we ate chili outdoors, around separate fire pits, with blankets on our laps, socially distancing across a brick patio. Merry Christmas! Like many, I was ready to forget.

But to these two mothers, the experience still felt close. They wanted me to understand why this set off a community divide and how its effects have lingered. They had been forced to make decisions contrary to the leadership in their state and those around them. This friction fed the anger that we saw unfold on TV at school board meetings, particularly in places like Brevard County where encounters grew heated, even violent. Leaders had pushed public health decisions down to individuals and called it "freedom" at a time when no one knew what to do.

This created a "with us or against us" political landscape that has stuck. Another mom I interviewed from the county noted that two years later, everyone still knew where families stood on masks and, now, vaccines. Her middle school daughter hangs out with friends from ardent anti-mask families, but wants to fit in. "I just don't say that I'm vaccinated when I'm at my friend's house," her daughter told her.[7]

During the 2020–2021 school year, this mom kept her daughter home the entire year. After nine weeks, however, she decided that her son, autistic and gifted, should attend third grade in person—but masked. When she, also masked, accompanied him into school, she faced sneers. "People would say, 'Why do you have that on?'" And they would *baa*, "like sheep."

DeSantis weighed the fears of the vulnerable against economic costs in a state whose economy needs tourism. The reality was that if you lived in Florida during the height of Covid, you had to make personal calculations. That continued into 2022, as DeSantis vowed not to require Covid vaccines for students to attend school. To the moms I met in Melbourne, this felt consequential.

For others, it was freeing. At the opening cocktail reception for the Moms for Liberty gathering, I strolled past the security detail and the live band to the outdoor patio overlooking Tampa's waterway. I happened upon members from Brevard County who quickly boasted that "we were the first chapter!" I asked one mom what drew her to the organization. Her answer: masks. She did not want face coverings to ruin her daughter's high school experience.

Masks became the visible symbol of the political divide. Many kids didn't care that much about wearing one, at least not as much as adults did. Some teens, in fact, appreciated the excuse to hide acne. A teen I interviewed in Tennessee in September 2020 saw a fashion opportunity and sewed over a dozen masks to complement her outfits. Others, particularly younger students, saw an all-purpose shield. Masked, they were "safe."

Parents who opposed masks made various arguments, some more credible than others, including that they were making students ill (for which there is no clear evidence); that they constrained their children or harmed those with hearing loss who needed visual cues, which was a genuine problem. Yet for a time masks were all we had. They offered clear benefits in lowering Covid transmission and other respiratory illnesses. It's why, even when masks vanished from daily life, they continued to be required in health-care settings.

For Moms for Liberty, the issue of masks was a tool to activate and build a following, which is what they have done. As they gathered in July 2022, the group's Twitter account said it had ninety-five thousand members in two hundred chapters in thirty-seven states. About five hundred traveled to Tampa for the first National Summit, a turnout likely lower than they had hoped given the group's rapid growth.

AN IDEOLOGICAL BOOT CAMP

It was plain from the first session at the Moms for Liberty event that despite the stylish body-hugging dresses in patriotic colors, summer heels, and freshly blown-out hair, this was a call to arms. As DeSantis approached the podium for the opening address, he was thanked for coming with a symbolic weapon, "the first-ever 'Liberty Sword.'"[8]

Soon after, cofounder Tiffany Justice gifted her audience an identity that made the room purr with pride and purpose: they were "war moms." For the next three days attendees marinated in the language of battle—even on Sunday, slipped in amid Bible quotations. It was strange at times, such as when Jeff Childers, an attorney and Moms for Liberty board member, explained the need to add to the framework of Florida's parental rights law, passed in April 2021, known as the "Don't Say Gay" law for its anti-LGBTQ+ rules.

"It's like the body of an AK-47," he said, "and you start mounting new accessories, flashlight and laser pointer." The audience didn't react negatively to his use of an assault-weapon metaphor in talking of children and schools. This was an ideological boot camp, and no one was challenging the language, no matter how troubling (even just weeks after the school shooting in Uvalde, Texas).

The conference's opening felt like a rally for DeSantis. Women jumped to their feet to wave bright red "Mamas for DeSantis" signs overhead. But it was also the start of a disciplined campaign with a call to action. The message: there are threats on the home front, and as it was for women during World War II, these moms' labor is urgently needed. Every speaker was introduced in relation to a familial role, identifying how many children or grandchildren they had. Female speakers joked about their husbands, even waving to them from the stage.

The conference marched the women (and a few men) down a winding road of bizarre far-right claims so oft repeated that they became familiar. The charge to the moms: speak out, run for school board, and challenge the threats to your values and, especially, your children. The drumbeat of fear was striking. Several speakers nodded to or quoted Mao Zedong, Vladimir Lenin, and Adolf Hitler as bogeymen aligned with current educational practices.

Parents were told that public schools are rooted in "Marxist ideologies" and seek to brainwash their children—and not "brainwash in some cute way," said one speaker, the far-right cultural critic James Lindsay. "I mean brainwash in the sense of 'she-now,' which is Mandarin, which is literally what the Maoist prisons referred to as their program of thought reform."

Lindsay did not let up. He paraphrased Lenin's quote "Give me four years to teach the children, and the seed I have sown shall never be uprooted," and followed it up with "Hitler said, 'What are you? You're going to pass away. I have your children,'" to press the urgency of halting what he claimed was happening in schools under the guise of Social Emotional Learning. (Social Emotional Learning actually offers children tools to help them learn how to learn, which includes skills like taking turns and managing their emotions in class).

"I want you to understand that education has been stolen from us," said Lindsay. He said schools were "sexualizing" children by including gender identity—what he and others on the far right have mutated into "gender ideology"—in library books and discussion. "When you sexualize children, you destabilize them," he said. "And it is not developmentally appropriate for children to have their fundamental categories of man, woman, whatever, boy, girl, complicated so they can't be understood unless you are telling them what the right answers are. That is what Social Emotional Learning is, by the way."

DeSantis had previously planted that seed. He boasted about drawing "a line in the sand," with the "Don't Say Gay" law that outlaws discussion of sex and gender identities in grades K–3. While such a prohibition seems reasonable on first blush, the reality is that it's rare for students in those grades *not* to discuss or make a drawing of their family—or notice others. The law effectively re-norms what we mean by "family" so some no longer count. DeSantis claimed that the law lets parents send a child to school "without having woke ideology" in which you "have some first-grader be told that yeah, your parents named you Johnny and you were born a boy, but maybe you are a girl."

What DeSantis described is not actually happening in schools. But that was, and is, beside the point. His goal was to rally this crowd, including many who identified as "stay-at-home moms" and were unused to or uncomfortable being on a public stage. To urge action, DeSantis, Lindsay, and others appealed to their patriotism. There were grave threats to democracy; this was an urgent battle that needed them, DeSantis said. The other side, DeSantis warned, is "trying to delegitimize the foundations of this country. They want people to believe that the institutions that it was founded on were rotten" and "were really not worth fighting for."

Lindsay outlined what the moms should fear and look out for; more detail was provided later, in strategy sessions. Regarding all of this information he stated: "I want you to sit with [it] a lot over the next weeks and months. If you knew you were sending your children for thirty to thirty-five hours a week to a Maoist thought reform prison, a Maoist brain-washing prison, what would you [do] differently? The answer to that question, whatever it is for you, is the answer to 'James, what should we do?'"

In case they missed his message, Lindsay pressed them to take "all lines of dedicated action to fix this system to get this crap able to be seen and identified for the crime against humanity that it is and pulled out of schools." And then, "You are War Moms. You've got this!"

NEW THREAT: SOCIAL EMOTIONAL LEARNING

The message that public schools are seeking to brainwash their children and separate them from their families and their faith would naturally be horrifying to parents. Oddly, no one, not in a single session I attended, raised even the slightest question about whether this was actually true. When Betsy DeVos, former US secretary of education, was interviewed as attendees lunched on vegetable bisque and chicken salad, she declared, "I personally think the Department of Education should not exist"—and received a standing ovation. It was included in her call for "educational freedom" (a new term for "school choice" that caught on around the country in the push for universal school vouchers), which, listeners were told, was a critical option because public schools were such a problem.

Many speakers of course went further, casting public schools as dangerous and those connected to them as conspiring to hurt children. They repeated these claims while positioning themselves as experts parsing apparent threats in plain sight. (One panelist's qualification: He is a dad who travels around Canada and the US wearing a sandwich board to engage in street conversations about puberty blockers for transgender youth).

While vilifying public schools, speakers targeted Social Emotional Learning as a particular evil. So, what is it?

Social Emotional Learning as used in schools is an approach that recognizes that academic, classroom, and life success are not purely the result of smarts but are also influenced by the ability to manage and channel our emotions in a productive manner. How we interact, work with others, and resolve conflicts shapes the quality of our environment and our personal success.

The idea of teaching children to treat others well in school is not new. Parents and teachers have for centuries urged students to "follow the Golden Rule." In the late 1960s, psychologists, including James Comer, a groundbreaking psychiatrist at the Yale Child Study Center, took note of the relationship between a child's school and home environments, their psychological development and academic achievement. The idea that these interrelationships mattered gained traction in the late 1980s, perhaps coincidentally or perhaps not, as education reform became a national focus. Suddenly it was not OK that some schools were troubled places with low achievement. Reform efforts focused mostly on things that could be measured, like test scores and funding inequities—and the relationship between them.

Yet, in seeking solutions, researchers, child development experts, policymakers, and school leaders also began to consider social aspects of learning and the differences between home and school environments, and the role of emotions in effective learning. Emotions were not the only answer to promoting effective learning but were viewed as a part of an overall recognition that learning happened in the context of relationships, that learning was social and developmental. You could not simply march through academic content in a systematic way; students needed to be ready to engage with the material to be learned.

At the same time, educators were developing programs such as the Responsive Classroom, in Greenfield, Massachusetts, and Open Circle, founded in 1987 by Pamela Seigle, a former classroom teacher who saw her class lessons go out the window because students were not ready to focus on learning. In early 2001, as I reported for an education column for the *Boston Globe*, I found myself with a group of fifth-graders in a West Roxbury elementary school in an Open Circle discussion.

The class had a conversation to identify and work through things that were bothering them. They tackled tensions created by popularity, peer pressure, stealing, and parents who they felt didn't understand them. Some offered confessions that might seem trivial, like that of a student, Marcus, who stole a classmate's glitter pen and blamed it on someone else. Talking through the issue let students process something that had distracted them, and others, in class. "Feelings drive attention and attention drives learning," Seigle told me. "For kids who come into school and are feeling angry and upset, unless they have the skills to manage those feelings, their ability to concentrate and attend to academic tasks is impaired."[9]

In psychology circles, interest in the power of emotions was taking off. In 1990, Peter Salovey, now president of Yale University, and John D. Mayer, a psychologist at the University of New Hampshire, published a foundational academic paper that identified the power of "emotional intelligence" and set out a framework to understand its dimensions.[10] It is now, of course, a full field of study with university centers and researchers developing tools, including for schools.

As interest in applying this in schools spread, a group of educators and researchers in 1994 formed the Collaborative to Advance Social and Emotional Learning, now known by its acronym, CASEL. The group aimed to apply emotional skills to academics as well as to problems that were showing up in schools, including violence, drug use, bullying, and—in what seems ironic now—concerns about a decline in civility. While this predated the rise of the internet and social media, it did foreshadow the cultural anxiety that was unfolding as technology was changing our personal relationships—and, we now see, fueling a political divide.

The idea that there was tangible value in learning to regulate our emotions went mainstream in 1995 when the science journalist Daniel Goleman published *Emotional Intelligence: Why It Can Matter More Than IQ*, which became a bestseller. Martin E. P. Seligman, a psychology professor at the University of Pennsylvania, framed the field as "positive psychology," which focuses on the strengths and tools that support well-being. Meanwhile, at Stanford University, Carol S. Dweck noticed in her research how preset student attitudes about intelligence affected performance and, critically, how activating a "growth mindset" could improve outcomes. Then Angela Duckworth, at the University of Pennsylvania, made the case for persistence and self-regulation as ingredients to success. She earned a MacArthur "Genius Grant" in 2013; in 2016 she published *Grit: The Power of Passion and Perseverance.*[11]

This scholarly work attests that harnessing not just *what* you learn but *how you feel about learning it* has become a foundational concept with consequences for schooling and teaching. Research now shows that Social Emotional Learning contributes to better academic performance and a decrease in anxiety and behavior problems among students. Meanwhile, it's practice has evolved from a spot conversation during the school day, similar to what I saw, to being woven into how teaching happens. A math teacher may give students two problems to do silently; when they finish, she might ask: How are you doing? The question is not simply about arriving at the correct answer, but also about checking in on the process of solving the problems and—yes—how they felt as they tackled them. Similarly, if the energy in the class is crazy and, as one teacher put it, "they are bouncing off the walls," she might turn off the lights and have students put their heads on their desks for a few minutes as a reset.

Teachers are now trained to consider emotions as part of what's on the table, along with the math lesson. Being able to be comfortable about making and admitting mistakes has become an important part of the learning process. The point is not to get the right answer, but to understand how to approach a problem, and specifically, where you tend to get tripped up. Being able to self-correct is profoundly important—and something that wasn't necessarily taught in the past.

Abby, a kindergarten teacher at a magnet school in California, told me that she does "a lot of Social Emotional Learning mixed with classroom learning." Such learning includes helping children learn to resolve conflicts. A common scenario: A child does not look where they are going and runs into a classmate, who interprets the bumping as purposeful. In a classroom of twenty-six students during the 2021–2022 school year, she said, this kind of thing happened a lot.[12]

In response, she led a Social Emotional Learning discussion that she introduced by saying, "I have been noticing that a lot of friends are getting upset that we are not being careful when we walk and then friends bump into other friends." They discussed it as a class and came up with solutions. There are also formal Social Emotional Learning lessons. In one, this teacher read a book about an alien from outer space and a child trying to get along. The alien wants to play outside, but the child wants to play an indoor game. Each gets upset, "but then they come up with a compromise": playing outside first, then playing a game afterward.

The value of Social Emotional Learning in class, she said, has been highlighted by the effect of the pandemic. Kindergarten benchmarks are prescribing more than just academic achievements such as that children must learn to read and count to one hundred. They must also learn how to operate in a classroom environment, taking turns and working with others. After being isolated for two years, often commanding a caregiver's total attention, many kindergarteners needed help with the social part of school. This included teaching students to be welcoming toward everyone in the class. Her class is composed of a racially diverse group of students, including some from nontraditional families. When you consider the on-the-ground reality of school, as opposed to amped-up rhetoric, creating behavioral norms in a classroom is a basic requirement. It has been for decades. Only now we are talking about it and giving students tools to use. And the far right is calling this Marxist.

A NEW RED SCARE

At the Moms for Liberty conference, Social Emotional Learning was the target of serious and confusing attacks that, if you knew what Social Emotional Learning actually was, made no sense. It was cast as a threat infiltrating schools and impinging on parental roles. One packed strategy session was led by Deb Fillman, a homeschooling mom with a sit-com vibe who has a YouTube channel called *The Reason We Learn*. Her presentation had participants gasping in horror. A woman in front of me clasped her head in distress. Agitated, she said what others likely thought: "Just get the kids out of the schools!"

Fillman described Social Emotional Learning as a tool "to alienate your children from who they might otherwise have been, from themselves, from, you know, whatever they would have grown up to be and from your family and from your values. And it is intentional." She said schools were overstepping their bounds by talking with children about emotions, developing healthy identities, and making responsible and caring decisions. "That's what parents are for!" she exclaimed.

"Who's defining what 'responsible' is, who's defining what 'caring' is? Well, guess what? The government!" she quipped. She stressed several things. One was that children should not be responsible for helping to craft a classroom or school culture ("They did not check with you and get your permission"). Another was that Social Emotional Learning might sound good and valuable, like "just a premise you are supposed to accept that is not only OK and not harmful, but desirable." But, she said, pausing for effect, "I personally disagree."

Fillman echoed fearful messages previously planted by other speakers claiming that children were being brainwashed. Social Emotional Learning was a socialist cabal, she said as listeners nodded. "SEL is aimed at redistributing power. There is your Marxism," she offered. "Anytime you see redistributing power and privilege you are talking about Marxist terms."

Parents had been tricked from the moment they enrolled their child in public school without an inkling of the evils within, she said. "You didn't stand there outside the school that first day and say, 'Well, don't listen to everything the teacher says because they might be lying to you, and they might make you feel uncomfortable, and that's because they're a secret Marxist.'"

The language in this session and others, similar to common rhetoric from the far right, was florid and extreme. And constant. It felt possible to get yourself indoctrinated into the idea that schools are indoctrinating children into Marxist ideologies. How did we get here?

This is not a new move. In fact, the technique of sowing fear around secret infiltration of Marxist ideas, of schools conspiring to spread anti-American ideologies damaging to innocent children by evil educators is precisely what swept across the country in the late 1940s and early to mid-1950s during the McCarthy era, also known as the Red Scare. At the time, charges were rooted in fears that Communists were infiltrating government and society.

What's more, the threat was in plain sight, infecting the very institutions we trust. Being suspicious became not only important but also essential as a demonstration of patriotism.

Now we see a reprise of that. What resonates as one digs into archives of government materials, civic organizations, popular media, and scholars' analyses is how infectious misinformation and propaganda can be. Social media amplifies this, but it was also a key part of the Red Scare. Yes, there are always threats, and we have a history of disagreements about the functioning of public school, including what is taught, by whom, and with what materials.

But while arguments surface in every era, they don't always feed sharp divisions. Yet at other times, every policy move, curricular trend, or action appears to provide evidence on one or another side of a divide. This polarization often coincides with destabilizing events, like wars and revolutions (industrial, digital, or governmental overthrow), that lead people to question the silent supports beneath our society. Trump's presidency, which undermined civil discourse and the sober function of government even before January 6, 2021, was its own revolution. The pandemic compounded the chaos, seeding fears eerily similar to what unfolded during the Red Scare.

At that time, schools and educators became targets "precisely because," as one scholar put it, "they wrestled with many of the issues that divided the country in the postwar era." Those issues, including federal aid for education, racial integration, and "progressive" teaching approaches, among others, might find parallels today in voucher-style funding efforts, the ways race is taught, and the incorporation of Social Emotional Learning into school lessons.

In the late 1940s and early 1950s, those who employed fear tactics and applied pressure to the schools championed values that look familiar today: states' rights, racial segregation in schools, a "traditional" education environment, and a nationalist approach to foreign policy. Those pressing the attacks at the time were far-right groups with funding who influenced or aligned with elected officials to translate their rhetoric into laws and policy.[13]

During the Red Scare, the National Council for American Education, founded by Allen A. Zoll in 1949, published and distributed anti-Communist propaganda in the form of pamphlets that appeared in communities across the US with provocative titles such as *How Red Are the Schools? Progressive Education Increases Delinquency* and *They Want Your Child*. A 1951 article in *The Education Digest* warned, "Right-Wing 'Front' Organizations: They Sow Distrust."[14] It included information on Zoll and others, with the author underscoring a point worth noting today, that these organizations—the story listed eight—crafted positive-sounding names that camouflaged their intentions. Zoll's National Council for Education, the author said, "appears to be a clever fusion of National Education Association and American Council on Education."

The group's stated purpose? "The eradication of Marxism and collectivism from our schools and national life," which assumed Marxism was a legitimate threat to public education. The article described another pamphlet, *How Red Is the Little Red Schoolhouse?*, which included on its cover the image of "a Russian soldier injecting a needle labeled 'Organized Communist Propaganda' into the little red schoolhouse. Below the picture is the statement, 'It's *high time* American parents knew the facts!'"

Such graphic fearmongering came in many forms and from many places, including the Committee for Constitutional Government, founded in 1937 by newspaper publisher Frank Gannett. The organization's name evoked wholesome values while hiding that the group was a powerful lobbying force that—again—fenced with ghosts, seeking to end "socialized education" and warning of "Marxist influences" in the public schools.

This is the identical overblown and fear-inducing language we hear today. Ironically, Russian social media and interference is a true problem—one that members of the far right ignore as they publicly laud President Vladimir Putin! Now, use of the word "Marxism" has become a reliable rhetorical device to induce fear and trigger allegiance to extreme conservative values— values that are then cast as patriotic. At the same time, words like "liberty" and "freedom" are co-opted and twisted to encourage blind obedience to a far-right agenda. Similarly, during the Red Scare, under the guise of protecting the nation, anti-Communist crusaders questioned the patriotism of those not in lockstep with their views.

They cast educators at the time as "enemies of America who infect the minds of the young." Such language was persuasive. According to a 1947 Gallup Poll, a majority of Americans believed that those in Washington should "bear down hard on 'Red' activities," with 61 percent agreeing that membership in the Communist Party should be "forbidden by law."[15] The same percentage believed that some American members of the Communist Party of the United States had allegiances to Russia rather than the US. And 67 percent said that American citizens who were members of the Communist Party should be barred from holding government jobs.

The McCarthy era, lasting from 1947 to 1954 and called such because of the high-profile hearings by Senator Joseph McCarthy, a Republican from Wisconsin (though he was hardly the only one), stands as one of the most politically repressive periods in US history. Republicans gained control of Congress in 1946 just as Korea, which had been under Japanese rule, was divided along the 38th parallel between Communist North Korea and the US-dominated South Korea. Tensions had been rising in the region, and at home, over the political and ideological threat these developments represented. In 1947, President Harry Truman enacted a "loyalty in Government order," praised by both parties but especially by Republicans. Carroll Reece, Republican National Committee chairman, said he hoped that it would "drive out those subversive termites who have been using positions of power and influence under the current administration to undermine our form of government." He also noted that a loyalty oath was "an important part of the program supported by the Republican party and its candidates in the 1946 campaign."[16]

By 1950, the Korean "conflict" had put the US and the USSR at odds. Although hostilities lasted only until 1953, the war cemented the distrust that would undergird years of turbulence and tensions between the two superpowers. Also, in 1949, mainland China fell to the Communists, escalating tensions and amplifying fear of Communist aggression. Republicans seized on this as an opportunity to frame their Democratic opponents as "soft on communism," a charge that would be replayed in political campaigns for years.[17] No one, however, was more effective in fanning flames of fear than McCarthy, who, without evidence, made claims that there were "traitorous" Communists in government and industry. He would eventually be challenged as peddling "barefaced lies" and face censure by the Senate, ending his anti-Communist crusade.[18]

This is not to diminish the importance of national security nor legitimate investigations of Russian spying, which continue.[19] But McCarthy's pursuit of Communist infiltrators was more stunt than substance, as the historian Beverly Gage suggested in G-Man: J. Edgar Hoover and the Making of the American Century, her book about the FBI director, J. Edgar Hoover. Hoover's FBI did surface some actual spies, as opposed to McCarthy, who "turned out to be noisy and reckless, a talented showman and propagandist."[20]

For a time, his televised hearings—along with those held by the House Un-American Activities Committee (HUAC)—made drama out of the quest to rid the nation of dangerous Communists. Screenwriters and Hollywood stars were blacklisted. Then, attention moved to schools. In early 1953, a *New York Times* headline announced "New Inquiry Seeks Reds in Education." Committees would probe "the extent to which Communists might have infiltrated their persons and philosophies into the educational system of the country."[21]

In the weeks that followed, newspapers featured reports of teachers and local educators being called to testify. The very act of being called could be career-ending. Once identified by HUAC, educators were typically then required to meet with their local school boards for additional questioning. Everyone, it seems, got in on the task of tracking down "reds." Many educators refused to answer questions—and were then suspended or fired. Typical was a fifty-three-year-old Somerville, Massachusetts, high school language teacher suspended after refusing to respond to queries of a Senate committee probe of the "Communist infiltration of Massachusetts schools." Yet in such a climate, who could blame her? How does one begin to answer such a question?[22]

Once named, there seemed no way to be found innocent because the force of the accusation branded teachers as traitors. Officials at all levels declined to halt this troubling momentum. In New York, a state Supreme Court justice upheld the right of a local Troy, New York, school board to dismiss six teachers who refused to be questioned about whether they were or had ever been members of the Communist Party. In Boston, several teachers, all identified as "Mr. X," were required to answer questions by the school committee after being called to testify by congressional committees. One scholar, Stuart J. Foster, found that in Philadelphia, twenty-six educators who invoked the Fifth Amendment or refused to respond to questions were later dismissed. He also cited a *Harvard Crimson* report estimating that by July 1953, just five months later, "over 100 school teachers had been dismissed for non-cooperation with congressional committees."[23]

A LIFE DESTROYED

At this time, in other words, there was no way to defend yourself once charges had been leveled—not unlike the dismissal of some teachers today, accused of teaching critical race theory, a law school construct that has become a far-right code for teaching about race, or librarians labeled as sexual groomers for including in their collections books that reflect LGBTQ+ voices.[24] Yet both now and then, a few educators have spoken out. In 1954, that person was Anne Hale Jr., a forty-six-year-old second-grade teacher in Wayland, Massachusetts. Her photo in the *Boston Globe* reveals a slight woman in glasses holding a book, standing in what looks like a library. On the evening of July 7, the local school committee voted 2–1 to dismiss her following a suspension "as a result of her one-time membership in the Communist Party." Interestingly, the board chair, who opposed her firing, stepped down from that position after the vote. The headline: "Wayland Ousts Teacher, Ex-Red."[25]

Following her dismissal, Hale released a statement that was published in the *Boston Globe* challenging her treatment and the red hunt as anti-American. "The issue here is whether the liberty our forefathers fought for is still worth taking risks for," she wrote. "Do we believe with Jefferson that free discussion of all views is the best way to have truth prevail?" She lamented that she "is very sorry that the Wayland School Committee was not able to make a decision more in keeping with the Declaration whose very anniversary we have just celebrated. The opposite philosophy is that which leads—has led in the past—so quickly from the persecution of Communists to the persecution of trade union leaders and liberals and anyone who thought for themselves—and from Jews to Catholics to Protestants."[26]

A history of the case was written in 2003 by Robert Mainer, who moved to Wayland in 1962 and sought to gather information before elders passed on. He wrote a very informed and detailed accounting for the Wayland Historical Society, drawing on interviews, local newspaper and town archives, and records from First Parish church, where Hale was a member. Mainer captures both the "hysteria" and fear leading up to Hale's public hearing and her thoughtful intellectual nature, interested in equity and new ideas.

She was a popular teacher, a Radcliffe graduate who had taught in prestigious schools before coming to Wayland. Yet these were tense times. Mainer cited an "absurd" rumor in town that certain residents, including Hale, had painted their homes red to "signify their support for the Communist cause." While we now may "shake our heads in wonder" at how people responded to perceived Communist threats, he wrote, "Such threats were taken very seriously. The Soviets had nuclear weapons. Their missiles were aimed at the United States." The nation's civil defense agencies were telling citizens how to prepare in case of nuclear attack; magazines offered instructions on building bomb shelters.

Hale had belonged to several organizations, including the League of Women Voters, First Parish, and, for a time, the Communist Party. In a statement to the school committee, she cited the many goals she had worked toward, among them, the improvement of schools, bringing more democracy into the classroom, expanding public schools to include nursery and kindergarten, seeking better wages and working conditions for teachers, and the end of racial and religious discrimination in employment, education, and social opportunity.

She also expressed an interest in "a fairer distribution of wealth through some form of planned economy" that would "eventually secure maximum production and the end of depression and war." One gets the sense that Hale was open-minded and curious, intrigued by socialist ideas, particularly as they related to matters of equity—but hardly dangerous. Reading the messages to her students upon her dismissal, one feels she was exactly the kind of person whom you would want teaching your child.

Yet Hale's dismissal haunted her for the rest of her life. Friends vanished; it became difficult for her to get work and support herself. At one point she got a job cleaning animal cages at a veterinary hospital but "had to leave when her name was discovered on a list of subversives," according to an account cited by Mainer. And it had a ripple effect. "Her brother, Mathew, was fired from his position as a lawyer in a Federal agency when it was discovered that his sister had been a member of the Communist Party."[27]

The velocity and volume of attacks that destroyed Hale's life also eroded trust in public education. Back in 1941, the National Education Association (NEA) had seen that this was happening. But it's efforts to push back and halt the momentum of the fabricated hysteria were late, weak, and ineffective, writes Foster. As early as 1941, according to Foster's research and analysis, NEA president Donald DuShane alerted delegates at the organization's annual meeting in Boston to a coming "crisis" and called for the group to "protect our schools from misunderstanding an unjust attack."[28]

Foresight only matters if people pay attention and act. Organized efforts to confront and halt the hysteria and disinformation were lacking then and, despite growing efforts, are insufficient today. Like the fabricated worries leveled against Hale and fellow teachers, we again see made-up and hyped-up fears of "indoctrination," "sexualization," and "grooming," all accusations that sound horrific but are completely invented. As during the Red Scare, those seeking power and control today, including far-right organizers, funders, legislators, and school board members, are pushing lies calculated to trigger emotional outrage.

A campaign mailer sent in spring 2022 in the Keller Independent School District in Texas would not have been out of place in the 1950s. It shows a darkened black-and-white photo of a child sitting on a tile floor with his head buried between his knees and comes with a frightening message superimposed in all caps: "KELLER ISD EXPOSED OUR KIDS TO EXPLICIT, 'WOKE' BOOKS/ THE FAR-LEFT AGENDA HAS INFECTED KIDS AND IT'S HURTING OUR KIDS." Then, in a friendlier typeface: "It's time for a new School Board."

Far-right messages aim to undermine the institutions we rely on to support our democracy. As they sow distrust in government at the national level, they also erode faith in our institutions at the local level, fracturing personal connections and a critical sense of community. The social fabric is being destroyed. But people are willing to risk this because the far-right has effectively promoted the Red Scare strategy of presenting an even greater threat: teachers and schools harming children. As I heard over and over at the Moms for Liberty summit, when your child faces danger, the response is obvious. You must push aside all hesitations and concerns to act. You might not think of yourself as political, but this is not a choice. You must fight. And maybe run for office.

TRAINING THE GROUND FORCES

There was no more powerful message at the Moms for Liberty summit than that they should run for school board. I lost count of the number of times that those who had declared their candidacy were asked to stand, to massive applause. Florida governor Ron DeSantis made the point that for the first time ever, he was endorsing candidates for school board because "the state is not going to be able to do all this stuff on its own and do everything right. It's really the local communities that need to be leading the way." And, yes, if he endorsed you, stand and be recognized. Of the thirty candidates DeSantis endorsed, at least twenty won their elections several weeks later. Five other campaigns went to a runoff.[29]

The other problem, DeSantis pointed out, was that because Florida's constitution requires that school board elections be nonpartisan, voters needed help. One wanted to avoid a scenario in which the "left wing interests get behind a candidate and package it a certain way" and then you end up where "these conservative counties will have left-of-center school boards."

His point, which he verbally danced around but which has become evident in Florida and across the country, is that long-ignored local school board elections are the foundation of far-right support for up-ballot candidates—and not the other way around.

The activism that started with Covid mask mandates, the visuals of angry parents packing school board meetings and holding signs on street corners, revealed something important about power to national politicians. Key support was not just about the gun lobby or anti-abortion funders. It would involve those issues, but it started at home, with parents and their children. The best way to win at the top was to support the army on the ground.

But DeSantis, along with other speakers and strategists, also knew that mobilizing a force of moms requires emotional preparation. Politics is mean. "There are a lot of threats to freedom. There are a lot of people who push back when you stand up and do the right thing," DeSantis said, adding that many "don't want to hear the truth, and you speak the truth."

"Many of you are going to take fire," he warned. "It is not just people like me that is a target because I am in an office, it is parents who go to a school board meeting. You go to that school board meeting, and you speak that truth" and the media "will try to smear you, they will dig into your background and lie about you." And when you are a candidate, he said, "when you are vying for some of these local offices, they will come after you."

In the Sunday-morning session, Ben Carson invoked Jesus: when asked about attacks, he said, "Yeah, well, there is no question you have to expect that. The Bible says that. Jesus says, 'If you follow me, you are going to be persecuted.'" But in the opening session, DeSantis framed their task as patriotic, a duty to country requiring sacrifice.

Running for office, being politically active, he said, echoing the Florida law invoked in the 2012 shooting of Trayvon Martin, "requires you to stand your ground. It requires us to understand now's not the time to be a shrinking violet. Now's not the time to let them grind you down. You've got to stand up and you've got to fight."[30]

We are facing a troubled time in which "woke-ism has gotten into our institutions," he said. If you show people that you are willing to fight, "they will walk over broken glass." People will have your back, he assured, adding that we have "a reservoir of patriots across the state."

What the conference effectively pulled off was, on the one hand, to celebrate femininity, motherhood, and traditional values; the A-line lemon-yellow dress that Descovich wore on Sunday morning was a clear nod to the 1950s. And on the other hand, this gathering activated the ruthless warrior bent on protecting her young. These moms were being deputized to fight—and given the language with which to do it—all without relinquishing their gendered familial role. What's more, it was happening now because America faced a crisis that demanded extreme and unusual action. Just as women were needed for factory work during World War II, moms were needed to seek local political office now. The framing was genius.

In practical terms, the conference energized these ultraconservative Christian moms while connecting them to a national far-right network that had, frankly, been dying for such an opportunity. As I perused the tables outside of the ballroom, chatting with those selling books and peddling ideas, it was clear that these Moms for Liberty attendees were valuable recruits.

The Leadership Institute, which was a lead sponsor of the conference, boasts that it has trained conservative activists since 1979. The organization hosted multiple strategy sessions, going into detail on subjects from vetting candidates and doing strategic research to media training and the details of running for office.

One session leader speaker who boasted about having Tea Party leadership cred said they would gladly travel to lead free trainings. That sounds generous until you pull the organization's 990, a filing required of nonprofit groups, and discover that their annual public donations and grants more than doubled between 2017 and 2021 to $29,817,694 a year. They can afford to come for free. Many people I interviewed mentioned, "Oh, I've seen their flyers." The institute also launched a free online school board candidate training program in August 2022. Bridget Ziegler, the director of School Board Programs, was a cofounder of Moms for Liberty, according to incorporation papers. She stepped down from a leadership role in Moms for Liberty in spring 2021 "due to its rapid growth and Bridget's limited bandwidth," but was very visible at the National Summit.[31]

Support for parent activism has become a busy conservative space for good reason. As parents during the pandemic began organizing anti-mask demonstrations, far-right groups saw the opportunity to bring their work—often focused on lobbying, drafting model legislation, and framing arguments, backed up by scholarly-sounding logic—from the control booth to the stage. Organizations have sought to equip parents in different ways. The goal is to engage them in their battle in ways that were simply not possible before Covid.

For example, Citizens for Renewing America has created a tool kit for parents (the banner is red with a hammer and sickle image) with detailed instructions on "how to stop critical race theory and reclaim your school board." It includes warnings on opposing "CRT activists" who "will come as sheep, pretending to be articulate, reasonable, and moderate thought leaders" but gain power to "implement destructive CRT." Parents must be on guard for those "who could do their children harm." It is scary stuff. Consider the warning that opponents, "are not trying to win an academic debate, they are trying to socially replace you."[32]

Thus, training moms and dads to run for school board is an extension of far-right political work that has been going on for years. It has required just a small pivot. Outside of the main ballroom, I chatted with Melvin Adams, the gray-bearded president and founder of the Noah Webster Foundation, whose website and materials offer a lot of room to move given its anodyne-sounding goal to "reclaim education and culture through foundational principles and sound policy." Adams excitedly reported that ten months earlier, they launched an online self-paced school board training program. He said that "hundreds" had already enrolled.

CHAPTER 2

HOW SCHOOLS ARE BECOMING PARTISAN AND POLITICAL

I N THE SUMMER OF 1996, Nancy Garrett was among ninety-seven Tennesseans chosen to carry the Olympic Torch on its journey to Atlanta for the opening of the Summer Games. Garrett, a compact package of competence and social energy who speaks with a warm Southern lilt, was six months pregnant with her son as she made the gentle jog, "a very short distance, right through the middle of District 12" in Williamson County, she recalled, referring to the voting map.[1]

It was a huge honor, but not really a surprise. Garrett has deep roots in this tony Nashville suburb of emerald-green fields and split-rail fences. She grew up here, the third of five girls. Her father, William Nelson, was a popular chemistry teacher at Franklin High School, where Garrett graduated in 1979. Her dad was so beloved that when he died in 2017, a former student, Bill Lee, who was elected governor in 2018, paused a bus tour he was making around the state to speak at the funeral.[2]

Garrett may be equally beloved. For decades she has been a relentless community, church, and school volunteer. She is also, importantly in this state and county, been an active Republican who has held signs, posted signs in her yard, canvassed, donated, and worked the polls for other Republicans as well as Republicans running for nonpartisan posts such as alderman. Sure, she has a serious paid job as a senior knowledge leader at a Fortune 50 company. But Garrett is one of those whom others count on to step up to the plate and lead.

And she has. She helped found an area service nonprofit, Hands on Nashville. She started a summer school reading program and held PTO leadership posts for a dozen years. In 2016, Garrett was appointed by the County Commission to fill a vacancy on the Williamson County School Board. In 2018, she was reelected; in 2020 she became the board chair.[3]

But when it came time to seek reelection in 2022, she faced a challenge. It wasn't directly related to the pandemic issues she and her board navigated. It was political. After Governor Lee in November 2021 signed a law allowing county political parties to have partisan school board elections, Williamson County for the first time had candidates aligned with a political party.[4]

Garrett was appalled. Suddenly she found herself carrying a different torch—this one for keeping politics out of school board races. Despite her Republican connections, Garrett decided to run as unaffiliated. To her, the choice was clear and principled.

"If you have grown up in education, there is no way you'll run as a partisan candidate," she told me, a stance she repeated often and made clear on her campaign website. "There is no way I would run as a Republican. It's a double standard. We expect our teachers to be nonpartisan in the classroom, and so why don't we hold ourselves to the same standard?"

"THE KEY THAT PICKS THE LOCK"

Nancy Garrett's stance is rooted in her deep sense of community and in the belief—one that so many have long shared—that public schools, and their administration, should be a local task, and that leading was about care for the next generation, about steering the ship and providing for young people what, especially in Williamson County, families had moved there to find.

But for many others, school boards have become something else entirely. They have become the means to a political end. Steve Bannon, who has a knack for spilling the beans and revealing far-right thinking, said as much in August 2022. In 2018, as a member of the Trump administration, he told the writer Michael Lewis, "The Democrats don't matter. The real opposition is the media. And the way to deal with them is to flood the zone with shit." Another share: "This is not about persuasion; this is about disorientation."[5]

In other words, Bannon tells you exactly what the far right is doing. No apologies. Just plain strategy. So when he did it again at the Conservative Political Action Conference (CPAC) in Dallas in early August 2022, it was hardly a surprise. Bannon hosted his show, *War Room: Pandemic*, on Real America's Voice, a far-right network, from the CPAC and conducted interviews.

In one of those interviews, he talked about education, specifically school boards. He spoke with Glenn Story, cofounder and CEO of Patriot Mobile, a Texas-based Christian cell phone carrier, and Leigh Wambsganns, executive director of Patriot Mobile Action, a PAC (political action committee) formed in early 2022.[6] Patriot Mobile Action had recently spent about $400,000 on campaigns that in the end won eleven school board seats.

As he approached Story, Bannon grew excited. "Now let's talk about PACs. As I said last night, one of the keys to these is school boards, right? The school boards are the key that picks the lock," he said. He then asked Story to "tell us about what you did in Tarrant County."

In case anyone doubted, Bannon made it clear: school board elections are not about kids, schools, and local communities. Rather, they are tools, the building blocks of party power. Story praised Wambsganns. "She puts hundreds and hundreds and thousands of hours of interviewing candidates" for the PAC to support, he said, adding, "We won every seat."

Wambsganns cast the win in even more strategic terms. Those eleven seats enabled them "to flip" four school boards. "In all four of those school boards, we did not have a school board majority," she said. The wins mean "that now North Texas has over 100,000 students that before May had leftist leadership. Now they have conservative leadership." Not only did candidates win seats, but they gained leadership posts—president, vice president, and secretary—on those boards.[7] Never mind that school boards in Texas are, theoretically, nonpartisan and all about serving the local community.

To be clear, the far right has not been quiet about its intentions to build, train, and support a ground army of school board candidates. School boards have been seen as sleepy local bodies that passed budgets, debated capital expenditures—does the high school get a swimming pool?—and voted on issues from school start times and the district calendar to teacher contracts. But they have also long made consequential decisions that got little attention—such as deciding whether a high school health clinic would provide contraception.

The old perception of school boards as a backwater of American politics was not wrong, but it is incomplete. There is a powerful history of women using schools and school boards to exert political influence before they won the vote. School boards were also flash points for confrontation following *Brown v. Board of Education of Topeka*, in 1954, and, later, during court-ordered desegregation. But it was during the 1970s that the Christian right most clearly saw and began to act on available opportunities they found in the American political system, particularly in schools.

THE POLITICAL RISE OF THE CHRISTIAN RIGHT

It is hard to consider current school board battles without revisiting the 1970s, when the Christian right movement began to crystallize. This crystallization was also marked by the founding of new think-tanks such as the Heritage Foundation (formed in 1973); the Libertarian Cato Institute, in 1977; and the Leadership Institute in 1979. Yet at the time, its growth was largely overlooked, according to Matthew C. Moen, a well-regarded scholar of the Christian right. Politicians and journalists were caught off guard, and scholars, he wrote, "ignored the Christian Right's infiltration of state Republican party organizations until the Reagan era was over."[8]

What's more, he observes, journalists tracking scandals of televangelists like Jim Bakker and Oral Roberts missed the distinction "between ministries and objectives." They failed to note that whereas Bakker was "bent on building the ultimate Pentecostal amusement park," the fundamentalist Jerry Falwell had a "mission to remake America."

It was this latter effort, specifically the growth of Falwell's Moral Majority, that laid the foundation for the current far-right movement. Initially, Moen observes, Falwell and others centered their work on expressing moral outrage. In their radio scripts and news organs, the organization portrayed a heathen nation that had lost its way. For instance, the March 14, 1980, issue of the *Moral Majority Report* ran a story trumpeting Falwell's national letter-writing campaign to "put voluntary prayer back into public schools." The campaign was a response to what the paper viewed as a travesty: during a White House visit with President Jimmy Carter, himself a born-again Christian, Falwell and several ministers were "shocked" when Carter said he "would absolutely never sign a bill" returning prayer to school.[9]

Moral outrage remained an animating force in 1987 when the January issue of the *Liberty Report* (the "newspaper for the Moral Majority") ran an editorial whose title charged, "What Was Wrong Is Now Right." The problem, the commentary argued, was that "our country has simply drifted too far from the Judeo-Christian principles of our Founding Fathers. The abandonment of these godly principles has left a void only too happily filled by the shrill sound of secular humanism."

The article pointed to the behavior of troubled youths as evidence that religious values should be enforced in everyday life. "Perhaps parents don't tell their children anymore to 'Return the money,' or 'Don't lie,' or 'Be careful what you do on a date.'" The commentary claimed that moral standards "went out when humanism came in." The writer concluded, "It is no wonder our society had thrown God out of our public schools" and "opens its arms to homosexuals," among other perceived ills.[10]

Although Falwell's moralizing attracted like-minded followers, it didn't gain political traction. By 1989 Falwell had shut down the Moral Majority. Yet other leaders were rising, including Pat Robertson, who hosted the popular show *700 Club* on his Christian Broadcasting Network. In 1981, he spun off the Freedom Council in a bid to involve Christians in the electoral process (it was disbanded in 1986 amid charges that the charity was improperly funding Robertson's run for president).[11]

Yet, around that time, the Christian right started doing a few things that one could argue set it up for future success, among them finding better financing sources (rather than relying on direct-mail appeals) and, through Robertson's candidacy for president in 1988, drawing together groups that had not been aligned and had often been at odds, including fundamentalists, evangelicals, and charismatics. Rather than focus on religious differences, the Christian right could expand its pool of recruits and supporters around political goals they could agree on.

But perhaps most powerfully, the movement transformed its messaging. As Moen observes, the Christian right recast its outrage into "the more familiar and widely accepted language of liberalism with its focus on rights, equality, and opportunity." That move, translating religious aims into secular terms, yielded framings that included opposition to gay marriage as homosexuals seeking "special rights," as school prayer reflecting "student rights," and objection to content in textbooks as the exercise of "parental rights." These same phrases are being employed today.

In addition, Moen writes, Christian right leaders used the "invective language of liberalism as a political tactic, blaming cultural elites for 'bigotry' and 'discrimination against traditional values.'" As Moen concludes in his 1994 article, "The strident campaign to 'put God back in government' has been replaced by a quiet effort to rally sympathetic citizens and win elections."

One could say that the Christian right figured out how to speak the language of American politics, to persuade rather than to preach. That strategic approach is still visible as efforts to insert Christian values into public schools are argued in secular, defensive terms such as "asserting parental rights"; censorship of library books is portrayed as seeking "to protect children" from "pornography." Strikingly, three decades ago Moen foresaw the activism we see now as he predicted the rise of the far right's interest in local politics with "issues of public education topping the agenda because of the school's key role in socializing citizens."[12]

When Pat Robertson ran for president in 1988, however, the focus was more top-down than grassroots. His broad name recognition was initially a benefit, but soon became a liability. Although he performed well in the Iowa caucuses, finishing second behind Robert Dole and ahead of George H. W. Bush, Robertson was not an effective candidate.[13]

In one opinion poll, the sociologist Steve Bruce notes, when asked which of six Republican candidates was "someone you can trust," respondents placed Robertson dead last, behind Bush, Dole, Jack Kemp, Pete DuPont, and Al Haig. "With the usual cautions about such poll data," Bruce marvels, "it is still significant that a leading religious broadcaster should be regarded as less trustworthy than four professional politicians and a career soldier who was Richard Nixon's Chief of Staff!"[14]

During his campaign, Robertson tried to distance himself from his past as a preacher. After polls revealed that voters opposed a minister as president, he resigned his ordination as a minister in the Southern Baptist church. But erasing his history was hard to do, considering that so much had been recorded. He had, after all, claimed that God performed miracles at his request, including healing a woman with "cancer of the womb" and diverting a hurricane, which he took as a sign that he should run for president. A December 21, 1987, report on NBC *Nightly News* included a montage of damning clips of Robertson making outrageous assertions and also insisting that he had never been an evangelist.[15]

BUILDING POLITICAL POWER, FROM THE BOTTOM UP

Following his failed run, Robertson turned the work of the Christian Coalition to other tasks, among them organizing at the grassroots level. In 1992, hundreds of "stealth" candidates ran for state and local offices, concealing their connections to groups like the Christian Coalition along with ambitions for, among other items, pressing for public prayer and teaching creationism in schools. As a story in the *Christian Science Monitor* noted at the time, "The religious right has thus emerged strongly as a force in Republican Party politics."[16]

The liberal group People for the American Way monitored five hundred races across the country with religious right candidates running in 1992 and 1993, and estimated that 40 percent had won election. Many of the candidates campaigned largely through church channels and avoided public appearances and questionnaires, a tactic alive today. According to the *Monitor*, "One woman was elected to a suburban school board reportedly without ever being seen in public until the day she was sworn in." A second *Monitor* story, some eight months later, found that religious right candidates had won school board races in twelve states. As a 1994 *Mother Jones* article put it, the religious right had a plan to "go local and build political power from the bottom up."[17]

The stealth strategy remains effective and has been evident in recent years. The problem is that it has an impact on the information voters have at their disposal. For example, if one candidate refuses to participate in a forum sponsored by the League of Women Voters, their opponent may not participate, a practice that is designed to promote fairness but that limits the exposure of candidates who want to share information with voters.[18] In some races, candidates decline requests to speak with reporters or to respond to community groups. Then it becomes a game of name recognition and turnout—both of which money and organization can influence.

On the other hand, some far-right candidates embrace a "pro-family" platform. Ralph Reed, the first executive director of the Christian Coalition, argued in a story in the *Christian Science Monitor* in 1993 that this helped them win votes. "For too long, people of faith have not fully exercised their rights and responsibilities as citizens," he argued. "Women, African-Americans, other minorities, gays, and union workers have all gone out there and increased participation and involvement of like-minded citizens. We're beginning to do the same thing."

In one New York City race, Reed told the *Monitor*, the Christian Coalition passed out five hundred pamphlets outlining "candidates' stands on such issues as voluntary classroom prayer and requiring parental consent for students to receive condoms in school." He boasted that the organization's involvement "doubled voter turnout from previous elections." As a result, he claimed, of eighty-nine "pro-family" candidates the organization had supported in 1992 and 1993, fifty-six were elected. Reed called it "a stunning success rate of 63 percent."[19]

In some ways, the Christian Coalition pioneered what would become a staple strategy decades later: bringing national organizations to local political debates. In the early 1990s, as school districts were revamping their sex education curricula to reflect the threat of AIDS, I found myself covering what was an odd battlefront: objections within the community to a new pilot sex-ed curriculum for ninth-graders in Newton, Massachusetts. It was odd because Newton was one of the most progressive and healthcare–conscious constituencies in the state.

The idea that a suburban community that was home to Harvard professors, scientists, doctors (and, some claimed, the state's highest per capita population of therapists) would not embrace frank discussion of sex, including abstinence but also condoms and homosexuality, was a stretch. Yet Newton—less so in nearby communities that were more conservative and religious—was where the battleground settled.

In May 1993, I attended a packed school board meeting in the Day Middle School auditorium, an anodyne brick building a few miles from where I lived. There were 430 parents in the auditorium while another 200 watched on a television in the cafeteria and still more tried to listen from the parking lot. Although I did not realize it at the time, the scene was a precursor to what is happening today. Members of the far-right Newton Citizens for Public Education objected to the pilot sex-ed program as an affront to parental rights and values. When similar objections arose in a few other communities, the Christian Coalition, in October 1993, tried to organize a training for school board candidates.[20]

Local progressive groups formed and pushed back. Whether because of that opposition or, more likely, because the Christian Coalition targeted the wrong time and place to ignite a movement, their message didn't catch on. Still, when far-right Newton leaders threatened to field candidates for school board, Martin Kaplan, Newton school board chair, raised the alarm.

"We must recognize that the religious right wing seeks control through the ballot box," he said. He underscored the importance of voter attention and turnout. He reminded residents of what has now become so obvious: "fundamentalist right-wing candidates win elections by receiving more votes than other candidates."[21]

By the time Election Day arrived, the far-right slate had fizzled. The sex-ed plan passed and was implemented without fanfare. (The leader of the far-right effort in Newton, Brian Camenker, then founded a national anti-LGBTQ+ organization, MassResistance, which the Southern Poverty Law Center has labeled a hate group.)[22]

Yet, Kaplan's message was prescient. Of course, it is critical to reach like-minded voters. Equally essential is getting them to show up and vote.

LOW VOTER TURNOUT, FAR-RIGHT ORGANIZING

The idea of activating voters to win local elections makes good sense, but historically many voters are not well-informed or engaged, which likely contributes to low voter turnout. Voting in national elections typically runs at about 60 percent of the electorate (in 2020 it was a striking 67 percent), and around 40 percent for midterms. But it is much lower for local elections, often less than 15 percent. It is not unusual for school board races to see a voter turnout of 10 percent or, as in Los Angeles in 2019, 8.7 percent.[23]

That means that even when races are hotly contested, a candidate may win or lose by a small number of votes. It also means that outside influences—PAC money and dark money, untraceable funds spent on behalf of candidates—can profoundly impact an election. For example, in May 2022 in the Frisco Independent School District (ISD) race in Texas, the candidate for place 2 (school board seats are designated by number), Natalie Hebert, a former teacher, mother of two, and an incumbent school board member, lost to a newcomer, Marvin Lowe, by fifty-one votes. Voter participation in Texas school board elections is often difficult to pinpoint because ISD boundaries do not fit neatly into the boundaries of cities or counties, which administer elections. For instance, the Frisco ISD includes towns in Denton and Collin counties—Frisco, Prosper, Little Elm, Plano, and McKinney—plus unincorporated areas. Furthermore, typically other county races are happening at the same time as the school board elections.

As a gauge, the previous municipal election in Frisco had a voter turnout rate of 8.91 percent. In the May 2022 Frisco ISD school board race, Denton County, where 40 percent of ballots were cast, had an overall 11.36 percent turnout. In Collin County, voter turnout across all races was 7.5 percent. A total of just 15,040 votes were cast in the race for place 2 on the Frisco ISD school board.[24]

Even in a district in which education is such a prominent issue, relatively few show up to cast ballots for the school board members. "People just don't pay attention to school board races. They just don't know who they are voting for when they are voting," Hebert pointed out when I met her a few weeks after the election at a busy Frisco eatery. "We are just used to being in our routine that everything is pretty and great. We are vulnerable because we don't have that fear of things going south."

But for a voter, parent, teacher, librarian, or school leader, not paying attention is costly. New laws shake up school routines and have had, for example, school librarians rifling through stacks to account for books that suddenly appear on a legislator's hit list (more on this later). "It is going to be vital to the success of public schools in the next ten years" for educators to pay attention to what unfolds in the state legislature, said Hebert. For many teachers, she said, "I don't think they realized that education is extremely political."[25] That may be changing.

Education certainly has become political in communities like Frisco. In late summer 2021 the Families 4 Frisco PAC was formed (Lowe was a late addition to its slate). Its creation was inspired by the Southlake Families PAC, which had formed a year earlier. The Southlake Families PAC was so effective in identifying, selecting, and supporting far-right candidates for school board (their candidates won) that its tactics were the subject of a flattering feature in the *National Review*. Other far-right groups across North Texas took note.[26]

The *National Review* feature told the story of how Tim O'Hare, a former chair of the Tarrant County (Texas) Republican Party, and a longtime political operative, Leigh Wambsganns, of Patriot Mobile Action, got to work in the summer of 2020 to halt a Cultural Competency Action Plan (CCAP) that was to be adopted by their Carroll ISD school board. The plan had been written by a community diversity council in response to two videos of students using a racial slur that went viral plus a broader concern about racism in the district. A Peabody Award–winning NBC podcast, *Southlake*, had chronicled the racial issues, creation of the plan, and the school board races.

The success of the Southlake Families PAC is that it revealed to far-right activists what you could accomplish by challenging (and taking over) a school board. The PAC's work effectively halted implementation of the Cultural Competency Action Plan, which O'Hare crowed about in December 2021, saying that he and Wambsganns had "founded Southlake Families in the summer of 2020 in response to Southlake Carroll ISD's Marxist, CRT-filled CCAP agenda. Southlake Families energized parents and encouraged them to take a stand and work together to take on the powers that be, and we prevailed. Critical Race Theory is now dead in Southlake Carroll Schools, and we know other districts in Tarrant County will follow suit."[27]

The legal unraveling of the plan came about because a parent, Kristin Garcia, a donor to Southlake Families PAC, obtained texts that a few board members had sent in advance of the August 2020 vote, and filed a civil suit which eventually yielded charges against the school board members for violating open meeting laws.[28] The county indicted the board members, and following unsuccessful appeals, the case ended in the settlement that O'Hare celebrated—which effectively killed the plan and barred its discussion.[29]

So as schools and districts around the country seek to use more inclusive language and practices in schools, that is not happening in Carroll ISD. It's worth noting, however, that the US Department of Education's Office of Civil Rights in February 2023 was investigating eight separate discrimination complaints against the district.[30]

The *National Review* article bemoaned the fact that in the CCAP plan "nearly everything, from curriculum to discipline policies to teacher training to hiring decisions, would be filtered through the prism of diversity, equity, and inclusion." Which is a mainstream practice everywhere, in schools and in corporate America alike. But it is not a conversation that interests leaders of the Southlake Families PAC in this wealthy enclave outside of Dallas. Some in Frisco took note. Others in North Texas also took note of how the PAC identified and funded candidates that shifted the composition of the school board.

The origin story of the Southlake Families PAC is important: It was formed after Wambsganns helped to organize a meeting of some four hundred people in August 2020. Notably, she invited Allen West, then chairman of the Texas Republican Party, to be the keynote speaker. The fledgling PAC raised $75,000 instantly, with thousands more to follow. Just halfway through the 2022 election cycle, the PAC had raised $172,012 and had spent thousands on behalf of local candidates. And they spent it with national campaign firms like Axiom Strategies, LLC (clients include Ted Cruz and Ron DeSantis), and Vanguard Field Strategies, which "helped lead the ground effort for President Trump in Pennsylvania in 2016, [and] Governor Glenn Youngkin in Virginia in 2021," among a string of listed successes.[31]

Clearly, the Southlake Families PAC is not a politically naïve organization. Rather, it is a savvy operation with national resources to deploy on local school board races. In inviting West to give the kickoff speech, organizers activated a figure well-known for trying to push the Republican Party further right. The PAC's message and ambitions could not be clearer. In fact, around the time of Wambsganns's gathering, West unveiled a new party slogan, "We Are the Storm"—which would be compared with language used by QAnon, although West denied any connection.

At the "We Are the Storm" event, on August 4, 2020, West trumpeted the power of local races. "One of the most important elections we got on November coming up is school board," he said, then called to the stage Muni Janagarajan, who was running for school board in the Frisco ISD. West then officially and publicly endorsed him.

Janagarajan lost his Frisco race, but months later he was listed as the treasurer of the new Families 4 Frisco PAC.[32] He kept his connection to West, who then spoke at a Families 4 Frisco "meetup" in February 2022 in a retirement community. West was joined there by two far-right Carroll ISD school board members, Hannah Smith and Cam Bryan, whom the Southlake Families PAC had screened and successfully helped to elect in May 2021.[33] (When Bryan ran, he raised $64,000, more than any Southlake candidate had ever raised, including for city council and mayoral races.)[34]

At the event, Smith—a lawyer who had once clerked for Clarence Thomas and Samuel Alito—boasted that in Southlake the diversity council's work had been "destroyed." According to a report of the event in the *Dallas Morning News*, Smith shared with the hundred or so people present that "she heard from a mother, now running for Frisco's school board, who told her, 'We want to do in Frisco what you guys are doing in Southlake.'" Presumably the mother Smith was referring to was Stephanie Elad, who had just taken out papers to run. Smith assured listeners that "having conservatives on your school board really makes a huge difference from curriculum to teacher trainings to what's in your kid's classroom."[35]

THE FRISCO PUZZLE

In some ways, Frisco is an interesting place for a cultural and political showdown. It is one of the fastest-growing cities in the country. The population, according to 2021 Census figures, is 210,000, but blink and it will be up 5 percent. The *Frisco ISD eNewsletter: June 2022* noted that the district was preparing "to open two new schools this fall and welcome an estimated 1,600 new students." This is because the city, just miles north of Dallas and Fort Worth, is a booming spot for corporate relocation. Drive through Frisco and you quickly lose count of the glass-sided high-rises under construction.[36]

Frisco is home to the Dallas Cowboys Merchandising and Distribution Center, and a headquarters for Keurig, Dr. Pepper, T-Mobile West, Teachers Insurance and Annuity Association (TIAA), PGA of America, and several dozen more members of a who's who of American sports and industry. It's a key site for mega players, including Federal Express, Home Depot, Oracle, Amazon, and others. Strikingly, a review of public-facing statements made by these organizations shows that they present themselves as eagerly embracing diversity, equity, and inclusion.[37]

Frisco's growth is not an accident. The Frisco Economic Development Corporation exudes a business-friendly vibe—rumor has it that a city official boasted that Dallas would one day be a suburb of Frisco. And the public schools are excellent. The Frisco EDC website highlights the enviable data, including a 99.4 percent graduation rate and 110 National Merit Semi Finalists. It also highlights the district's diversity, noting in large font that there are "83 languages served."

Since 2010 the school population has grown dramatically in size and become more diverse. In 2010, according to data from the Texas Education Agency, the district had 33,757 students of whom 61 percent were white. Ten years later, the number of students had nearly doubled, to 62,571, of whom just 39 percent were white and 31 percent were Asian; Hispanic and Black students were the next two largest groups.

Not surprisingly, rapid growth has increased racial and political diversity—including, as one longtime resident put it, companies "coming in with their California values." Add in Covid learning challenges since 2020 and you have a paradigmatic image of that moment: frustrated parents packing school board meetings to object to, at first, mask mandates and, later, issues such as the selection of library books. Families 4 Frisco grew as those parents found one another. But what started as communion over education issues—Was the middle school English pilot effective? Was the grading system fair across the district?—soon was transformed into the embrace, according to a former Families 4 Frisco member, of a "full-blown radical right agenda."[38]

The former member identified herself as a proud conservative and gun owner. She feels the Republican Party has become something she can no longer align with ("I carry a nine-millimeter [handgun] every single day, but I do not think my eighteen-year-old should be able to buy an assault rifle. That makes me a RINO," she said, referring to the derisive label "Republican in Name Only").

The former member sees plenty that needs addressing in the schools, but Families 4 Frisco became something else entirely. As she attended gatherings, she noticed that "there are QAnon stickers on people's cars and I was like, 'What in the actual hell is going on?' Everything we didn't want to be, by February we were," she said, referring to the start of the group in August 2021 and its activities by February 2022. "We are blasting teachers on the stage, threatening school board members with guns on social media. I said, 'Y'all, I'm out.'"

The group doubled down on its aggressive tactics. Stephanie Elad filed papers to run for a spot on the school board in January. Marvin Lowe filed in February. The two campaigned together and became the de facto Families 4 Frisco slate. Leading up to the school board election in May, Tracy Gamble, a longtime politically active Frisco resident, saw far-right activists, whom she nicknamed "hatriots," "flooding" people's Facebook pages. According to her review of city records, she claimed that some of them did not even live in the district.[39]

At the same time, State Representative Jared Patterson (R-Frisco) took to social media to attack school libraries, claiming they contained "pornography" (this has become a favorite activity of far-right elected officials and activists to gain attention and stir up parents). His most inflammatory texts have since been deleted. But Patterson engaged in a public feud with the superintendent, who had adjusted the review process for books and sent a sober, explanatory two-page letter to parents.[40]

Amid the vitriol, the *Dallas Morning News* published an editorial with the headline "Attention Frisco Residents: Your Schools Are in Trouble." The commentary said the problem is "not because of the books in the library. And it's not because of the teachers in the classroom. It's because a devoted and misguided group of zealous activists have decided that schools are the place to bring the frontline of the culture wars, and they are winning the day in Frisco."[41]

In a campaign mailer put out by Lowe and Elad, they sounded alarms, claiming, "This 'Critical Race Theory' nonsense is happening right here in Frisco schools." They urged parents to "take a stand against this radical indoctrination. Vote for a new school board!" Candidate forums were rife with sharp exchanges and campaigning was heated.

Elad and Lowe were also spending money, but it is difficult to track. For example, the national 1776 Project PAC lists Elad and Lowe as candidates they "endorsed" and likely funded—along with far right candidates in Florida, New Jersey, Colorado, Ohio, Virginia, Minnesota, Kansas, and Pennsylvania—but there is no record of any such donation on either Elad's or Lowe's campaign finance reports filed on either of the required days, eight and thirty days prior to the election.[42]

According to Transparency, USA, during the 2022 election cycle, the Families 4 Frisco PAC spent $7,528 to boost the visibility of their candidates: with Premier Mobile Billboards (presumably for the box truck with their faces that drove around the city), with Facebook, for marketing, and other expenses. Notably, the Families 4 Frisco PAC, which received donations from Allen West and a far-right Carroll ISD school board member, doesn't have to reveal which, if any, candidates benefitted from the expenditures. Still, Lowe's campaign filings, at $18,814.75, show him outspending Hebert three to one, including $3,757 paid to Axiom Strategies, the Kansas City, Missouri, national campaign outfit. (Lowe also donated $1,000 to Elad's campaign.) Elad spent $22,403.18, according to filings.

Again, Elad and Lowe likely benefitted from much more spending, but there is no way to track this dark money. But just considering the reported spending and campaign messaging, this was not a traditional, local race. "Frisco got a huge wake-up call" when Elad and Lowe won, said Gamble, the longtime local political observer. "Frisco just got Southlaked."

Gamble was not alone in interpreting the result as she did. Steve Bannon said as much when he interviewed Elad a few days after her win. Elad observed, "This movement is just the beginning. This is just the beginning in Frisco." Bannon took it from there. "I tell you what, this is just the beginning in the *nation*," he declared. "And this is how we are going to take the nation back, village by village, school district by school district election. You're representing something much, much larger."[43]

LOCAL SCHOOL BOARDS, NATIONAL INFLUENCERS

It is not surprising that school boards have become highly contested races, worthy of national attention and PAC money. But it is alarming. That's because it is rearranging the terms of our democracy, and the relationships we have with those governing our local communities. What does it mean when school board members answer not to neighbors, but to party leaders who direct the language, the policy platforms—and the donations—that shape their agendas?

Influence and spending by outside interests seeking to influence public education is not new, but its nature is changing. Maurice T. Cunningham, a retired University of Massachusetts, Boston, political science professor who has spent years tracking and writing about dark money, has long worried about what it means when oligarchs (he often cites the Kochs and the Waltons) favoring market-based solutions used their dollars to tilt "the legislature toward the privatizers' idea of reform."[44] Cunningham has tracked ballot initiatives and PACs with "buoyantly nonpartisan names like Educators for Excellence or National Parents Union." By hiding "the true powers" behind campaigns, he argued in *Dark Money and the Politics of School Privatization*, such names present "a misleading picture to the public."

The origins of the tangled and misleading picture we now face are rooted in the late twentieth century, when some of the wealthiest Americans, often through their foundations, focused on a genuine challenge: How do we make public schools better? How do we raise achievement for all students? The year 1983 marked the appearance of a landmark report, *A Nation at Risk*, by the US National Commission on Excellence in Education, which decried the failing state of American public schools. Not unlike the Sputnik launch, it set off a race on the part of business leaders, educators, and politicians to seek solutions. They convened roundtables and committees, which in the 1990s gave rise to a spate of local, state, and eventually federal education reform efforts and laws.

The focus fell heavily on two goals: finding innovative ways to provide students a quality education, regardless of zip code, and funding public schools more fairly. Not surprisingly, much of the energy centered on low-income and urban schools. This spurred the rise of charter schools, new approaches to teacher training, fresh pedagogical methods, and new curricula. Education became a booming landscape for social entrepreneurs—and for people interested in funding them.

This is still happening. But we also can trace the current nationalization of education politics in part to the invitation that the education reform movement offered. Recently, Jeffrey R. Henig, Rebecca Jacobsen, and Sarah Reckhow, in *Outside Money in School Board Elections*, looked at how income inequality in the US has increased the political influence of the wealthiest Americans. The authors found that even before the *Citizens United* decision in 2010 opened the spigot of dark money spending in political campaigns, "contributions from the top 0.01 percent of households began in the 1990s and grew steadily through the 2000s." They also cited data from the Center for Responsive Politics showing that "the total cost of congressional elections grew from $2.3 billion in 2000 to $4 billion in 2016 (adjusted for inflation)."[45]

Their analyses, like Cunningham's, looked at how billionaires across the political spectrum have donated to education causes in ways that concealed their political agendas from the public. Cunningham drilled down into campaigns seeking to lift the cap on the number of charter schools permitted to open in Massachusetts that featured families of color to make ballot questions appear to be grassroots efforts. In fact, by tracing the money he found that campaigns often hired firms to collect signatures, canvas, and phone-bank. It was very much a professional job. So there is a long-standing precedent for people with money using their dollars, sometimes in deceptive ways, to support their favored approaches to educational challenges.

What we have now is a somewhat different matter—even though at first glance it may look similar. Today, the spending is not about seeking better school performance for the underserved. It is not about a philosophical divide over how to address educational access, quality, or outcomes. Rather, the money aims to draw school board elections into the same antidemocratic partisan ground fight that is infecting state legislatures and, of course, Congress. The push for charters and vouchers uses the tactics that Cunningham identified to remove taxpayer dollars from public schools under the guise of "choice" for low-income students.

This very issue of outside interests and money—well chronicled by Jane Mayer in the *New Yorker* and David Pepper in his book *Laboratories of Autocracy*—is why legislators from gerrymandered districts pass bills that a majority of people in their states oppose. That is the threat to local school boards: when the concerns of the people in a local community are less important than the far-right agenda that has been legislated at the state level.[46]

As Jacob M. Grumbach, an assistant professor of political science at the University of Washington, put it in his book, *Laboratories Against Democracy: How National Parties Transformed State Politics*, the rising power of state governments has "collided with nationalized party coalitions, supported by highly coordinated networks of political organizations, national media, and a racially sorted electorate" that are reshaping the landscape for Americans.[47]

Noting the likelihood of politically similar states to emulate one another's legislative moves, he sees state government power as a threat to democracy. "The nationalization of the parties has upended the role of states as 'laboratories of democracy' that customize policy based on local conditions, converting Republican states in particular to laboratories *against* democracy," he argues. He notes that "state governments are playing a greater role in the lives of their residents," economically and socially, than they did a generation ago, yielding broader differences in "how much you pay in taxes as a millionaire," "how generous your welfare state is," and "your ability to obtain an abortion, use marijuana, or own a gun."

To do his research, Grumbach created a tool to analyze the level of democracy in each state, using sixty-one variables that included such factors as policy responsiveness to public opinion, gerrymandering, voting registration laws, and voting wait times. He found that states with Republican leadership have seen a steep decline over the past decade or more in levels of democracy in state government. The big problem, he observes, is that instead of looking at what policies work, elected officials look to political parties to signal what will help them win.[48]

This same mindset has taken root in public school boards. Because schools are where parents gather and their children's education is a focus of a lot of parental emotion, the far-right has through state leaders and political networks deployed the Republican Party's extreme political vocabulary to manipulate them into mistakenly believing that their children are in danger. One hears the same phrases repeated over and over. This is not to ignore the failings of public education. But the fears being hyped—of children being "indoctrinated with Marxist ideologies" and sexually "groomed," among other claims—are utter fabrications.

Wealthy education reformers once sought to use education PACs to see their theories of school improvement realized. Today, far-right power brokers are using political PACs both to elect far-right candidates to school boards and to activate them as members of a national far-right network. It is ingenious, given that there are some 82,423 elected school board members in the US, probably the largest single category of elected officials in the country. Their influence is powerful; they serve 13,194 school districts responsible for 56.6 million public school students.[49]

It may be hard to believe now, but in the recent past, some school board elections have been uncontested; seats were left unfilled. Now, according to Ballotpedia, which follows school board elections in 470 districts, including the 200 largest (by student enrollment), the percentage of unopposed school board seats in the nation's 100 largest districts fell from 40 to 24 percent between 2018 and 2021. Incumbents won between 51 and 61 percent of seats each year. And when incumbents sought reelection, between 79 and 89 percent won each year.[50]

But other data reveal a contentious landscape. Despite the fact that most school boards are nonpartisan posts, as of October 2022, Ballotpedia identified 1,331 districts in 49 states in which candidates took stances on controversial issues with strong political overtones. Those included the role of race in curricula, responses to Covid (including mask mandates), and issues of sex and gender identity in schools.[51] In reality, many school board races are becoming nonpartisan in name only, as money pours into campaigns of candidates whose views align with funders'. Of course, several states have recently voted to let school board races actually be partisan (candidates run as members of a political party). One of them is Tennessee.

"A COUNTY DIVIDED"

By the time Nancy Garrett was appointed to the Williamson County School Board in November 2016, political divisions were already well-entrenched in the district, just south of Nashville. Garrett had been tapped to fill the vacancy created when Susan Curlee resigned in August 2016. Curlee had been among a group of candidates favored by a local Tea Party–aligned group; her 2014 race was aided by the Tennessee chapter of Americans for Prosperity, a political lobbying group founded by Charles and David Koch.[52] The group was a 501(c)(4) nonprofit, which means that it could not donate to or seek votes for candidates.

But in the summer of 2014, the Tennessee chapter, known as the 9-12 Project, found a way around the rules. The chapter's head, Andrew Ogles, told *The Tennessean* that it spent $500,000 in six weeks with the goal of "bringing the issues with the Common Core to light in Tennessee." That spending included supporting four Williamson County school board candidates, but the trick was that voters were not asked to cast ballots for them. Rather, framing the Common Core as federal overreach, the group sent out mailers that asked voters, according to the news story, to *thank* the four candidates for their efforts to "stop Obama's radical agenda." (Each ran on an anti-Common Core platform.)[53]

Another mailer asked, "Should Obama exert even more control over our schools?" The same story in *The Tennessean* noted that "different versions had board candidates [Beth] Burgos, Dan Cash, Susan Curlee and Candy Emerson each saying no. All four won their races." And in a phrase that should have been a warning, Ogles proclaimed, "This is just the beginning."[54]

The Americans for Prosperity effort unfolded amid rising opposition to the Common Core.[55] The Common Core standards were created starting in 2009 by teachers, education researchers, content experts, and state policy advisers (along with public feedback) as a guide of what students should learn in each subject and grade level each year. They flowed from a goal to give all students, regardless of zip code, access to learning that would ready them for college or career upon graduation. Given the long-standing tug of war between federal and local control over education, however, the Common Core was soon vilified as federal intrusion and a "one-size-fits-all" approach, which especially energized the far right.

The Common Core was made an issue in the Williamson County school board races in 2014. But states—not local communities—are the ones that voted on adopting it (Tennessee did but dropped the Common Core in 2015). Generally, key curricula and standards are decided at the state level, which is why state legislatures have become an education battleground. Despite Tennessee's adoption of the Common Core, during an October 2014 meeting, the newly seated Williamson County School Board voted 12–0 to stand "in support of locally derived educational standards and decision making."[56]

It was purely a symbolic vote. Yet over the next eighteen months, new board members sought changes that got people riled up. They proposed changing what was labeled "semester break" in the district's school calendar to "Christmas and New Year Holiday." They proposed having prayer rather than a moment of silence at school board meetings. Neither proposal passed.

"There also was a proposal to allow teachers and the public to review state tests and classroom materials for religious bias, and concerns that an art history textbook did not show American history in a positive enough light," according to a story in *The Tennessean*. "The proposals yielded little or no change."[57]

There was so much political posturing, that, as one parent put it at a school board meeting on January 20, 2015, every time the Williamson County

Schools were mentioned on the nightly news, "I half expect the story to lead with circus music playing in the background."[58]

By the time Curlee resigned in August 2016, she had had a rocky tenure. Local news outlets described her as "controversial." She had been criticized for using the word "retard" on social media, had called for the resignation of the Williamson County director of schools, and had filed suit against Williamson Strong, a local parent group, which she charged was acting as an unregistered political action committee. (The group was fined, appealed the decision, and was then found not in violation of election rules.)[59]

Curlee was also named in a threatened lawsuit after improperly reacting to a fight at Heritage Middle School. The district paid a $36,500 settlement to the plaintiff. There was, of course, more, including petitions and reprimands proposed against various people, plus "Williamson Secrets," a gossipy, anonymous tell-all on *Medium* that included damning emails and tweets by board members, including Curlee, and local political figures. It revealed a community both highly engaged and in conflict.[60]

This was the world that Garrett entered. As a professional well versed in corporate communication and governance as a result of her day job, Garrett was a steadying force. She is not impulsive nor prone to going with her gut. She does her homework. Yet she is outgoing and interacts warmly with people she encounters in public. Garrett was built for local politics.

The Williamson County schools are a source of local pride, yet there are issues requiring leadership. In 2019, the district made national news after two teachers created a classroom activity in which students pretended to be slave owners. In the summer of 2020, problems with racial harassment and bullying of LGBTQ+ students came to light when students described hundreds of alleged discriminatory incidents on an Instagram site, @dearestWCS.

In February 2021, the district commissioned a firm called Fostering Healthy Solutions to lead diversity, equity, and inclusion workshops, evaluate district culture, and provide a plan. At the same time a group of parents founded a group, One WillCo, to focus attention on racial issues in the district. When the Fostering Healthy Solutions report was issued in the summer of 2021, it pointed out the existence of contradictory sentiments: "support for diversity initiatives, opposition to Critical Race Theory, praise for their voices being heard, and a push to stop diversity efforts immediately." The report concluded that "multiple perspectives exist" and that they "manifest into the current culture of WCS, a county divided."[61]

That division has not gone away. It has shown up, for example, as battles over masking and curriculum. In fact, two months after the state legislature in May 2021 passed a law to withhold funds from schools that teach about white privilege, the Moms for Liberty Williamson County chapter became the first in the state to file a formal grievance. They challenged the district's use of the state-approved Wit & Wisdom language arts curriculum, claiming that it violated the "anti-CRT" law.[62]

The divisions reached an apex on August 10, 2021, during a special meeting at which the board set Covid protocols for the start of the school year. One year later, Garrett sat at the dining room table in the modest, well-kept brick home that she shares with her husband, a hospital administrator, and recalled the nearly four-hour meeting. "It was traumatic," she said. "It was a horrible, horrible night and a horrible night for our community."[63]

Video of the evening went viral, attracting national and international attention, including mention by President Biden.[64] People had lined up two hours before the 6 p.m. meeting. The room with its upholstered auditorium-style seating facing the semicircular wood-paneled dais where board members sat, each with a desktop computer and microphone, quickly filled to capacity. People brought signs. Those unable to enter stood outside and chanted, "No More Masks!" There were thirty public speakers. Some parents and health-care workers spoke in favor of masking (case numbers had spiked in the schools and region). Others spoke in opposition.

The anti-mask attendees were vocal, interrupting with clapping and outbursts despite Garrett's gaveled reminders for quiet. Security escorted several people from the meeting. Just prior to the vote, Garrett stated that there were many with strong views who did not feel safe attending a crowded meeting. She had received a flood of emails and had tallied them. Garrett then unfurled a scroll of attached papers and shared the results: she had heard from 781 individuals wanting the board to approve a mask mandate and from 348 opposing it.

The board voted 7–3 to require masks in elementary schools where students were too young to be vaccinated, but only through September 21. Protestors erupted in anger, creating a chaotic scene. In the parking lot, chants of "Will not comply!" rose up. Video captured protestors threatening health-care workers who had supported masking as they tried to reach their cars, saying "We know who you are," "We will find you!," and "You'd better watch out!" Law enforcement officials gingerly parted the mob so that the workers could exit in their cars.[65]

NANCY GARRETT'S GAMBLE

Election Day, August 4, 2022, was sultry and hot. Temperatures reached 90 degrees. As I stood with Garrett in the parking lot of the massive white Church of the City, the conveniently located polling place not far from the Murfreesboro Road, I saw her grappling with the reality of her decision to run as an unaffiliated candidate in this newly partisan race.

As Garrett waved her cerulean blue campaign sign overhead, she told me that this was her "Liz Cheney moment." She greeted voters, many by name. Several sauntered over to chat. She offered to help with an effort to secure a playing field for a school's club lacrosse team. She asked after children. Some gave her a hug; others a hopeful "Good luck" or "I voted for you."

But the challenge was right there in plain sight. She spotted others who wanly waved from a distance or made quick small talk and slipped away. People she had known for years had turned their backs, people whose allegiance to party, she discovered, mattered more than her competence or her dedication to the schools and the community. Or their relationship.

Across from the grassy island where we stood, pop-up tents of poll workers for various Republican candidates, including her opponent, held signs in a kind of team effort. County commissioners, state representatives, and judges were also being elected. At other polling places, there were sample Republican ballots. Here, they held signs with the names stacked one atop another to simplify the task for those heading into the air-conditioned space to vote: Just go straight Republican.

It was a message that Garrett and her volunteers, who included retired teachers, church and community friends, and even a former school board member, had been working feverishly to counter. This was about that most precious public good, the schools. Garrett is an active voice on social media; she received scores of endorsements that she posted on Facebook.

The overall race for school board had been contentious. Garrett's opponent had received donations from prominent Republicans, including $2,500 from Senator Marsha Blackburn, according to campaign filings, but during the campaign he had kept a low profile, said little, and declined to join a League of Women Voters forum. That kept Garrett from being able to participate.[66]

The most contentious race was between Eric Welch, a wiry veteran and father of two, who had served alongside Garrett and was also seeking re-election, and William "Doc" Holladay. Holladay sought to frame as lessons learned a troubled past that included addiction and rehab plus indictments on nine counts of prescription drug fraud and four counts of forgery.

Welch ran as a Republican; Holladay ran as an independent—but was clearly not happy about it. He was endorsed by Moms for Liberty, and during the campaign relentlessly attacked Welch as a "RINO." At one point he posted on Facebook that Welch "has tested positive for Covid, but reportedly tested negative for being a conservative or a Republican." Meanwhile, Holladay positioned himself as the real conservative in the race—and also, according to his campaign banner, a "Patriot."[67]

As the polls closed, Garrett and her volunteers gathered in downtown Franklin on the top floor of the Americana Taphouse. The loft-like space was decorated with red, white, and blue balloons. There was a buffet with chicken wings and hot snacks, pitchers of iced tea, and a cash bar. As the night wore on, before results were in, Garrett went around the room, sharing nicknames ("Mother Teresa") and expounding on the virtues of each person present by name. The crowd included Republicans, Democrats, neighbors, the president of the Chamber of Commerce, a friend from elementary school, and her nephew Brannon, a college student who was her campaign manager.

Welch arrived with his wife, Andrea. Like everyone there, he kept peering into his phone in anticipation of election returns. The early voting results were tallied and released first. The news was good for Welch: he was ahead in his three-way race, with 47 percent of votes, and would easily go on to win when the day-of votes were counted. But Garrett was ten percentage points behind in early voting. She was experienced enough to know that it didn't look good. She would lose by eighteen percentage points when all the votes were tallied.

Every other incumbent school board member was reelected. Every single office on the ballot went to a Republican. There had been election nonsense like yard-sign stealing and people posting other signs next to Garrett's and Welch's signs that read, "Voted to mask your child."

Welch said the election result was not about Garrett's performance as board chair. "This is simply about her having the wrong letter at the end of her name," he said, as the evening wrapped up. "Had she had an 'R' at the end of her name, she would have run away with it. Would have been a shoo-in. But it was a matter of principle for her," he said, and sighed. "So, those are the results."

The next day Garrett was up early. She had made arrangements to volunteer at a school, which she had done on a regular basis for years. When I met her back at her home, we sat again at the dining-room table. She wore her official black-collared polo shirt embroidered with the phrase "Be Nice" and "Williamson County Schools" in red stitching. Her lanyard with her official WCS badge still hung around her neck. Over sandwiches she walked through it all.

"It feels like a betrayal," she admitted. "I knew that it would be a more challenging road for me as a nonpartisan candidate, but I did not anticipate that people who supported me would not come alongside me based on my record of service and my work ethic." It hurt, but she would not have done it differently, she said.

It is hard to know what Garrett's loss really means. Turnout was about 20 percent of registered voters. There were a lot of races on the ballot. Was this a meaningful rejection? Or voter laziness? Confusion? Just vote for every Republican on the ballot? Garrett has long been an active and informed voter. But not everyone is.

One of her suspicions is that as education issues get politicized at the state level, inserting party politics into school boards is "designed to weaken public education so that all these people who run with a party affiliation will not stand up when things come from the state that you know are not good for our high-performing district. It's all about weakening public education."

Ken Chilton, an associate professor of public administration at Tennessee State University who also ran for school board as an independent and lost by a wide margin, noted the big wins up and down the ballot by far-right candidates. Christian nationalism, he observed, "is growing here."

CHAPTER 3

WHEN LIBRARIANS COME UNDER ATTACK

A S A SCHOOL LIBRARIAN with over two decades of experience, Lindsey Kimery was incredulous at where she found herself, and what she was hearing. On March 2, 2022, she was seated at a long walnut-colored table with a spindly black microphone arching toward her as she faced members of the Tennessee House Criminal Justice Subcommittee.

Kimery, the coordinator of library services for Metro-Nashville Public Schools, past president of the Tennessee Association of School Librarians, and, at the time, the cochair of the association's legislative task force, was there to testify against HB 1944. The bill, its sponsor, Representative Scott Cepicky, explained in his opening remarks, would remove an exemption for K–12 schools from state laws governing the possession or distribution of "pornographic or obscene materials" to minors. The bill's effect was that teachers and school librarians could face criminal charges for possession of books deemed inappropriate. They could face fines, convictions, even prison time if found guilty. What's more, said Cepicky, the state would create only a "skeletal process" that "will fill in from the local level," letting school boards be the arbiters of appropriate content. "I can't think of anybody better to represent the community standards," he said. Then, in a puzzling twist that undercut his point, he said reporting and compliance mechanisms would require that books found in violation be reported to the Department of Education, and then removed from schools statewide.

When the Tennessee Senate took up its version of the bill, its sponsor, Senator Joey Hensley, introduced it as "dealing with obscenity and pornography in the school libraries," stating this issue as an established fact. A representative from Governor Bill Lee's office suggested the bill might run into conflicts with the US Constitution. Later in the debate, Senator London Lemar, from Memphis, noting the potential constitutional issue, made a motion to send the bill to "summer study," effectively killing it with a 6–3 vote.[1]

What was striking about the bill—and the hours and attention it consumed in both chambers—was how willing legislators were to consider applying criminal consequences to educators and librarians; and how easily they ignored the fact that the law sought to censor and limit access to books with racial and LGBTQ+ themes. Many who testified quoted or paraphrased the Bible. One expounded on the dangers of pornography.

Just before Kimery testified, Andrew Maraniss, a *New York Times* bestselling author and one of the few to speak against the bill, also cited the Bible, but he offered an alternative to what had become a common practice of far-right activists at school board meetings: reading lurid lines from books they wanted banned. Maraniss read from the Bible, Ezekiel 23:20–21: "There she lusted after her lovers whose genitals were like those of donkeys and whose emission was like that of a horse. So, you longed for the lewdness of your youth, when in Egypt your bosom was caressed and your young breasts fondled."[2]

It didn't take much imagination to see his point. "Would anyone argue that the Bible is a work of pornography? Certainly not," he said. "So, let's not cherry-pick."

By contrast, Kimery's testimony was plain. She gave a dry explanation of fact and experience. She reminded representatives that the 1982 Supreme Court decision in *Island Trees Union Free School District v. Pico* found that students' First Amendment rights limited school officials' ability to remove school library books on the basis of their content.[3]

Then she pointed out that HB 1944 proposed "a solution we already have." There are existing processes for reconsidering library materials, she said. "Despite careful selection of library resources and the qualifications of those involved in the selection process, objections to library resources that are deemed offensive or inappropriate may occur." There are steps to follow. In years as a school librarian when a parent raised a concern, "We were able to work together to meet the needs of their child and no further action was needed."

Kimery, who "grew up in the Southern Baptist church," offered something that has eluded politicians. She was talking about working through differences. She shared how she responded to an objection and found a solution. That is no longer what is happening in Tennessee and many other states. Rather, legislatures and school boards are passing laws or local policies to censor and control materials in libraries and classrooms that they don't personally like.

And they have done it in a clunky way, like Cepicky's "skeletal process," that lets politicians score political points for "protecting" children. HB 1944 died, but a similar bill became law in Missouri in August 2022.[4] In Tennessee, the Age-Appropriate Materials Act of 2022 did pass, as did one on "obscene materials" in K–12 online resources, which followed a so-called "anti-CRT law" passed during the previous session.[5] Bills similar to HB 1944 were introduced in Indiana, Idaho, and Iowa during the 2021–2022 legislative session. None passed, but in 2023, many more such bills were introduced seeking to hold librarians (and in some cases, teachers) criminally responsible for "pornographic" books in their collections. In Florida, a 2022 law took a slightly different tack, but with a similarly chilling effect. The "curriculum transparency" law—part of Governor Ron DeSantis's "Year of the Parent"—requires that all library and classroom books be reviewed by a certified media specialist to ensure that no content is "pornographic" or "inappropriate for the grade level." It drove some teachers to remove or cover classroom libraries; librarians were required to undergo state training to instruct them on curation of collections (already required as part of their professional graduate training). But the new state training instructs them to remove books that include prohibited subjects such as race, social justice, culturally responsive teaching, and Social Emotional Learning.[6] This new climate has teachers and librarians fearful, confused, and stressed. Some have quit or lost their jobs doing what they believed was right, often by protecting students' First Amendment rights.

"Right now," Kimery told me, "I have an email I need to respond to from a librarian in east Tennessee who is in a district where the elementary-school assistant principal told the librarian to remove any books that mentioned LGBTQ because 'that is the new state law.' There is a lot of misinformation and a lack of support and fear of backlash."

People become librarians because they love to read, Kimery said. "There is no hidden agenda other than that reading was my favorite thing." Having books by, about, and for LGBTQ+ students "does not mean we are out there promoting it. It just means we have books for those readers, too. What I try to convey is that a library is a place for voluntary inquiry."

Kimery, the mother of four boys, does not restrict what her own children read. "I just want them to read and get off [video] games," she said. "I let them navigate it. I have told them, 'You are welcome to check out anything in the library that interests you. If there is anything that comes up, I would love to talk about that with you.' I am not going to set any parameters. That is a key part of helping kids grow up into successful adults, letting them explore, but letting them know you are here if they need you or if they have a question."

KRAUSE'S LIST

It is unclear how the latest book ban fervor got started. Certainly, a former Texas state representative, Matt Krause, deserves some of the credit.

On October 25, 2021, using his position and powers as chair of the Texas House Committee on General Investigating (yes, there is such a body), Krause sent a letter to the Texas Education Agency and to school districts listing some 850 books. He demanded that districts (1) identify how many copies of each title they possessed and where they were located, including which campuses and classrooms; (2) say how much the district spent to acquire the books; and (3) identify books not on his list that dealt with topics such as AIDS, sexually transmitted diseases, or other subjects that "might make students feel discomfort, guilt, anguish, or any other form of psychological distress because of their race or sex or convey that a student, by virtue of their race or sex, is inherently racist, sexist, or oppressive, whether consciously or unconsciously."[7]

Districts had until November 12, less than a month, to respond. Not surprisingly, this alarmed librarians. At the time, Mary Woodard, president of the Texas Library Association, was also in charge of school libraries in the Mesquite ISD. She recalled receiving the letter. "I was actually at home. My superintendent forwarded it to me. It was in the evening," she said. "I just felt a cold chill. I was beyond shocked that somebody from our state government was asking what books were available in our school libraries. I never thought I would see anything like that."[8]

Krause also wanted to know which books were in classroom libraries (in addition to school libraries). Unlike librarians, who are trained to select and update collections and advise students, Woodard told me, teachers "buy things they think their kids will like." She was also puzzled by the language about "discomfort," which echoed the so-called "anti-Critical Race Theory law" that went into effect in Texas in September 2021. The challenge, she said, is that such a measure is very subjective and wide-ranging and therefore difficult to apply to books. "What causes discomfort for one person may not cause it for another," she said.

Like librarians around the state, Woodard was quickly called into a meeting with her superintendent. "We talked about what we were going to do," she said. Ultimately, they gathered the information Krause asked for, but decided not to send it unless it was specifically requested. It wasn't. "We never did anything with that information," said Woodard.

The lack of follow-up by Krause was interesting, to say the least. Krause has repeatedly refused to say how he compiled the list or what he was trying to accomplish. But it doesn't take much creativity to see that it may have been a ploy to appeal to far-right voters. Around the time the letter gained attention, Krause was running for state attorney general. He failed to make it onto the Republican ballot in March 2022, but then instead decided to run for district attorney in Tarrant County as a "Faithful, Conservative Fighter," according to his campaign website. He lost that Republican primary on May 24, 2022, and his legislative term ended on January 10, 2023.[9]

In fact, the list was probably the most newsworthy thing he did as a state legislator—it caught fire. It certainly got a boost from Governor Greg Abbott, who around that time called on the Texas Education Agency to launch criminal investigations into the availability of "pornographic books" in school libraries.[10] Suddenly, Krause's list was a state resource and was being discussed in the national media. Some of the writer Andrew Solomon's books were on the list, prompting him to write an essay titled "My Book Was Censored in China. Now It's Blacklisted—in Texas." Solomon, also a professor at Columbia University and a lecturer at Yale, wrote, "Finding my work thus blacklisted disturbingly evoked a childhood during which I was shunned and abused for being gay, in which I felt ashamed, defenseless, sad and epically vulnerable. I had written my book to help people, and now it was being held up as derelict and unpatriotic."[11]

Actually, Krause's list was quite sloppy. Media outlets dove into specifics and unearthed a ridiculous assemblage. Danika Ellis of *Book Riot*, a podcast and website about books and reading, sifted through the entire list. Among the problematic titles were books about teen rights. "To be clear," wrote

Ellis, "I'm not even counting books about reproductive rights or your rights as an LGBTQ person in particular." Krause had included *The Legal Atlas of the United States* and *We, the Students: Supreme Court Cases for and About Students*.

Of course, books that mention LGBTQ+ students or are about sexuality (even from the 1970s) or race were well represented. But there was a lot that was puzzling. "Almost one in five of the books listed, I have no idea why they're included," wrote Ellis. "They're average YA novels (with no LGBTQ content), as far as I can tell, or they're nonfiction about innocuous topics. Probably the one that has me the most stumped is '*Inventions and Inventors*' by Roger Smith from 2002. What's controversial about a book on inventions??"[12]

Other outlets shared similar head-scratching reactions. The *Dallas Observer* named their "10 most absurd" books on the list, including *The Year They Burned the Books*, by Nancy Garden; *Wonder Woman Unbound: The Curious History of the World's Most Famous Heroine*, by Tim Hanley; and *The Gale Encyclopedia of Medicine*, by Jacqueline L. Longe. Yet many educators treated the list like an instructional manual. Chris Tackett, a political campaign finance expert, tweeted a photo of a man in a hoodie leaving the high school library in Granbury Independent School District pulling a dolly of cardboard boxes labeled "Krause's List."[13]

It turned out that Granbury ISD's superintendent, Jeremy Glenn, was eager to comply, as a leaked audio recording showed. He gathered librarians in January 2022 and told them that students didn't need access to books about sexuality or transgender people. A secret recording of the meeting was shared by the Texas Tribune–ProPublica Investigative Unit and *NBC News*. It revealed a stunning disregard for students' First Amendment rights. Yet when Glenn addressed the librarians, there was clearly no room for disagreement.[14]

Glenn started by stating that school board trustees had been in touch with him. "I want to talk about our community," he said in a firm but syrupy drawl. "If you do not know this, you have been probably under a rock, but Granbury is a very, very conservative community and our board is very, very conservative." He warned, "If that's not what you believe, you'd better hide it because it ain't changing in Granbury. Here, in this community, we will be conservative." He then detailed what that meant, including not having books about sexuality or LGBTQ+ or "information on how to become transgender." Then, Glenn revealed his personal discomfort with gender-fluid individuals, saying, "I will take it one step further with you and you can disagree if you want. There are two genders. There's male and there's female. And I acknowledge that there are men that think they are women and women that think they are men. And I don't have any issues with what people want to believe, but there is no place for it in our libraries."

He told librarians that he was forming a review committee of parents and educators and that "we are going to pull books off the shelves, especially the 850 books that were put forth by what [sic], Representative Krause. We will pull any of those books from the library plus any we feel that don't conform." He finished with a directive that camouflaged the seriousness of what he asked them to do. "When in doubt, pull it. Let the community sign off on it, put it back on the shelf. You're good to go."

CONTROVERSIAL COLLECTIONS

Books and reading materials have always upset people. In fact, discomfort seems to be partly the point of publishing books. Not surprisingly, the matter of what should and may be included in school libraries has long been a source of contention, often influenced by the political climate of the time.

In "School Boards, School Books and the Freedom to Learn," published in the *Yale Law Journal* in 1950, amid the fervor of McCarthyism, the authors wrote that book burning had experienced "a modern revival. Its new setting is an American public school where the local school board is playing Censor with controversial ideas in books and magazines." The situation it outlines (it wasn't a legal case) is interesting—and has some resonance today. After *The Nation* published articles critical of Roman Catholic church doctrine and dogma, the New York City Board of Education at its meeting on June 24, 1948, "without hearing or notice," voted to remove *The Nation* from school libraries.[15]

Notably, the board did not remove issues containing the offending articles but voted not to include the politically left magazine on future lists of approved periodicals. Over the next several years, as the board repeatedly refused to reinstate the magazine, *The Nation* appealed twice, unsuccessfully, to successive bodies, one of them the state department of education. The acting state commissioner, Dr. Lewis A. Wilson, said the school board "has not merely the right to determine the periodicals to which it will subscribe or accept for deposit"—*The Nation* offered a free subscription—but also a responsibility to use its best judgment to determine what would best benefit "the educational welfare of its pupils."[16]

Was it censorship, as the *Yale Law Journal* and *The Nation* defense suggested? Libraries cannot subscribe to every periodical. The schools did not remove existing materials but chose not to include new issues. *The Nation* at the time declared it would pursue the matter further, but there is no evidence that it did so, leaving us without a more final resolution.

Yet the example hits on a problem in public school libraries today. We have seen the push to remove materials already on the shelves in the library. But there is also the question of what should be included in the first place. Did removing *The Nation* also remove an important viewpoint?

Already, there are signs that rather than face controversy, some librarians simply choose not to purchase some books. A book survey that was labeled "controversial" conducted by *School Library Journal* in Spring 2022 received input from 720 school librarians, 90 percent of them from public schools (all were anonymous). It found that 97 percent said they weighed the impact of controversial subjects when making purchases. "The presence of an LGBTQIA+ character or theme in a book led 29 percent of respondents to decline a purchase," the survey report said. Forty-two percent admitted removing a "potentially problematic" book that had not faced challenge or review.[17]

Such forms of "soft" censorship are concerning. School library collections include books that complement what's taught in classrooms. But they must also support independent reading and personal learning, said Kathy Lester, president of the American Association of School Librarians and a librarian at East Middle School in Plymouth, Michigan. That means having books that "serve that full population with different backgrounds, needs, and interests," she said. "It is really important that we do that."

Yet, doing so has become charged. Lester, who spoke with me during a break from her state's annual conference for school librarians at the Kensington Hotel in Ann Arbor, said there was a lot of talk about book bans. "I just came from a session that was from a school district that has received challenges," she said. When leaders asked who had faced challenges, hands flew up, she said. "And if they haven't received challenges, they are concerned" that they will.

What worried Lester, who said librarians are facing attacks on social media and having criminal reports filed against them, is the impact on students. It is not only about the need for LGBTQ+ and students of color "to see themselves and feel affirmed" in library collections, but about other students seeing them as well. "If all they ever see are the same sorts of materials and books, what are they learning?" she asked. "How are they building that understanding of other cultures, of people different from them?"[18]

For years, of course, some students were not represented in books geared to their age group. As a young reporter in the early 1990s, I met with a high school student in Canton, Massachusetts, for a series I wrote for the *Patriot Ledger* on gay life in the suburbs. We met in the public library. I will never forget sitting across from this lanky, red-haired student as he told me he was starved for information. He said that he would look up the word "homosexual" in the dictionary to feel that he existed.

Although the conversation about book banning is often cast as "protecting" students from the harms of graphic or detailed information, it reinforces a narrow definition of human experience. It may exclude those seeking to understand themselves, not for a frame they fit, but for what they can bring to the world once they feel included.

OBJECTIONS REFLECT TIMES, PERSONAL VIEWS

Book banning is a chaotic and illogical business. How a book is received or understood is often subject to the historical moment—and the tastes of individuals. The notion of an objective measure or checklist to decide what is "appropriate"—something far-right school boards have worked to police and enforce—has long been slippery to define. In the late 1930s, the children's book *The Story of Ferdinand*, about a bull who would rather smell flowers than fight a matador, was interpreted as carrying a pacifist political message. But in a whirl of confusion, it was marked as both pro-Franco and anti-Franco—and also as "communist, anarchist, manic-depressive, and schizoid," according to an analysis of children's book censorship in the *Elementary School Journal* in 1970. In other words, everyone saw what they wanted to see.

That also happened to *Sylvester and the Magic Pebble*, a children's book by William Steig about a donkey who finds a magic pebble and, frightened by a lion, wishes himself into becoming a rock. The book also contained images of police officers dressed as pigs. In 1971, the International Conference of Police Associations took offense at that portrayal of police as pigs—"pig" being a derogatory term for law enforcement officers. Then, as now, some viewed it as problematic and requiring a response. According to the author of the journal article, school librarians who agreed with the police association view of the drawings and "considered [the portrayal] a political statement" pulled the books from their shelves in numerous cities, including Lincoln,

Nebraska; Palo Alto, California; Toledo, Ohio; Prince Georges County, Maryland; and several cities in Illinois.[19]

Books often get singled out because they make someone uncomfortable. Lately far-right activists have particularly objected to graphic images, including of intimate body parts. Which is what happened in the 1970s with Maurice Sendak's *In the Night Kitchen*, which I read to my kids many times. The problem was that the book included drawings of the toddler hero's penis on several pages. School and public libraries quietly devised a solution: They used white tempera to paint diapers on Mickey, the main character. At a meeting of the American Library Association in Chicago in June 1972, some 475 librarians, illustrators, authors, and publishers were outraged at the practice of painting over the penis and signed a petition denouncing it as a form of censorship.[20]

Books that involve drugs, violence, sex, and sexual orientation can attract fierce opposition, regardless of the intended message, literary merit, or value. Sometimes these books offer windows into other worlds and experiences, which in 1971 is exactly what bothered school board members and a few parents in a white middle-class section of Queens, New York City. The city's Community School District 25 voted to ban *Down These Mean Streets*, by Piri Thomas, in which the author shares his tough story of survival in Harlem as the dark-skinned son of Puerto Rican immigrants.

The five members of the school board who voted to ban the book did not have children in any public schools governed by the district.[21] At a meeting that drew some five hundred people and lasted for six hours, at which sixty-three attendees spoke, most objected to the ban. The few in support took offense at "vulgarities and descriptions of sexual acts." According to a *New York Times* account, "Book Ban Splits a Queens School District," the five school board members who favored the ban had been nicknamed "The Holy Five" or "The Faithful Five." Four of the five had run on a slate sponsored by the Home Schools Association, a support group for Catholic parents homeschooling their children. That slate of like-minded school board candidates foreshadowed present-day political practice at a time when this was notable and not the norm.

In a parallel to the present moment, some questioned the motives of the board members who voted for the ban, concerned that they were reflecting personal interests and not the district's, which was "confirmed when the board called for aid to nonpublic schools," the *New York Times* story said.

According to the story, board member Edna Turner, who actually had five children in the schools, opposed the ban. Turner called *Down These Mean Streets* "a beautiful book—full of feelings." It was "a learning tool" because "the author was willing to expose his gut feelings so that we could better understand the problems he faced. It promotes understanding."[22]

A few years later, in December 1975, the board of Community School District 25, composed of different and recently elected members, voted to repeal the ban. The board president said the new board considered the act of book banning "abhorrent" and "undemocratic."[23]

At the time the controversy erupted in Queens, Thomas's book, published in 1967, had been out for several years and had received positive reviews. It had also already sparked conflict elsewhere, stirring tensions between students and parents in the wealthy New York City suburb of Darien, Connecticut, and had been covered in the *New York Times*. Things were especially heated in the spring of 1969 after a parent, Mrs. Donald E. Hill, wrote a letter to the local paper, the *Darien Review*, with phrasing we might today see on social media. It began: "Darien parents wake up! Why are our seniors reading filth and smut purchased from the Darien High School?"[24]

It was designed to get attention—and did, spurring additional letters to the *Darien Review*. Thomas's memoir was among readings in a required course for seniors, "Contemporary Social Issues." Critics of the book appeared before the school board in February asking for it to be removed, but no action was taken. Yet tensions grew. (Sales also soared, it was constantly checked out of the library and, according to students, "almost everyone in the school has read it.")[25] Parents objected to the vulgar language and depictions of pot smoking and homosexuality. By April 1969, students had raised money and invited Thomas to Darien High School to meet with them. Said one student, "We're defending our right to know about things our parents refuse to recognize."[26] In his report on the visit in the *New York Times*, John Darnton wrote that Thomas "walked into a morning assembly period to a standing ovation, and remained for four hours, reading his poetry, answering questions and talking to large clusters of students, many of whom cut classes to hear his views on racism, slums, prisons, politics and literature." Later he spent hours more answering questions from parents. Students said they found Thomas "humorous" and "sarcastic." Said one student, "He really communicated, just like his book."

For his part, Thomas told Darnton, "It seemed like the adults were trying to put up a force field around their children to keep out the world. It's like living under glass. But maybe some of these students have found a glass cutter."[27]

BOARD OF EDUCATION, ISLAND TREES UNION FREE SCHOOL DISTRICT V. PICO

Thomas's book would also go on to play a role in a case on which the Supreme Court ruled in 1982. It began in September 1975, when several board members of the Island Trees Union Free School District on Long Island, New York, including its chair, Richard J. Ahrens, attended a weekend education conference in Watkins Glen, New York, organized by a far-right group, Parents of New York United, Inc. (PONY-U. Inc. for short).

At the gathering, Island Trees Union Free School District board members mixed with representatives from the Heritage Foundation and parents opposed to school desegregation in Boston, among other attendees. The keynote speaker, Genevieve Klein, a member of the New York State Board of Regents, advocated for adoption of a voucher system for education. She complained that other regents had not taken up this cause.

"If you are a parent who believes that reading, writing, spelling and arithmetic are basic tools necessary for developing into a contributing member of society, then you know that parental control is an immediate necessity," she told the group. "If there is to be any hope for saving another generation from becoming functional idiots the time to act is now."[28]

PONY-U. Inc. was not just a local group eager to talk about schooling. Headed by Janet Mellon, a far-right activist, the group had spent several years orchestrating opposition to sex education and human relations education in schools and to student busing across Upstate New York. In 1970 Mellon claimed in an interview with a reporter from the *Buffalo News* that PONY-U. had two thousand members. Yet books were top of mind leading up to Watkins Glen. A few weeks prior, on July 10, the group had hosted a talk titled "Book Censorship in Our Schools" at the Central Fire Station in Ithaca, New York.[29]

The Watkins Glen conference also came on the heels of one of the most violent and divisive school textbook battles in history. For six months in 1974 and 1975, bitter conflict had roiled West Virginia's Kanawha County after a new school board member, Alice Moore, sought the removal of textbooks that she found objectionable. She had won her seat by convincing voters that schools were "destroying our children's patriotism, trust in God, respect for authority and confidence in their parents."[30] Moore also mobilized other conservatives, locally and nationally, attracting Mel and Norma Gabler, education activists whose crusade against textbooks included specific instructions spurring conservatives to "excise the rot from the nation's schoolbooks," as Adam Laats writes in *The Other School Reformers: Conservative Activism in American Education*.[31] That "rot" included teaching evolution; communicating a "liberated" sexuality; "graphic accounts of gang fights; raids by wild motorcyclists; violent demonstrations against authority; murders of family members; of rape" and "books that denigrated traditional patriotic stories" in favor of popular subjects at the time, including Bob Dylan, Janis Joplin, Gertrude Ederle, Bobby Jones, Joan Baez, W. E. B. Du Bois, "and many others dear to liberal hearts."[32]

As protests in Kanawha County grew, others joined, and violence spread. Reverend Marvin Horand, a fundamentalist minister and former truck driver, called for school boycotts, arguing that "no education at all is 100 percent better than what's going on in the schools now. If we don't protect our children from evil, we'll have to go to hell for it."[33] The controversy ultimately resulted in two shooting deaths and multiple bombings. Reverend Horand was charged and ultimately found guilty in connection with the dynamiting of two elementary schools.[34] The Heritage Foundation was also on the ground, providing legal support and helping a local group hold a "series of 'Concerned Citizen' hearings on discontent with the public schools." Mellon of PONY-U. was one of their "expert" speakers.[35]

At the Watkins Glen conference—with the memory of Kanawha County still fresh—board members of the Island Trees Union Free School District received a list of thirty-two books described as "anti-American, anti-Christian, anti-Semitic and just plain filthy." A few months later, in February 1976, the board ordered the Island Trees Union Free School superintendent to remove eleven books from the district's junior and senior high schools, including nine from school libraries.[36]

The move stirred outrage, but the board held firm. In March, it defended the banning, claiming that the books contained "material which is offensive to Christians, Jews, blacks and Americans in general." Two of the books—*The Fixer*, by Bernard Malamud, and *Laughing Boy*, by Oliver La Farge—had won the Pulitzer Prize. At a press conference, school board member Frank Martin read aloud from *Slaughterhouse-Five* by Kurt Vonnegut, citing sentences in which Jesus is called a "bum" and a "nobody." Martin said that "even if the rest of the book was the best story in the world, I still wouldn't want it in our library with this stuff in it."

The other books were *Down These Mean Streets*, by Piri Thomas; *The Naked Ape*, by Desmond Morris (whom I would get to know when a new edition was published in 1986); *Soul on Ice*, by Eldridge Cleaver; *Black Boy*, by Richard Wright; *Best Short Stories of Negro Writers*, edited by Langston Hughes; *Go Ask Alice*, by an anonymous author; *A Hero Ain't Nothing but a Sandwich*, by Alice Childress; and *A Reader for Writers*, by Jerome Archer.[37]

Opposition to the ban grew. In April 1976, five hundred people jammed a local school board meeting to discuss it; it was estimated that speakers were "around 10 to 1 against the board." The board sought to sway audience members by distributing excerpts that board members found offensive. People objected, saying that it was important to read the whole book. Among the attendees were many juniors and seniors in high school. Said one, "These books are very tame. It's nothing you can't hear in the sixth-grade school bus."[38]

Nonetheless, the board upheld its decision. Then, several months later, in July 1976, the board again voted to continue the ban, excepting *Laughing Boy* and *Black Boy* from the list. At the July meeting, Ahrens, the board chair, said that the board "will not answer any of the questions on the merits of the books" posed by the audience. Board members had read the books and pronounced them "educationally unsound."[39]

By September 1976, the matter had attracted some notice, and Piri Thomas, the author of *Down These Mean Streets*, wrote an essay for the *New York Times* arguing for "the right to write and to read." In it, he mentioned the visit to Darien, noting students' "ignorance" of "life outside of their hothouses," but "their sincerity in wanting to learn." He also wrote about the banning in Queens. He quoted a youth who had told the board that if the book "is as dirty as you who are banning it say it is, please go down to the boys' and girls' bathrooms here in this school and you'll really see something dirty written on the walls."

In a message that resonates today, Thomas in his essay made a case for the tough truths he wrote about, explaining that the book "was not written to titillate but to bring forth a clarity about my growing up in El Barrio in the 1930's and 1940's." As long as that "truth" exists, he wrote, it is important for the book to stand. "Since the horrors of poverty, racism, drugs, the brutality of our prison system, the inhumanity toward children of all colors are still running rampant, let the truth written by those who lived it be read by those who didn't."[40]

When the books were first removed, Steven Pico, at sixteen, was vice president of the junior class and a member of the school newspaper's editorial board. The following year, as student council president and a liaison to Island Trees Union Free District Board of Education, he often attended school board meetings. In the midst of the ongoing debate, Pico attended a meeting organized by the American Library Association and decided to mount a challenge to the ban.[41]

At the time, however, most of his peers either did not support his position or were apathetic. Many were "preoccupied with getting into colleges" and didn't want to get involved with a controversial issue. Teachers "were worried about tenure and their jobs." Pico eventually connected with lawyers from the New York Civil Liberties Union. Four other students joined the suit, which was announced on January 4, 1977, at a press conference held at the Association of the New York City Bar Association. Vonnegut, who appeared at the press conference, exulted that bans helped book sales, but said, "As an American, I am distressed that this sort of thing can happen in my country."[42]

It took years for the case to make its way to the high court. Pico went off to college, spending about half of his weekends away from campus raising awareness about the dangers of censorship. He earned his BA from Haverford College in 1981. A little over a year later, on June 25, 1982, the Supreme Court handed down its decision.

The Court ruled that the First Amendment's guarantee of free speech limited the discretion of public school officials to remove books they considered offensive from school libraries. The *New York Times* ran its story on the ruling on page one. Linda Greenhouse, who covered the Supreme Court beat, noted that Bruce Rich, general counsel to the Freedom to Read Committee of the Association of American Publishers, "called the ruling 'marvelous' and said it 'sends a very important message to school boards: Act carefully.'"[43]

"THAT IS NOT HOW BOOKS WORK"

The decision in *Pico* was taken as a victory by those opposed to banning books in school libraries. But as Greenhouse's story also stated, it was a complicated win. It was a plurality ruling, which included a four-justice majority and two concurring opinions, that recognized school officials had violated students' rights when they removed library books they didn't like (it sidestepped the question of curricular authority).

"Our Constitution does not permit the official suppression of ideas," wrote Associate Justice William J. Brennan Jr. But, as Greenhouse noted, "The Court did not define the precise limits of the Constitutional right it recognized."

School board members in *Pico* wanted to remove books whose content they disapproved of; but what if books were removed as a result of a restrictive policy? Or if state legislatures or school boards passed rules that explicitly or implicitly restricted library materials? Would that run afoul of the law? Or would it provide cover for de facto book bans? What if a district made a process for approving books so onerous that it led to "soft" censorship in which librarians simply stopped ordering books with certain types of content?

These and other questions are playing out in real time across the country as parents and organizations battle over what should be allowed in school libraries. Keller ISD, near Fort Worth, Texas, is one district that has faced its share of controversy.

Even before Representative Matt Krause sent out his list of 850 books, before Governor Greg Abbott announced plans to investigate school libraries amid reports of "pornographic" books—he specifically targeted Keller ISD—librarians in the district were on the defensive. After the Texas Legislature passed House Bill 3979, "Relating to the Social Studies Curriculum in Public Schools," in June 2021 (to come into effect three months later), librarians started combing through their holdings. Did they contain books that violated the vaguely written law?[44]

The language of the law is so tangled, in its ban on race and sex-based concepts, that it would seem to require surgical-level care to include history topics that grapple with inequality or bias. Plus, it demands that no "individual should feel discomfort, guilt, anguish, or any other form of psychological distress on account of his or her race or sex," which is tough to control.[45] The bill had been dubbed "the anti-critical-race-theory law," even though it doesn't mention critical race theory. "It was the confusion of that bill that out of the gate had us at a disadvantage," said Audrey Wilson-Youngblood, who was at the time a key administrator and librarian in Keller ISD. "We were wanting to make sure that we were walking the line and following policy." For example, was Jason Reynolds's young readers' adaptation of Ibram X. Kendi's book *Stamped: Racism, Anti-Racism and You*, now illegal?[46]

On August 16, 2021, the superintendent announced a review of materials "to ensure compliance with House Bill 3979." Quickly, however, concerns shifted from race to sex and gender identity. Parents strode into school libraries stating that they wanted to check out books for younger siblings, said Wilson-Youngblood.[47] Others said things like "'Oh, I just want to come in and take a look. My daughter is having trouble finding something,' which to a librarian is like a dream," she said.

But then Wilson-Youngblood "started to hear from librarians about parents taking pictures of books on shelves." Soon, they confronted librarians with questions like "Did you know there was smut in your library?" Some threatened to file criminal charges. Library staff were on edge. Then a parent, Kathy May, tweeted graphic images from *Gender Queer: A Memoir*, a graphic novel by Maia Kobabe, and wrote, "Welcome to Keller ISD" where "legitimate visual porn, a felony offense, is in one of our libraries." In a story in the *Fort-Worth Star-Telegram* May was quoted as saying that she "moved here from California to get away from this."[48] In a companion tweet, May complained, "Our district has a ton of leftist teachers, librarians and counselors who push this plus SEL/CRT. It's literally a district run wild."[49]

It ignited a firestorm. The book—the most challenged in 2021—was removed from Keller ISD and from school libraries around the country in a move that has bewildered the author. (As of September 2022, it had been banned in forty-one school districts.)[50] Kobabe, writing in the *Washington Post*, said the book aimed to help young people struggling with the confusion of being nonbinary. Kobabe, who uses gender-neutral pronouns, came out as bisexual in high school, but "it took almost a decade to also come out" as "nonbinary, even though I had been questioning my gender identity since I started puberty at age 11."[51]

The graphic novel shows drawings of menstrual blood and sexual scenarios, including a strap-on fake penis. But the story *was not about* lusty, florid sex; in fact, it was nearly the opposite, and described a lack of sexual interest amid the stress of coming to terms with one's gender when it may not fit visible categories. Kobabe described details that other nonbinary youth may relate to, such as attending a San Francisco pride parade and "thinking that the asexual group HAD THE BEST SIGNS." She illustrated this with drawings of signs such as "Why Have SEX when you can have CAKE?" and "How About We Just CUDDLE?"[52]

Kobabe wrote that when she was asked "'What age of reader do you recommend this book for?' I would generally answer, 'High school and above,' but the truth is, the readers I primarily wrote it for were my own parents and extended family. When I was first coming out as nonbinary, I kept getting responses along the lines of, 'We love you, we support you, but we have no idea what you are talking about.'"[53] Supporters of the book have argued that it is a "lifeline for students" facing the same sense of confusion that Kobabe wrote and drew about.[54]

Gender Queer created an uproar in Keller ISD, but it was not the only book to be singled out for removal. The list of challenges included the graphic novel *Anne Frank's Diary: The Graphic Adaptation*, by Ari Folman and David Polansky (returned to circulation); *The Bluest Eye*, by Toni Morrison (removed from circulation); *Relish: My Life in the Kitchen*, by Lucy Kinsley (removed from circulation); *Flamer*, by Mike Curato (removed from circulation).[55]

As tensions rose during the 2021–2022 school year, Wilson-Youngblood found herself being harassed on social media and was made the target of a barrage of requests for information under the Texas Public Information Act. "It is one of their most debilitating weapons," she said. "It is masterful."[56] She was suddenly tied up responding to demands for all training materials, PowerPoints, notes, agendas, and materials that she had supplied to Keller librarians, from August 2021 to February 2022. Plus, attendance records for all librarians at all meetings.

By spring 2021, after serving the district for nineteen years, she resigned. "My health and well-being and my family's well-being was not worth the trauma of what I was choosing to endure," she said when we spoke over Zoom a few weeks after she left her job.

Wilson-Youngblood told me that it became impossible "to unravel legitimate concerns" from "attacks and the misinformation and the mal-information being presented in this big bundle of knots of nerves and pain." What she noticed was that "the ones who are most passionate" in raising concerns about books "are not readers or they have not had that experience of losing themselves in a book or connecting with characters not like themselves. They misunderstand that there can be more than one truth and that someone's truth can be different than your own," she said.

They also misunderstand how children and youths read. Just because someone reads about sex or drugs or foul language does not mean they will go out and mimic it. People have told her, "'I don't want a child to pick up this book and think it is OK to use that word,'" said Wilson-Youngblood. "That is not how books work."

NEW SCHOOL YEAR, NEW POLICY, NEW PROBLEMS

In April 2022, following on Governor Abbott's instruction from months earlier, the Texas Education Agency released new guidelines for how districts should avoid "obscene content" from entering school libraries. The guidelines lacked the power of law but were suggestions for districts, which urged them to involve parents in book selection and "encouraged" librarians to find out from parents if there were books that they did not want their child to read. It was a bid for wholesale changes in how books were acquired for school libraries, bypassing the graduate training that is part of being a librarian. It gave school boards made up of citizens elected for whatever reason to have final approval of new book purchases and to create a process for parents to object to specific books, even though a challenge process was already in place. The guidelines included the language of the Texas Penal Code §43.24(a)(2), which states that "no library material shall be used if it contains content that meets the harmful material standard." This language was a clear and political statement, and a not-so-veiled threat.[57]

In most states, K–12 schools and public libraries are typically exempt from obscenity laws; it is recognized that items that may clash with the language of those standards—art, biology, literature—involve creative and educational works that seek to deepen understanding of the human experience. In fact, removing that exemption was the goal of the failed Tennessee House Bill 1944. What happens when far-right activists apply standards of obscenity to art and books in which the intent is not prurience but insight? And who decides that?

Unsurprisingly, the Texas Library Association and the Texas Association of School Librarians (a division of the Texas Library Association) had something to say about the new guidelines. In a shared statement, the groups said, "The policies as outlined raise significant concerns" about the burden on librarians, superintendents, and school boards to read and review thousands of titles. That was the gentle part. It acknowledged the difficult task of honestly reviewing thousands of titles above and beyond other educational demands, especially for people who lack training as librarians. Basically, such a process means relying on the personal views of elected officials and other untrained people, which could sound like the very situation that got the Island Trees Free Union School Board in trouble.

The Texas Library Association statement also sought to remind people that the dispute over books was not about required reading for class assignments: people needed to understand the actual role libraries play. "School libraries are for *all* students but not all students are the same—they have diverse interests, abilities, and maturity levels, and varied cultural and socioeconomic backgrounds. The school library collection, developed by highly trained and educated certified school librarians with input from students, teachers, parents, and administrators, must be relevant to the students and campus it serves." The statement also pointedly rebuffed Abbott's charge, adding, "Furthermore, school libraries do not collect obscene content."[58]

In May 2022, in Keller ISD, three new school board members were elected who had been backed by the far-right Patriot Mobile Action PAC (created by the conservative cell-phone carrier Patriot Mobile), which took credit for flipping the board so that it had a far-right majority. This new board was only too happy to take up the rhetoric and task of removing "obscene content" from school libraries. On July 8, 2022, the board passed an updated book policy that largely mirrored the new state guidelines. During a board workshop, a new board member suggested rating books like films, affixing a color code to alert parents and librarians to concerning content. The far-right Keller ISD Standing Strong group later promoted this idea on its Facebook page. A veteran board member observed that students would quickly discern any secret color code.[59]

Then, on the eve of the 2022–2023 school year, there was an apparent book emergency in Keller ISD. The first day of school was August 17, and on August 16 principals received an email ordering them to remove forty-one titles from school libraries; some of them had previously been challenged and returned to shelves, whereas others, including *Gender Queer*, were long gone. The email, from Jennifer Price, the executive director of curriculum and instruction, said, "By the end of today, I need all books pulled from the library and classrooms. Please collect these books and store them in a location (book room, office, etc.)." She requested confirmation of receipt of the email, then added, "I apologize for the late request."[60]

The move made national news. Among books pulled were the Bible and *Anne Frank's Diary: The Graphic Adaptation*. The American Civil Liberties Union called on the board and school superintendent to return the books to the library shelves, stating that the districts should "not re-review books that have already gone through the challenge process" of acceptance into school collections and should "ensure that books remain on the shelves during review," as is standard practice. In a tweet, it warned that removing the books "is a violation of the First Amendment."[61]

The regularly scheduled school board meeting a few days later, on August 22, 2022, was packed, fiery, and long, going on for more than five and a half hours. Two hours of public comment—each speaker was allowed three minutes—were punctuated by clapping and whooping from both sides. Most of those speakers expressed outrage at the far-right board, including the re-review of books, at a proposal to lift a $50,000 cap on payments for outside legal counsel for the board, and at the move to institute prayer at the start of school board meetings, led by Christian pastors.

A few did stand up to praise the board. One read from the Bible and assured trustees, "You have a wall of people behind you." One mother stated, "It is my space to teach my child about sexuality and that there are two genders." She added that "it is now clear that extreme content is OK with some brainwashed parents who are spreading a socialist agenda."[62]

Several speakers opposed to the book removal commented on an op-ed that Sandi Walker, a newly elected far-right board member and board vice chair, had published a few days earlier in the *Dallas Express*, a conservative outlet, in which she described parents who opposed her as "the Woke mob." She cast herself as protecting children, charging that "nothing in the First Amendment requires minor children to read obscene, sexually explicit content. In fact, Texas's penal code forbids it. We are setting boundaries, not banning."[63]

One dad, a barrel of a man wearing a gray scaly cap with sunglasses dangling from the front closure of his white button-down shirt, approached the stand-alone mic and, referencing the op-ed, asked, "How can you honestly say that you want what's best for our kids when you despise a portion of our kids because of their beliefs, religious ideologies, goals and lifestyle choices? How can I as a parent trust that you will make mature and professional decisions?"

A Christian pastor from a local church said he "could not sit idly by" while the board passed policies that targeted LGBTQ+ individuals by removing books from the library. "I know some of you think you are protecting our kids, but the policies many of you are considering are harming our kids and perpetuating messages of hate," he said.

One of the most moving statements came from a high school senior named Cameron who said he was gay. In middle school he was told by peers that he "was too girly," that he was "a freak," and "I began to agree with them." He would sit alone at lunch and read a book from the library. Then, "I found a book about boys that felt the same way as I did. Soon, I found that feeling different is actually very normal." In high school he gained confidence. Now he saw harm in the removal of LGBTQ+ books. "The fact is that marginalized students in Keller ISD feel attacked by the school board," he said. "This pervasive censorship is about more than politics. It is about lives."

The public comments and meeting revealed a sharply divided community—and an elected board doing nothing to heal that divide. When it came time to vote on the new content guidelines by which books would be judged, votes fell along partisan political lines. The proposal passed 4–2 with one member abstaining because she found the content checklist confusing.

She was right—it is confusing. Books were now to be judged according to how often certain items appeared in the pages of a book, and ill-defined terms like "prevalent," "common," "some," or "minimal" would indicate which different amounts would be permitted at different age levels. Content would be judged and challenged according to the amount of profanity, kissing, horror, violence, bullying, drug or alcohol use by minors, drug use by adults, the glorification of suicide or self-harm or mental illness, brief descriptions of nonsexual nudity, and sexually explicit conduct or sexual abuse. Books would also be assessed on the basis of illustrations or descriptions of nude body parts, as well as passionate or extended kissing and detailed sex scenes or sexual activities.[64]

In discussing the content review guidelines at the board meeting, one veteran board member, Ruthie Keyes, puzzled over how to apply them. In talking about violence, "Are they talking about military combat?" She had spoken with teachers who estimated they would need to remove two-thirds of their classroom library books—"that's a lot. And none were talking about explicit sex scenes." And if an adult character smokes a cigar in a book, is that a strike or a disqualifier? She voted against the guidelines. In November the board would vote to add one more category to its restrictions: no books could mention or discuss "gender fluidity."[65]

As a result of the new policy, mirroring the new Texas Education Agency guidelines, books now face a more rigorous selection process that requires more layers of librarians to review books proposed for purchase. The books are then put on a list, which is open to review and challenge by members of the community for thirty days. Then the board must approve the purchase of each book. When the books are received, they are reviewed again by librarians. Once shelved, they can still be challenged and face review by a book challenge committee.

It did not take long for the new policy to have an effect. At the October 24, 2022, Keller ISD board meeting, Melissa Brewer, a librarian from the Bear Creek Intermediate School, made her way to the mic, her hair piled in a messy swirl, glasses affixed to her face, and paper in hand.

She spoke calmly and respectfully but was clearly burdened by the new policy, which she considered an affront to the training she and her peers had undergone. The board "has shown by its actions that Keller ISD librarians are not respected at all," she said. "We are not even allowed to order the newest *Diary of a Wimpy Kid* or the latest *Guinness World Records* unless the board gives express permission for those specific titles. We can't get any new nonfiction books about camels or squirrels or football without specific approval of the school board."[66]

Brewer described "a huge environment of fear" among librarians and a "an overwhelming climate of hopelessness among educators." She said librarians "are not even trusted to order a new alphabet book like *ABC Cats* for pre-K students." The result is that students keep asking why there are no new books in the library. Some of her biggest readers have resorted to re-reading books. Brewer said she tells students that books will be coming soon and makes excuses for the lack of new books. What she doesn't tell them is the truth: "I certainly don't mention the role that politics is playing in our libraries and our district."

But in a reminder that this *is* political, the far-right Keller ISD Family Alliance PAC, in late August 2022, used the new policy and book removals to fundraise, complaining that "left wing activists" are angry because "they hate the Board's new common-sense policy designed to prevent pornographic materials from being available to our children. . . . Parents and concerned community members stood up against the left's woke agenda in schools, now we MUST hold the line and protect our hard-earned victories and our children." Then it asked, "Can we count on you today to support our school board with a donation of $25, $50, $100, $250 or even $500?" Below the text and the "donate" button was a reminder: "We cannot let a Woke mob destroy our schools."[67]

At first blush library books seem like an easy enough target for extremists. Yes, books may be graphic and explicit, but it matters how that is done and what message is embedded in the text. Not every book should be read by every child at any age. Yet the key question is not what information exists in books, but why are we letting people with a political agenda disrupt our school libraries? Why are we letting them use school libraries as a tool for attacking students who may need to understand a story that is either different from their own, or to understand exactly what they feel but have never before seen acknowledged?

CHAPTER 4

HOW WEAPONIZING
CRT DISRUPTS LEARNING

MATTHEW HAWN WAS THE TEACHER who between classes at Sullivan Central High School in Sullivan County, Tennessee, would be in the hallway, bantering with fellow teachers and with students about TV, music (he wore a Pearl Jam T-shirt when we first met), and nonsense such as "What, exactly, qualified as 'soup'?" He coached baseball and taught courses on personal finance and, for juniors and seniors, two sections of a class titled "Contemporary Issues."

Hawn, as students called him (or Coach Hawn), would pause a lesson to let a kid show off a new tattoo. When he taught, he pulled up a chair or sat at a school desk. He was not about podiums and lectures, but conversation. Even about provocation. He nudged, but also listened. Class was about learning to question, to research, and to evaluate what you thought.

"Kids wanted to take that class because they wanted to talk, they wanted to learn, they wanted to argue in an academic setting," one student, who took Hawn's "Contemporary Issues" class—twice—told me.[1] A former student who was studying to be an early-childhood educator, said, "He was our teacher, but he was our friend, too. You could talk to him about anything."[2]

And students did. When I visited Hawn's home, a ranch house in Kingsport, Tennessee, it was jammed with vinyl records, posters of rock bands, books, and family photos. The dining table was crowded with artwork and notes from students. One thanked him for "being the one teacher I can imagine being a real person outside of school" and joked that "I'll remember you when I start my cult!" Some notes were humorous or flip. One student with a difficult home life wrote that he was "a blessing. . . . You are truly a role model" in curly black ink letters. "Long story short, thank you for positively impacting my life. It means more than you know." Another thanked him for "always being the one to invoke important conversations that help everyone understand each other a little more."[3]

Conversations I had with students about Hawn's class reminded me of a conversation I had had decades earlier with Walter Beavers, the head of the English Department and a beloved teacher at Weston High School in Massachusetts. After watching him conduct a class like a piece of music, leading an experience that was fun and fizzy, yet also layered, I interviewed him as he explained his philosophy. "My job is to have a relationship with the students," he said. "Shakespeare is what comes up in conversation. Hemingway is what we talk about. But *my job is the relationship.*"[4]

It is one of the most true things I have ever heard about how education should work. Learning happens in the context of relationships, which may look like trust in a teacher or in the culture that a teacher builds among students in a class. It is within this shared time and space that understanding evolves. It lets students test ideas—and even change their minds.

Which is what Kyle Simcox, who graduated from Sullivan Central High School in 2018, did in Hawn's class. Simcox was raised in a conservative Christian household where he sat with his grandmother each night and watched Bill O'Reilly on Fox News as she drank decaf instant coffee. When Simcox took Hawn's class, he had joined the Tennessee Army National Guard.

In class they discussed President Donald Trump's fascination with the display of French military hardware during a Bastille Day celebration in 2017. Trump then sought to have "a really great parade to show our military strength" down Pennsylvania Avenue. Simcox, too, liked the idea. But Hawn pressed him to notice which countries—North Korea, China, and Russia—embraced such displays. Simcox grew furious and stormed out.

"I ended up leaving the class and calling him a snowflake, and to get the hell away from me," Simcox recalled. Then, he said, "I did a little research and found that it was not very customary for democracies to do" military parades. Now, he said, he and Hawn "look back and laugh. But that is the whole point of having that type of class."[5]

In fact, as someone who grew up in Sullivan County—which is nearly all white and where 75 percent of voters in 2020 cast ballots for Trump—Hawn believed a class that exposed students to varying perspectives was valuable. It would prepare them for college and life.[6]

After all, as a high school student himself, Hawn had embraced the Confederate "rebel" flag and listened every day to Rush Limbaugh and then parroted his far-right views. "I picked up on the stereotypes and the blaming of the liberals for all the problems," he said. As a student at Tennessee Tech University, Hawn recalled that at first, when he "talked about race or LGBTQ and women's issues and stuff like that, I was your typical northeastern Tennessee conservative white male. I had never been exposed to competing ideas."

That changed as he became friends with people different than him, including Black students in his dorm. He heard fresh perspectives on life and history. "Racism and racial equity and even the Black experience in the United States wasn't anything I had ever learned," he said. He had grown up believing "the Lost Cause" interpretation of Southern history and the Civil War, including the myth that slavery benefitted both Blacks and whites. By the time he graduated, first as a finance major and then, a few years later, after earning a teaching certification, Hawn was eager to return to Sullivan County and teach students like himself.

In 2005 he began at Sullivan Central High School teaching economics and in 2008 became part of the permanent staff. His mom helped him set up his classroom. He was "head over heels" with excitement about having his own classroom, he recalled. Different years, Hawn taught different courses, including personal finance, a rock 'n' roll elective, and "Contemporary Issues."

"Contemporary Issues" had no prescribed syllabus or standards and tackled current "hot-button" topics, Hawn said. Which is what, in the 2020–2021 school year—after he had been teaching the course for more than ten years—became a problem. Hawn was teaching both online and in person and the things he was teaching about—including racism and white privilege—were the very issues animating far-right activists. In Tennessee this showed up in the state legislature in the form of a law regulating the teaching of "divisive concepts" in K–12 public schools around race and sex, including limiting teaching about institutional racism. It, like similar laws being passed around the country, was widely described as an "anti-CRT" law.[7]

It passed both houses of the legislature on May 5, 2021, and was signed into law by Governor Bill Lee on May 25. Hawn had felt the charged climate all year long, but on the day the bill was signed into law, Hawn was called into a meeting with district leaders and was handed a draft of a document dismissing him. In the document he was charged with "unprofessional conduct" and "insubordination." At the June 8, 2021, school board meeting, trustees voted 6–1 to proceed with his dismissal, marking the start of a long and painful legal battle.

Dozens of Hawn supporters stood outside the June 8 meeting with signs, then packed the room, clad in light blue T-shirts with "#IstandwithHawn" in white lettering. After the director of schools, Dr. David A. Cox, detailed the charges, he addressed the anger around Hawn's firing that people had expressed online. He insisted that he did not oppose discussions of white privilege and that Hawn's dismissal was unrelated to the new law and had "no relationship to that bill or that language." Yet it was hard to see how the claims of "unprofessional conduct" and "insubordination" suddenly arose this academic year wholly independent of the heated political environment.[8]

THE BIRTH AND RISE OF THE "ANTI-CRT" CRUSADE

The summer of 2020 was chaotic. Following the murder of George Floyd and deep into the pandemic with no vaccine as yet, there was fear, frustration, and mounting evidence that racial inequality was embedded in our institutions. It had always been there, but Covid made it obvious. Researchers would later confirm that low-wage front-line workers, disproportionately Blacks and Latinos, got sick and died at strikingly higher rates than whites.[9]

One could see who stocked grocery shelves, worked in takeout restaurants, and delivered goods to people who could stay at home and order stuff online. At the same time, we had seen, over and over, Black men, women, and even children shot and killed at the hands of police. There was a bigger and deeper problem that America was finally talking about.

It had been laid out in books like *The New Jim Crow*, by Michelle Alexander; *Caste*, by Isabel Wilkerson; and *Stamped from the Beginning*, by Ibram X. Kendi. It had shown up in the opening of the Equal Justice Initiative Legacy Museum in Montgomery, Alabama, which in a compact space in a humble building traced a direct line from slavery to mass incarceration. Along with the National Memorial for Peace and Justice, a sculpture, and a park whose name belies its visual recounting of the racialized terror of lynching, it had opened April 26, 2018, with a weekend of events. It offered a clear and powerful statement of our history of racial injustice.

On August 14, 2019, the *New York Times Magazine* published "The 1619 Project," led by journalist Nikole Hannah-Jones. The project, which marked the four-hundredth anniversary of the beginning of American slavery, was clear about its goal. "It aims to reframe the country's history by placing the consequences of slavery and the contributions of black Americans at the very center of our national narrative." It was bold and unapologetic in its bid to be a corrective to a white-centric history.[10]

Trump responded with his own President's Advisory 1776 Commission, which reframed history in a very different manner. Nicknamed the "1776 Project," it now includes a PAC supporting far-right school board candidates. Larry P. Arnn, president of Hillsdale College, an influential conservative Christian college in Michigan, was appointed to lead the commission.[11]

It was Arnn who, during a meeting with Tennessee governor Bill Lee in 2022, said that teachers were "trained in the dumbest parts of the dumbest colleges in the country." Arnn, who has worked to gain state support for his Christian charter schools, which embrace the 1776 Commission version of history, has also influenced new history curricula in several states, including Florida and Virginia. Interestingly, the commission did not include a single historian.[12]

None of this, however, was visible during the summer of 2020, when the country seemed to be reevaluating how the US operated, including the practices, procedures, and assumptions of government and culture. Protestors took to the streets. Some gatherings were peaceful; others were not. TV news showed smashed store windows, looted shops, and things set on fire, but it also displayed the grieving family members of Black people killed in ways that revealed a deep racial bias that could no longer be explained away.

As a Seattle resident, Christopher F. Rufo, a documentary filmmaker-turned-conservative-political-journalist and activist, did not have to search for material. It was right in his backyard. When protestors drove police out of a precinct near Cal Anderson Park, erected barricades, and established the Capitol Hill Autonomous Zone, or CHAZ, Rufo was ready. He penned pieces and recorded podcasts for *City Journal*, the media organ of the far-right Manhattan Institute, with headlines like "Anarchy in Seattle" and "CHAZ to CHOP: Seattle's Radical Experiment."[13]

Then, in July 2020, Rufo zeroed in on something that would change the conversation and elevate his national profile. He learned of a program in Seattle "inviting 'white City employees' to attend a training session on 'Interrupting Internalized Racial Superiority and Whiteness.'" It was "designed to help white workers examine their 'complicity in the system of white supremacy' and 'interrupt racism in ways that are accountable to Black, Indigenous and People of Color.'" His story about the training program was titled "Cult Programming in Seattle."[14]

Rufo tapped into a particular moment in which white Americans realized that they were white, that whiteness carried heavy historical baggage, and that white people needed to understand how this history impacted people of color. I attended two such trainings in the summer of 2019. I understood the point was to disrupt assumptions. When you are white you don't have to think about race because things are set up in ways that are suited to you. The trainings were uncomfortable; some exercises felt contrived. But they provided a structure for conversation and reflection.

The experiences also made clear to me that it doesn't take much spin to make such trainings *sound* absurd and troubling, and that was just what Rufo did, laying the groundwork for his rise in popularity on the political right. In "Cult Programming in Seattle," Rufo described a "racial-justice shakedown" in which white employees were made to "abandon their 'white normative behavior' and learn to let go of their 'comfort,' 'physical safety,' 'social status,' and 'relationships with some other white people.'"

And then Rufo mentioned James Lindsay, who at the Moms for Liberty event had compared public schools to Maoist prison camps. He quoted Lindsay as saying that such trainings employed "the language of cult programming—persuading members they are defective in some predefined manner." Rufo warned that this was "part of a nationwide movement to make this kind of identity politics the foundation of our public discourse."

On July 18, 2020, he pressed harder. In "'White Fragility' Comes to Washington," Rufo claimed that diversity trainings at several federal agencies were part of "the creation of a new, radical political consciousness."[15] He also mis-defined this new consciousness as CRT, writing, "Critical race theory—the academic discourse centered on the concepts of 'whiteness,' 'white fragility,' and 'white privilege'—is spreading rapidly through the federal government." The erroneous definition of CRT caught on. Rufo tweeted about it. Then, on August 17, 2020, Rufo was a guest on Fox's *Tucker Carlson Tonight*, where he described critical race theory as spreading "like wildfire" across American institutions. Carlson knitted his brows. "People," Carlson puzzled, "have said nothing about this."[16]

Of course, that would soon change.

Rufo continued to tweet about critical race theory, and Carlson continued to have Rufo on his show.[17] By late August 2020, Rufo tweeted a "SCOOP" about FBI trainings and warned, "Let me say it plainly: critical race theory is a toxic, pseudoscientific, and racist ideology that is taking over our public institutions—and will be weaponized against the American people. Time to fight back."[18] Critical race theory, or Rufo's version of "CRT," was catching on.

On September 2, 2020, on Carlson's show, Rufo rang the alarm bells, warning that "conservatives need to wake up that this is an existential threat to the United States." It was so dire that even within the Trump administration CRT was "being weaponized against our core American values." Then Rufo did something bold: he addressed the president directly. "I would like to make it explicit," he said, looking into the camera. "The president and the White House, it is within their authority and power to immediately issue an executive order abolishing critical race theory training." Then, in an utterance I still find scary, Rufo said, "I call on the president to immediately issue this executive order."[19]

And guess what? He did. A few days later, on September 4, 2020, Russell Vought, director of the Office of Budget and Management, sent a memorandum to heads of all agencies and executive offices stating that "the President has directed me to ensure that Federal agencies cease and desist from using taxpayer dollars to fund these divisive, un-American propaganda training sessions." It directed agencies to identify all spending related to sessions that involved "critical race theory" or "white privilege" or "any other training or propaganda effort that teaches or suggests either (1) that the United States is an inherently racist or evil country or (2) that any race or ethnicity is inherently racist or evil."[20]

That language construction—particularly the modifier "inherently"— would show up in the wording of legislation introduced in state houses around the country. "Critical race theory" and "CRT" had become household phrases. And, true to Rufo's intent, it had become a useful shorthand tool quickly taken up by far-right pundits and ultra-conservative school board candidates.

Actually, though, critical race theory is not what Rufo says it is. Rufo lifted the name and the connection with race, but critical race theory is actually a graduate-level legal framework. Critical race theory grew from observations in the 1970s and 1980s by legal scholars, including Derrick Bell, a professor at Harvard Law School, that there were structural problems within the law itself. Despite court decisions, civil rights laws, and desegregation policies, racial injustice continued. In fact, it was embedded in the laws that governed the United States.

"The cessation of one form of discriminatory conduct soon appeared in a more subtle though no less discriminatory form," Bell wrote. The problem, in other words, did not arise with one specific law or regulation, but from an elemental condition and the fact that racial unfairness is embedded in American legal culture and in our institutions.[21]

Moreover, it is essential to understand not just what critical race theory is, but also how it is used. Critical race theory is a theory, a body of thought, that is used to analyze the complexities and contradictions of racial inequality within the law and offers the legal profession a way to think about the problem. Peggy McIntosh, a researcher associated with Wellesley College who is known for enumerating her experiences of "white privilege," said CRT helped law students look beyond individual cases by offering the idea that the law "is not apart from all the other racial dynamics of the culture." Thinking in such a systemic way about the law has "no equivalent in schools," said McIntosh. "K–12 schools are not doing CRT."[22]

What's more, critical race theory was not developed as a tool to blame specific individuals or groups of individuals. It was not about diminishing some and raising up others, but about applying an intellectual frame to a complicated issue. Yet, Rufo baldly distorted it into something else entirely. And he knew exactly what he was doing.

In March 2021, he bragged on Twitter, "We have successfully frozen their brand—'critical race theory'—into the public conversation and are steadily driving up negative perceptions. We will eventually turn it toxic, as we put all of the various cultural insanities under that brand category." In a second tweet, Rufo set out the plan: "The goal is to have the public read something crazy in the newspaper and immediately think 'critical race theory.' We have decodified the term and will recodify it to annex the entire range of cultural constructions that are unpopular with Americans."[23]

CRT, in Rufo's words, was not actually the scourge he claimed it was. Rather, it was a "brand category," a misnomer to collect "an entire range of cultural constructions" that people didn't like and then deploy them for political effect.

It should be no surprise that critical race theory has become shorthand for anything that upsets people in teaching that involves race. Of course, Rufo's formulation not only skirted the matter that Bell raised but effectively flipped the concern. Instead of inquiring about why and how racism persisted, the focus was on how talking about it was "divisive" and how that might make white children feel. Suddenly, history was not about history but about how history might be received by those with the most power.

LAWS, CONFUSION, CANCELLATION

Back on August 17, 2020, Rufo had vowed on Fox News to launch "a one-man war on critical race theory." He would not have to go it alone. He soon had an army.[24]

NOW (Corpus) News on the Web is a database of articles in established newspapers and magazines used by academic researchers. Using this database, Robert Frank, a professor of linguistics at Yale, did a month-by-month analysis for me for 2020 of the prevalence of mentions of "CRT" and "critical race theory" in the database. It showed "a small bump in June" and "an explosion in September." Data by year from 2010 to 2022 revealed what you might expect: a small rise in prevalence of the two terms in 2020, then a dramatic increase in frequency starting in 2021.[25]

It did not take long for state legislatures and school boards to embrace Rufo's CRT messaging and then craft laws and policies in response, regardless of whether they knew what CRT was. The rebranding had succeeded: CRT = bad. In many cases, the laws were so vague—most didn't mention CRT—that nearly any discussion of race could be construed as problematic. North Dakota passed a law that was so sweeping, noted Judd Legum of *Popular Information*, that it prohibited "any instruction 'related' to the idea that 'racism is systemically embedded in American society' or the American 'legal system.' That means the bill bans any instruction or written materials referencing these ideas, whether or not they are endorsed by the teacher."

Given such constraints, Legum asked, "How can a teacher discuss slavery, the civil rights era, or the history of redlining?" What's more, he said, "on its face, any discussion of the new law itself would be banned in North Dakota's K–12 schools."[26]

In what would turn out to be a repeated scenario, state legislators passed laws in hopes of getting ahead of what felt like the next big controversy. Even though critical race theory was not taught in North Dakota classrooms, Republican state senator Donald Schaible told a local news reporter that the law was "more preemptive to try to make sure that it doesn't come to our schools." (Much research has shown CRT is not taught in any K–12 classrooms.)[27]

Nevertheless, Schaible made teaching about race in schools—which has been part of curricula for decades—sound like the new viral variant. And in Florida, just as he had boldly stood up against Covid, Governor Ron DeSantis did not intend to fend off CRT quietly. Rather, he made a headline-grabbing splash. On December 15, 2021, DeSantis announced a "Stop the Wrongs to Our Kids and Employees (W.O.K.E.) Act." He sold it as "the strongest legislation of its kind in the nation" that would take on *both* "corporate wokeness and Critical Race Theory."[28]

The law was passed in early 2022 (it was also renamed the less dazzling Individual Freedom Act) and signed into law by DeSantis on April 22, 2022. Attendees at the press conference included Rufo, who had a new title at the Manhattan Institute as director of the Initiative on Critical Race Theory.[29] Several months later, DeSantis appointed him to the board of trustees of New College in a move to transform the liberal arts campus into "the Hillsdale of the South," in reference to the Michigan Christian college.[30] In his role as a DeSantis advisor, Rufo also began launching attacks on diversity, equity, and inclusion programs, including unleashing a Twitter storm directed at Florida State University—on February 2, 2023, his tweets drew over seventy-one thousand views in twelve hours.[31]

This effort was not brand new but rather a fresh front on the war DeSantis had declared at the Moms for Liberty National Summit in Tampa in July 2022. There, he had touted his new law, calling it by its more dramatic nickname, the "Stop WOKE Act," which played well with the crowd. "At the end of the day," he told the packed ballroom, "we should not be spending tax dollars or using our energy to teach our kids to hate our country or to hate each other," as if learning about and acknowledging racial injustice was the ill. Yes, he said of the law, "we are getting sued on it," but he insisted, "We will win eventually. We'll get it done."

That is far from clear—but it may not matter. Multiple lawsuits have charged that banning certain categories of speech violates First Amendment rights, including those of professors and companies in Florida. In November 2022, Mark E. Waller, judge for the US District Court for the Northern District of Florida, blocked enforcement of a regulation that limited what college professors could teach about or say regarding race in their courses, calling

DeSantis's effort "positively dystopian." The libertarian magazine *Reason* even weighed in with a story headlined "The Problem with DeSantis' 'Stop WOKE Act,'" noting, "The state can't really banish ideas. And it's dangerous to try."[32]

Yet DeSantis—with Rufo's aid—may have found a way to make an end-run to achieve his goal. In early 2023, ahead of the spring legislative session, his office ordered public colleges and universities to "provide a comprehensive list of all staff, programs and campus activities related to diversity, equity and inclusion and critical race theory." The move was in preparation for an effort to prohibit state funding for such programs.[33] It sent an immediate chill across campuses—even private ones: at Palm Beach Atlantic University, an English professor, Samuel Joeckel, was fired in March 2023 over the teaching of a unit on racial justice. He blamed DeSantis for the loss of a job he had held for twenty years. "The timing of this is not a coincidence as we are dealing with an 'anti-woke' crusade from Governor DeSantis and other far-right politicians and activists," he told a reporter, adding that his university "was clearly influenced by this toxic political ideology."[34]

In Florida and elsewhere, so-called "anti-CRT" laws applied to K–12 public schools have had an almost immediate effect as teachers worried that something they said or did could get them attacked or fired. After a law in New Hampshire banned teaching that people in one group were inherently superior or inferior to people of another group, a tenth-grade history teacher in Hollis, New Hampshire, told the *Washington Post* that she was confused about definitions of "inherently," "superior," or "inferior."

"We asked for clarification from the state, from the union, from school lawyers. The universal response is no one's really sure," said Jen Given, who teaches at the Hollis Brookline High School. "It led us to be exceptionally cautious because we don't want to risk our livelihoods when we're not sure what the rules are."[35]

Such scenarios undermine trust in teachers to be the professionals they are trained to be. Yet in many places, heightened surveillance has been brought to bear on everyday educational activities. That happened to J. Michael Butler, the Kenan Distinguished Professor of History at Flagler College in Florida. In addition to teaching undergraduates, Butler also likes helping K–12 teachers deepen their knowledge. In November 2021, when asked by the National Council of History Education to lead a teacher training for the Osceola County School District, he told me "it was a huge pleasure and a huge honor." It was also "nothing out of the ordinary."[36]

It was to be a full-day program, from 8 a.m. to 4 p.m. on January 22, 2022. Butler spoke to the director about what would be useful for K–8 teachers to know. The broad focus, they agreed, would be on "the long civil rights movement." Said Butler, "What I wanted to emphasize more than anything else is that the civil rights movement is not one event, one organization, or one person."

Three presentations would be offered, covering three periods of American history. The first would cover 1896 and the Supreme Court decision *Plessy v. Ferguson*, in which the court ruled to permit separate railroad cars for Black and white patrons as long as the cars were "equal" (ignoring that separate accommodations reinforced a racial hierarchy). This ruling became the basis for a raft of separate spaces that, one scholar noted, was "an attempt to make black people disappear from white sight."[37] This panel would cover the years 1896 through 1945 and the end of World War II.

The second presentation would focus on the years from 1954 to 1964, during which the "Master Narrative" held sway. The "Master Narrative" is a term coined by the activist Julian Bond for the attitudes toward civil rights that prevailed in that period. Hasan Kwame Jeffries, associate professor of history at the Ohio State University, in the volume he edited on teaching the civil rights movement, described the "Master Narrative" as a "fiction" that racial equality had been achieved by the Supreme Court's 1954 *Brown v. Board of Education of Topeka* decision and the nonviolent protests led by the Reverend Dr. Martin Luther King Jr. and Rosa Parks, which led to the Civil Rights Act of 1964, which prohibited discrimination on the basis of race, color, religion, sex, or national origin. Taught in classrooms and written into school social studies standards, Jeffries wrote, "The Master Narrative reinforces the myth of perpetual racial progress. Yes, racial discrimination existed, but Americans, as is their custom, rallied to defeat it."[38]

The third presentation, "The Movement Continues," would pick up after the death of Dr. King in 1968 and include some of Butler's own research about protests in northwest Florida in the 1970s. A Black man had been shot by a sheriff's deputy in Escambia County at a distance of three feet; Butler wrote, "Despite substantial evidence that suggested foul play, a grand jury quickly declared the incident 'justifiable homicide.'"[39] The goal, he detailed in a follow-up email to me, was "to have teachers understand the importance of not presenting the death of Dr. King as the *end* of the civil rights movement, but rather a transition into de facto forms of racism. In other words, the struggle for racial equality in America had not ended but had evolved into areas beyond the end of discriminatory laws." He would use his research "as an example of police brutality as a continuing civil rights issue."[40]

Butler had prepared his material and was looking forward to the training. Then something strange happened. On Wednesday, January 19, 2022, three days before the Saturday program, he received an email, then a phone call telling him the session was canceled. The subject matter, Butler was told, "raised red flags within the district in light of all the conversations we are having about CRT." He was baffled that "they linked" his sessions "directly to CRT."

It also didn't make sense. "No one from the school board, no one from the district reached out to me to see the slides," said Butler. "They just assumed that somehow critical race theory could have been involved." In fact, "it was not. Unequivocally. Critical race theory played no role" in the planned presentation.

LEADING WHILE BLACK

Since late 2020, the distorted notion of critical race theory has become a broad and powerful weapon wielded by the far right to halt teaching about or acknowledging the role of race in society. For Dr. James Whitfield, the first Black principal of Colleyville Heritage High School in Colleyville, Texas, it also became a tool to push him out of a job.

Sitting at the dining-room table in June 2022 in the family room of his home, Whitfield was still puzzled by the velocity of events, but well rehearsed at walking through them. His story received national attention, covered by the *Washington Post*, the *New York Times*, CNN, and NBC News, among others. He testified before a congressional committee and has spoken with other educators facing fire, including Matthew Hawn.[41]

The public side of things unfolded quickly. During a meeting of the Grapevine-Colleyville ISD school board on July 26, 2021, Stetson Clark, who had just run for a seat on the board and lost, stepped up to the mic during public comments. Violating rules about publicly airing a grievance about an employee by name, he accused Whitfield of "the implementation of critical race theory" and of promoting "the conspiracy theory of systemic racism."

Soon after, Whitfield was put on paid administrative leave. At a meeting on September 20, 2021, the board voted 7–0 to move forward on a proposal not to renew Whitfield's contract for 2022–2023 and to schedule a hearing on the issue. No hearing would take place. On November 8, the board voted

7–0 to accept a separation agreement that would pay Whitfield through August 15, 2023, at which time he would formally resign. (The terms of the agreement prohibit him from discussing details.)[42]

But what happened before, around, and at these meetings revealed how critical race theory came to represent a constellation of objections to a Black principal by the far right. It came in the face of what had been a successful tenure. Whitfield was hired in 2018 as assistant principal at Colleyville Heritage High School and was promoted twice. In 2019, he was tapped to lead Heritage Middle School and a year later he became principal of Colleyville Heritage High School. It was a rapid rise.

While he was outwardly successful—praised for knowing students by name and building a supportive culture—a few in the community didn't like his unapologetic talk about equity and inclusion. In 2020, after the murder of George Floyd, Whitfield wrote an open letter reflecting on the problem of racism, noting that people had come together seeking progress. He urged all to "commit to the work and the hard, vulnerable and uncomfortable conversations we must have." At the time he did not receive a single negative response.

But the letter was soon seized upon by those organizing against him. At the start of the 2020–2021 school year, Whitfield was flooded with Freedom of Information requests. In September and October, he told me, he received "upwards of fifty to sixty" seeking all of his emails, texts, and social media posts containing terms such as "racial equity," "race," "inclusion," "diversity," and "George Floyd."

No one contacted him directly with concerns, but friends and supporters texted, warning that activists were attacking him on social media. Whitfield said that those who had issues or questions "could have asked me any of this, just send an email saying, 'Are you teaching CRT?' I would have brought you into the office, got you coffee. We could talk."

Whitfield tried not to let the requests or attacks shake him. "I just tried to talk myself out of it, like this is not anything that is going to have any bearing on anything," he said. "I would always tie back to my purpose. I had to tell myself that 'I'm here for a bigger reason.'"

But of course it did have a bearing on things. After the July 26 school board meeting outburst by Stetson Clark, parents rallied to support Whitfield. Laura Leeman, a mom of two in the district, created a petition to support him; within days nearly two thousand people had signed it.[43] This activity would spur Leeman to become even more active in supporting public education and against the extremist threats to it.

After Whitfield was placed on paid administrative leave, students walked out of class in protest. Under pressure, on September 1, 2021, the district issued a statement saying it had "received numerous questions" about the actions against Whitfield. But in a strange twist, the letter described what *was not a factor* in his removal: it "was not a result of statements made by members of the public, including those who spoke at recent meetings of the [Grapevine-Colleyville] ISD Board of Trustees. Nor was the decision made in response to allegations that Dr. Whitfield was teaching Critical Race Theory, or because of the photos on his social media account that were brought to the attention of the District in 2019."[44] (The decade-old photos were of him and his wife embracing on a beach in Mexico, taken on their fifth wedding anniversary. He had been asked to take them down; while upset at the request, he had nonetheless complied.)[45]

It was a puzzling statement. It provided little insight but stirred anger among parents and students. During a packed school board meeting on September 21, dozens lined up to speak in support of Whitfield. One student charged that "the mistreatment of our principal is merely an indication of a deeper problem." Parent Stacey Silverman reflected a sentiment echoed by others, saying "His ability to forge real connection with his students was rare and unparalleled" in the district. Further, she charged, "The abysmal racist treatment he has endured at the hands of this administration is unconscionable and nothing short of a witch hunt."[46]

Whitfield also spoke, saying that "every student, regardless of race, religion, sexual orientation, whatever bucket you put them in, I believe they all should have access to an excellent, equitable education. And yes, I said those words," he said. "Unfortunately, my unapologetic stance of those things has brought us here tonight."

Then, Whitfield threw it back. "I am still the same man today," he said to the board. "I ask you, What has changed since July 26?" when Stetson Clark called for his firing at the school board meeting. What *had* changed? An attack from the far right.

Whitfield asked that proceedings, normally held in executive session, be public. By the time a district official read aloud the charges against him, at a meeting on September 20, 2021, it appeared that the reasons for his non-renewal stemmed from the controversy itself. He was criticized by leaders in the district for speaking to the media, of having "deficiencies in situational awareness," a phrase that a parent would accuse the board of during a public comment period. He had not followed policy when he shared criticisms on social media. Some charges were met with laughter by the crowd, who found the charges ludicrous, including that "he has failed to maintain effective working relationships with the parents, the community or colleagues." To the charge that "he has diminished his effectiveness by dividing large sections of the community," someone shouted, "You are all full of shit!" to which the chair pounded the gavel. But it was, in essence, what made his reinstatement impossible.[47]

In a striking acknowledgment of the situation, board member Coley Canter addressed the room from the dais "to express personal regret." She admitted that she had failed to speak up when she saw Whitfield "being unjustly attacked. I had a moment, and I didn't do it and I regret that," she said. "And my kids are watching. And learning from your mom, I am changed by this moment. Our community is changed by this moment. Some moments you don't get to take back. I want to publicly express my regret."[48]

It was too late. A few weeks later, the board met and voted to accept a separation agreement that had been negotiated with Whitfield's lawyer.[49]

Then, in June 2022, information emerged suggesting that a more concerted campaign against Whitfield had taken place. The Republican National Committee sponsored a "school board discussion" event for North Texas school boards, to take place on June 26, 2022, in Coppell, Texas.[50] A newly elected school board member, Tammy Nakamura, who had been backed by the Patriot Mobile Action PAC, took the microphone and claimed that she had read Whitfield's personnel file and that he "was a total activist" who was "pushing a movement through." She cited information from Freedom of Information requests and said the open letter he had written following the murder of George Floyd "was the straw that broke the camel's back."

She also insisted that educators like Whitfield must be halted. "If we don't stand up now, it is not [yet] in all of the classrooms, it is not everywhere," she said, of critical race theory. Eerily, she added, "We have a list of those it is in and it must be stopped now . . . We cannot have teachers like this in our school because they are poison, and they are taking our schools down." It was an odd warning that some parents read as a hit list. The video was removed from the Republican site but remained on a Facebook page of Colleyville Citizens for Accountability, a parent and community group.[51]

THE NEW SEGREGATION

It is no secret that we have a dearth of Black educators, even as the percentage of students of color rises in public schools. Black students are 15 percent of students nationally. Black teachers are about half that; and 11 percent of principals are Black.

This situation can be traced to *Brown v. Board of Education of Topeka, Kansas.* Following the ruling, the ranks of Black educators fell. Between 1954 and 1964, 38,000 of an estimated 82,000 Black teachers and administrators left the profession. Between 1975 and 1985, the number of Black students majoring in education declined by 66 percent.[52]

Brown v. Board of Education was an important ruling. The Supreme Court ruled that separating children in public schools on the basis of race was unconstitutional. It signaled the end of legalized racial segregation in the schools of the United States, overruling the "separate but equal" principle set forth in the 1896 *Plessy v. Ferguson* case. But it didn't fix segregation. As Hasan Kwame Jeffries, the Ohio State history professor, pointed out in a lecture titled "Teaching Race and Slavery in the American Classroom," the very things the ruling was supposed to fix weren't suddenly changed after *Brown*. Jeffries told conference attendees he always asks students, "How long after the court ruling were schools desegregated? The students will invariably say, 'Immediately?' They are always saying in the immediate aftermath." Even Thurgood Marshall, who argued the case before the Supreme Court as a leader of the NAACP Legal Defense Fund, when asked how long it would take, "he said 'two years,'" said Jeffries.[53]

In fact, said Jeffries, "The immediate response to the court ruling was to double down in the white south." So-called "segregation academies"— private schools where white families sent their children to avoid integrated schools—proliferated. As a result, "10 years after the Supreme Court ruled that segregated education is unconstitutional, nearly all Black children in the south attended nearly all Black schools" and white children attended nearly all white schools. To be fair, he quipped, a goal of the civil rights movement is sometimes mistaken to be "not educational equality but [Blacks'] proximity to whiteness." (Despite *Brown*, he said, many Blacks had no interest in sending their children to school with the same white people who were trying to kill them.)

By the 1970s, segregation academies were rebranded as Christian schools that "dot the landscape and are still with us today." The push in the 1980s,

1990s, and at present to gain taxpayer support through voucher or "school choice" programs is the new face of an old effort "to find public dollars to promote, to support, to expand segregationist schools. So, what does race have to do with how we have structured our educational system today and over the last 50 years? Absolutely everything."

Jeffries's point is that de facto segregated academies maneuvering for public support have been with us for years. In August 1970, Senator Walter Mondale claimed that the Nixon administration was quietly granting tax-exempt status to southern white schools that continued to segregate in violation of IRS rules. He charged that this spurred "a dramatic, unquestionably new movement in education, the creation of all-white, tax-supported segregation academies flowering throughout the area where the courts have ordered desegregation."[54]

Today it boldly continues. In January 2022 Governor Bill Lee of Tennessee announced a "partnership" with Hillsdale College and its American Classical Education network. He hoped to open fifty to a hundred Hillsdale College–affiliated Christian charter schools that would be part of public districts and get public money but would operate independently and be free of the accountability measures required for traditional public schools.

The effort was stalled, however, by Arnn's comment about teachers in these schools being from "the dumbest parts of the dumbest colleges." In the three counties in which the charters were proposed, the school boards voted to reject them. Before it could be appealed to the state Public School Charter Commission, which can overrule local school boards, American Classical Education withdrew its application. In December 2022, ACE submitted applications to open five charters in other counties.[55]

In several states, vouchers have been rebranded as "education savings accounts" and marketed as tools to give choice and control to parents who have been frustrated by the hardships of Covid schooling. The education savings accounts have gained traction in places like Arizona, which in fall 2022 began offering parents enrolled in the new "Empowerment Scholarship Account" program $6,000 to $6,500 per child to spend on private, religious, or home schools.

The average annual private school fee in Arizona is $12,650.[56] So without additional resources these educational savings account dollars do not come close to covering private-school costs. Yet the program, like vouchers, diverts money from public schools, which typically serve poorer students, those with special needs, and those who live in rural areas. In effect, the programs offer a boost to those who can afford or are already paying for private school.

Such programs also lay the groundwork for economic and racial segregation in schools, which is already a problem. As a reminder of how persistent an issue this is, the K–12 world was watching as the Supreme Court took up two cases considering race and affirmative action in college admissions: *Students for Fair Admissions, Inc. v. President and Fellows of Harvard College* and *Students for Fair Admissions, Inc. v. University of North Carolina, et al.* In response, the Council of the Great City Schools filed an amicus brief. The council represents seventy-eight of the nation's largest K–12 urban school systems, with over 7.6 million students, more than three-quarters "from minority backgrounds."[57]

In the amicus brief, the group reminded the Court that in 2003 Justice Sandra Day O'Connor supported the use of racial preferences in admissions in *Grutter v. Bollinger,* "famously express[ing] her hope that '25 years from now, the use of racial preferences will no longer be necessary to further the interest approved today.'" Unfortunately, the brief stated, "Despite the best efforts of school districts like the Council's members to create more diverse schools, racial segregation has increased over the last two decades. [Progress toward desegregation] has faltered since the late 1980s, and much of that progress has been reversed. Today, public schools across the nation are nearly as segregated as they were five decades ago." The brief also cited a report by the US Government Accounting Office, released in June 2022, that found more than one-third of students attended a public school in which 75 percent or more of the student population was of the same race or ethnicity. "This de facto segregation is present in every region of the country," the report said, including urban, suburban, and rural areas.[58]

While we have a public debate over whether CRT is taught in schools, many American students of color attend under-resourced and underachieving public schools. They are living proof that inequality is indeed embedded in the very institutions that *Brown* saw as central to reversing the problem.

CHALLENGING YOUR COMMUNITY, LOSING YOUR JOB

Sullivan County, Tennessee, where Matthew Hawn grew up and lives, is not racially diverse; it is 95 percent white. US Census and other federal data present a picture reminiscent of the 1950s: Most people own their homes, which are modest, as are incomes. People drive solo to jobs; commutes average twenty-two minutes. At home almost no one speaks a language other than English. (The area does suffer from the modern problem of opioid addiction.)[59]

It is little surprise that Hawn has thirty relatives living within a few miles. Every winding road, school building, church, ball field—and the massive Eastman Chemical Company that twinkles at night like a small Dr. Seuss–inspired urban oasis—carries meaning for Hawn. Kingsport, Tennessee, and the Tri-Cities area that includes Johnson City and Bristol is not a throw-back locale in the Appalachian highlands. It is the place he, his family, his friends, and the people he knows and loves, have long called home.

The nature of the community also makes Hawn's situation feel personal. Randy Gilmore, one of the six school board members who voted for Hawn's dismissal, was his high school AP US History teacher and baseball coach. A 1995 team yearbook photo shows Hawn sitting cross-legged in the front row in his #7 Raiders uniform, and Gilmore, #10, at the top right. "That bothered me," said Hawn of Gilmore's vote. He recalled being a brash conservative in class and Gilmore "waving his arms and fed up with my nonsense." Now, Gilmore was helping to remove him from teaching and coaching.[60]

Hawn's problems were certainly amplified by Covid-19 and the need to juggle hybrid, remote, and in-person teaching that was the 2020–2021 school year. His trouble began on August 27, 2020. He showed his "Contemporary Issues" class a video of the family of Jacob Blake, who a few days earlier had been shot seven times in the back and side by police in Kenosha, Wisconsin.

Hawn contrasted it with Kyle Rittenhouse, the white teen who shot three people, two fatally, with a semiautomatic rifle at protests following Blake's shooting. (Rittenhouse would be acquitted after a jury found he acted in self-defense. He would become a far-right hero and start a YouTube channel to talk about firearms and the Second Amendment.)[61]

Hawn held up the fact that both were wanted by the same police force, yet Blake was shot and paralyzed while Rittenhouse was taken into custody peacefully. "Now my question to you is this, and this is a tough one," he said. "How is that not a definition of white privilege?"

Hawn then answered his own question. "This is what privilege looks like. Whenever you can fire into a crowd of people and kill people and then you can walk to the police without fear of being shot back, that is the definition of privilege. Of white privilege."

He said unequal treatment had been happening to African Americans for four hundred years, and listed slavery, Jim Crow, the war on drugs, and police brutality as aspects of unequal treatment. "America is not equal to everybody," he said. And then he said something that would turn out to be very problematic: "There is no counterpoint to this. It is what it is. It is a fact. So, I guess, the question should be, What should we do?" Hawn posted a video of himself leading the class, because some students attended remotely.

Hawn didn't realize it, but his assertion that white privilege was "a fact" would trigger anger—and a cascade of events. The next day he arrived to serve as a water boy for the football team's Friday night game (during Covid, adults dispensed water). Just as he stepped through the gate and past the white cinder-block ticket window, the principal approached to ask why he was discussing white privilege in "Personal Finance" class.

Hawn was stunned and puzzled, until he checked via his phone and saw that he had mistakenly posted the "Contemporary Issues" class video to the Personal Finance Google site. "It was an honest mistake," he said.

It probably also cost him his job. At the football game, from his phone, he removed the video and apologized. The "Contemporary Issues" class conversation was intended to be the start of a unit on racism. He decided to suspend the subject until later in the year, when all students would likely be in school in person.

That pause did not halt the momentum. A dozen days later, Hawn received an email from an administrator reminding him that under the state Teacher Code of Ethics he "must not unreasonably deny students access to varying points of view." Hawn was told that "using a statement like 'This is a fact,' leaves little room for discussion."[62]

Then, on October 2, 2020, Chad Conner, whom Hawn does not know, posted a video showing seventeen minutes and three seconds of Hawn's lecture on his Facebook page with the comment: "Local teacher teaching kids about why they have white privilege and why the cops should be defunded. Is this acceptable behavior for someone responsible for shaping the minds of our children? Feel free to share!"

Several comments saw Hawn "teaching kids to look at current events, challenge their own viewpoints and think critically. If that's not education, what is?!?"

Others, however, were "furious," and soon deduced that the teacher was Hawn. Some said they were contacting administrators. Hawn "was terrified" after reading the comments, some of them from people he knew and had grown up with. One commenter, Stan C. Edwards, shared the date of the next school board meeting and stated that he would attend to speak "in general" about his outrage. In his post he said, "It is against BOE policy to allow public discussion/mention of any BOE employee by name." (This was also true in Grapevine-Colleyville ISD in Texas, but Stetson Clark ignored it.) Edwards urged others to "please come if you can. Let's try to keep it civil, at this point in time."[63]

At the October 8 meeting, Edwards approached the mic clad in a brown polo and jeans. Like everyone present, he wore a mask. He acknowledged the policy of not naming a specific employee, then described a "potential scenario" in which "a teacher displays political bias in the discussion with his or her class." He asked, "What disciplinary actions are available to be levied against a teacher in the offense that I have laid out?"[64]

On January 6, 2020, rioters breached the US Capitol. This was a prime topic for the "Contemporary Issues" class, but Hawn sat tight. Soon, however, he said, it became clear "that we had to talk about the insurrection." One could argue that it would have been derelict not to talk about it in such a course. Yet there was a problem: class was remote. He would not be in the same room with his students.

Because of that and because there was so much evolving information, Hawn instead had students consider how the US could have elected someone who might try to overthrow the government. He assigned his fourth-period "Contemporary Issues" class a piece written by Ta-Nehisi Coates, "The First White President," about Donald Trump, which had appeared in *The Atlantic*.[65]

He said the article represented "just one viewpoint" and asked them to come up with a list of factors that might have led to Trump's 2016 victory, suggesting Russian interference, social media, Trump's being a good businessman, Clinton campaign failures, the Electoral College, and the fact that Trump wasn't a politician.

A few days later a parent complained about the article. On February 3, 2021, that complaint led Ingrid Deloach, assistant director of schools, to send Hawn a formal letter of reprimand. She said that the parent objected to the article, "specifically the language," which the parent "did not believe 'should be introduced to our children by a high school teacher.'"[66]

Deloach's letter cited Coates's use of the N-word, a Steve Bannon quote that used the words "cuck" and "whore." "Cuck" is short for "cuckold," but in Bannon's use is a derogatory term for a weak man with progressive or moderate political views. (In *The History of Troilus and Cressida*, Shakespeare slips both of these "inappropriate words" into a single line given by Thersites: "All the argument is a whore and a cuckold; a good quarrel to draw emulous factions and bleed to death upon.")[67]

It was not mentioned in the Deloach letter, but Coates had also written that Trump was "the first president to have publicly affirmed that his daughter is a 'piece of ass'" and that Trump had "introduced the phrase grab 'em by the pussy into the national lexicon." Both were examples of problematic language that would come up in legal proceedings.

The Coates article *is* provocative. The use of the N-word is central to his argument, which is that Trump is a white supremacist and used this stance to win election. Much of the piece is historical analysis with arguments bolstered by demographic and economic data.

Hawn appealed the reprimand, arguing that in sixteen years of teaching he had never faced any disciplinary action. He also charged that the district violated board policy by failing to follow its own due process procedure. On March 4, 2021, the board voted to reject Hawn's appeal and let the letter of reprimand stand (Gilmore, citing a conflict, abstained).[68]

MORE TROUBLE FOR HAWN

By mid-April, students were back in school in person. The class discussed the trial of Derek Chauvin, who had killed George Floyd, as the trial unfolded. Oddly, 2020–2021 would seem to have been a dream year for teaching "Contemporary Issues"; there was no lack of material. During class, one student raised the issue of "white privilege." Hawn assigned the classic 1989 essay by Peggy McIntosh, "White Privilege: Unpacking the Invisible Knapsack." Then he showed a video of a recitation of the poem "White Privilege," by Kyla Jenée Lacey. It contained seven curse words.

Before showing the video Hawn joked to the class, "I will probably get fired for showing this," which he said was an effort at humor "to diffuse a very difficult situation." Hawn claimed that he tried to mute out the curse words, but several were heard by students. To provide an alternative view, Hawn asked students to consider whether "Black privilege" existed and "what it would be and look like." He posted a related article by John Blake of CNN, "It's Time to Talk About 'Black Privilege,'" to the class site.[69]

The video reignited Hawn's troubles. A few weeks later, a group of administrators, including Deloach and David A. Cox, the director of schools, met with Hawn to share a letter laying out grounds for dismissal. Hawn responded in a letter, stating that he was "not taking lightly issues of insubordination and conduct unbecoming of the profession and can assure you that I have reflected deeply on these and will do better in the future."

It made no difference. On June 8, 2021, Cox read the dismissal letter aloud at the school board meeting. The Sullivan County Board of Education voted 6–1 to proceed with firing Hawn, Gilmore also voting in favor.

A hearing on the dismissal was held August 16–18 and included testimony by the poet Kyla Jenée Lacey, who showed up to support Hawn, and several of Hawn's students. In one exchange a student was asked, "If you learned something that was a different viewpoint . . . did you feel free to bring that into class?" According to a transcript, the student answered, "Yeah." Hawn was grilled as to why he did not seek parental permission before assigning the Ta-Nehisi Coates article or why he did not print out the article and redact curse words or slurs, despite many students being remote at the time.[70]

But what stood out to me in reading the transcript, including Deloach's testimony, was what you might expect: This was not really about curse words. The real issue was political.

Administrators saw Hawn as offering a "liberal" political view. They felt that he should literally offer a "conservative" counter. Under questioning, Deloach said that if a student believed that the Holocaust did not exist, that the teacher would "have to treat it as a valid viewpoint" in class. She admitted that having students do research to explore their own views would meet the required ethical standard. This was Hawn's approach.[71]

But none of this mattered. Hawn had upset people—and he had done it at a moment when political division was seeping into personal relationships and pulling communities apart. Hawn himself felt the change. He said he was used to parents who "would come up to me at basketball and football games and talk about what we were discussing in class." It might be climate change or women's rights. "There were things they disagreed with, but they were OK with me discussing them with their students." In class, he joked about taking away people's guns. "They would joke right back."

But a different atmosphere had swept in. Schools and classrooms were no longer about the relationships teachers built with students. There was less room for the carbonated prodding and ribbing that was a staple of high school learning. Now, people who were not part of a classroom's culture were dropping in and applying judgments.

This has bothered some of Hawn's former students, including Drew Robinette, who considers himself a conservative. Along with Kyle Simcox, in Johnson City I met Robinette, a recent college grad working at Eastman Chemical as a logistics planner. He graduated from Sullivan Central High in 2018 and had had Hawn for Economics and Personal Finance.

He said Hawn was engaging and got students to question their views. "I like him more because I do disagree with him," said Robinette, who recalled sparring over taxes. He valued being forced to defend his stances—and to listen. "I am a conservative," he said, "but I am not cocksure."

Robinette liked that Hawn "didn't think the way 90 percent of the students did." He would challenge students to research what they heard on TV or from those around them. "For a lot of kids, the first time you are hearing a different side is with him."

As these two young men, with similar amounts of loosely groomed auburn-colored facial hair, sat side by side, scooping up meat and pepper-topped slices, they told me they hold opposing views on most things—but were still best friends.

"We disagree on literally everything," said Simcox, who wore a Los Angeles Lakers lanyard; Robinette is a Boston Celtics fan. They ran down "bests" in basketball (Robinette: Michael Jordan; Simcox: LeBron James) and music (Robinette: Morgan Wallen; Simcox: Garth Brooks). When it came to political party, Robinette leans Republican and Simcox, Democrat.

The two love to debate, but are not driven to trounce the other. "We don't feel the need to change each other's minds," said Simcox. Their genuine regard for one another matters more than winning. Both also like being challenged—and are unafraid to change their minds.

When it came to Hawn's case, however, no school officials were reconsidering. In an October 2021 ruling, the hearing officer affirmed that "the Sullivan County Board of Education met its burden of establishing its grounds for terminating Matthew Hawn."

It found that he failed to follow the Teacher Code of Ethics "and in doing so acted unprofessionally." It also found him "insubordinate in that he failed to follow the reprimand that prohibited him from using materials with inappropriate language" and of "failing to present varying viewpoints, despite knowing he was to do so." On December 14, 2021, the school board voted to uphold the hearing officer's ruling (Gilmore was no longer on the board).[72] Gloria Oster, a veteran teacher who had taught Hawn AP English and had shown up at hearings to support Hawn, said she was not surprised, "given the political environment and the area we live in. This is a tough place to talk about anything other than conservative ideas and values at this point."[73]

On January 25, 2022, Hawn's lawyers filed an appeal with the Chancery Court of Sullivan County.[74] His sisters started a GoFundMe page to provide money for living and health insurance (he's a type 1 diabetic). When I first arrived in the region, I met Hawn in Food City as he shopped for basics like Gatorade, raisins, crackers, and peanut butter. Over three days we cruised the area in his white Subaru Crosstrek. We drove up a service road beside his old classroom. We sat at his mom's dining table, visited his father's townhome, picked up his niece Mae, a chatty and precocious kindergartner in a Minnie Mouse T-shirt and colorful Crocs, from school.

As Mae and Hawn kicked a soccer ball one afternoon, I spoke with Hawn's sister Laura, a supervisor at Pal's Sudden Service, a storied fast-food chain started in Kingsport in the 1950s. She had just gotten home. We stood in the garage. She wore a sweatshirt with images and words from Kyle Jenée Lacey's poem "White Privilege."

Laura said most of the teens who have worked for her at Pal's had him as a teacher or otherwise knew her brother. "They are super supportive," she said. "They say things like 'It's dumb what they are doing to him. He is one of the best teachers we have ever had.'" Laura felt that in sharing works by Lacey and Coates her brother had "showed the other side."

"We have learned one side since we were in kindergarten, and I'm forty-two years old. And that is what my parents learned." Of Lacey and Coates she said, "They *are* the varying viewpoints. Kids around here have never heard that."

Some in the community have expressed support for Hawn, but what stings are close family friends who don't even ask how he is doing or offer to pray for him. "We live in the Bible Belt. Most of these people say they are good Christian people," she said. "Their silence speaks more than anything else. I notice it."[75]

WHITE PRIVILEGE

Technically speaking, the two things that got Matthew Hawn into trouble were his failure to scrub curse words from class materials and—perhaps most frustrating to those opposing him—his assertion that "white privilege" is "a fact."[76]

In the present moment "white privilege" has taken on a judgmental sheen that it was not intended to have. Rather, Peggy McIntosh, the Wellesley College researcher credited with exploring the term in the late 1980s, came to it as an observation about unearned advantage in her own life. It grew from something she first noticed relative to gender.[77]

McIntosh had been leading a seminar at what was then the Wellesley College Center for Research on Women to help faculty from many campuses see how new research on women might be incorporated into academic disciplines. Although men attended these seminars, she noticed that even after several years, women's perspectives were still not showing up in many of the men's courses—and that men felt no urgency to change things.

"I found myself going back and forth in my mind over the question, Are these nice men, or are they oppressive?" McIntosh said in a 2014 interview that was published in the New Yorker. "I thought I had to choose. It hadn't occurred to me that you could be both."

These men, she came to see, were indeed "nice," but also possessed unacknowledged privilege that was powerful, but unconscious. Yet they could exercise it to keep courses as they preferred, which was not to include "the soft stuff" that incorporated women's perspectives. McIntosh then recalled the "frequent charges from women of color that white women whom they encounter are oppressive." She made a connection.

"I began to understand why we are justly seen as oppressive, even when we don't see ourselves that way." Further, she realized, "I had been taught about racism as something that puts others at a disadvantage but had been taught not to see one of its corollary aspects, white privilege, which puts me at an advantage."[78]

McIntosh then went about exploring "white privilege" as "an invisible package of unearned assets" that she tapped into on a daily basis but about which "I was 'meant' to remain oblivious. White privilege is like an invisible weightless knapsack of special provisions, maps, passports, codebooks, visas, clothes, tools and blank checks." In her best-known essay, "White Privilege: Unpacking the Invisible Knapsack" she made a list of twenty-six examples of white privilege she encountered in her daily life, such as "I can do well in a challenging situation without being called a credit to my race" (#14); "If a traffic cop pulls me over or if the IRS audits my tax return, I can be sure I haven't been singled out because of my race" (#19); "I can be sure that if I need legal or medical help, my race will not work against me"

(#24); and—interesting for this time—"When I am told about our national heritage or about 'civilization,' I am shown that people of my color made it what it is" (#6).[79]

I met with McIntosh at her home overlooking the Charles River on a Monday morning in October 2022, a few days after I had visited with Matthew Hawn. I am an admirer of McIntosh, whom I have come to know because we are both connected to the Wellesley Centers for Women (plus we served on a panel together several years ago). She appeared at her door in a green Thai silk jacket and her familiar tornado of white hair. We made our way to a long table beside a stretch of windows that looked like a favorite working spot, outfitted with a row of pens, paper, and two print newspapers. She had baked Linzer bars and placed a plate of them within my easy reach.

McIntosh is one of those scholars who is precise with language and firm about clarity, but who is also curious, hip, and generous. We quickly fell into conversation about what was happening in schools, as she was deeply involved in them for decades. In 1987, she founded what became the National SEED Project (SEED stands for Seeking Educational Equity and Diversity).

The project, which often works with schools and educators, helps groups design seminars that promote conversation and reflection that "acknowledge systems of power, oppression and privilege." The seminars guide community members to listen to one another—including hearing one another's stories—and to build relationships based on principles of social justice and racial equity. As one current codirector put it, "You share your story. I share my story. We both move a little bit. It's a long process." McIntosh codirected SEED for its first twenty-five years.[80]

McIntosh sees attacks facing public schools coming from "critics who just don't understand how classrooms work." A class "is a mix of students"; if the teacher has good relationship skills, it enables discussions "in which different students say different things about what they think and feel—and nobody wins. A teacher who is companionable to the students often says, 'Let's toss some ideas around' or 'Why don't we throw some ideas around.' And that is part of the aim of education," she said. "There are rules of decorum and politeness, even gentleness." When students get to know one another, "They have a better chance of building community than [if the school is] trying to muffle discussion of everything that involves power."[81]

It is that topic, in fact, that McIntosh said is key to understanding what is going on. "The new dynamics have to do with power," she said. "Citizens trying to get power over the schools. But also hating the school subjects that touch on power," which typically involve topics of race, gender, and sexuality.

"If you think through your own K–12 schooling, were you encouraged to look at how power works in your community, in your country, or in the world? My experience says we were not taught to touch power as a subject," she said. "The parent protests and interventions have to do with the times when power is finally being addressed by the schools."

Interestingly, while the work of the SEED Project has gone on for decades, helping people understand one another's perspectives seems especially urgent now. In some districts where they are working, said Emmy Howe, a SEED codirector, almost all administrators are white, even as the student body is racially and ethnically diverse.[82]

Gail Cruise-Roberson, another SEED codirector, said interest in SEED "continues to grow," but the work has come under fire in some places.[83] After the summer 2022 training, one facilitator described rigid rules about how conversations in their state could unfold: "No talk about Justice unless it's brought up by the attendees and we are supposed to steer the conversation in a different direction. We can't use words and terms like privilege, implicit bias, can't talk about blame. We have to do trainings in an 'objective' manner without endorsements of the concepts. It's been a challenge for sure."[84]

In spring 2021, a small group of activists in a small rural Minnesota school district ignited a firestorm in response to a video the superintendent made celebrating their work with the National SEED Project. Chris Lindholm, the superintendent of Pequot Lakes School District, had made the video in March 2021 to appreciate SEED. He said the project was "designed to help educators cultivate healthy dialogue and learning work that leads to an appreciation of diversity and making positive change happen. We have conversations on power, privilege, race." In the video, he also said he imagined that "life would probably be pretty lonely here if I was a student of color or a student that was gay or a transgender student or living in poverty."[85]

Soon a group of angry parents shared the video on Facebook and organized opposition. The private Facebook group, Parents for Pequot United was formed on April 11, 2021, and states on its "about" page: "United in our fight against Critical Race Theory in our schools!"[86] One parent told a local reporter that students were being indoctrinated in critical race theory and that, as a result, teachers "would be less empathetic" toward white students. Lindholm took the video down a few weeks later, in April 2021.

A school board meeting in May at which the video was on the agenda was packed with 150 people. It was so raucous that, according to a local report, "The officer had to call for backup from the Pequot Lakes police."[87] Lindholm resigned that month. He insisted it was not because of the backlash around SEED or the video.

Cruise-Roberson said that forging real understanding among people is hard and not always smooth. "The work we do is over time, building relationships with people that go through in some cases very uncomfortable places with themselves and each other, but they come out the other side still in relationship because they have built a level of trust." In many cases, problems that have arisen across the country surface when people "watching someone teach on a Zoom link for an hour or two" then go and "make some snap decision about the quality of education." What's needed is sustained dialogue. "If people are willing to engage with each other over difficult topics and listen as opposed to arguing and bashing each other, this is a hope. That does not seem to be the preferred mode of communication in the public sphere right now."[88]

A HISTORICAL MAKEOVER

As a culture we struggle with how to discuss and teach children about race and its role in our history. There is no shortage of stories about shocking school lessons featuring mock slave auctions, students asked to pick seeds from unprocessed cotton, Black students cast as slaves in plays, or first-grade field trips to a plantation.[89]

The answer should not be to ignore race or injustice. But that is what is starting to happen in schools. Rather than grapple with difficult truths, state lawmakers have tied themselves in knots over how to soften the dark chapters of history. Some seek to gloss over racialized horrors and instead focus on the perceived impact of tough truths on students. In some places that has limited what may be taught and what teachers can say aloud.

In Texas, the "critical race theory law" demanded that lessons avoid making students "feel discomfort, guilt, anguish, or any other form of psychological distress on account of the individual's race or sex." It banned "The 1619 Project." It required that slavery and racism not be described as "anything other than deviations from, betrayals of, or failures to live up to, the authentic founding principles of the United States, which include liberty and equality."[90]

Lessons had to steer clear of presenting facts that might complicate or
taint the rosy picture of America's founding. The push to make history fit a
specific viewpoint has seeded confusion. It had teachers in Carroll ISD in
Texas mistakenly thinking they had to offer an alternative perspective to
the Holocaust. And a summer 2022 working committee of the Texas State
Board of Education tried so hard to soften history that second-grade draft
standards used the phrase "involuntary relocation" instead of "slavery," until
a flood of outrage forced the board chair to release a statement conceding
that "the draft description 'involuntary relocation' for African people who
were sold into slavery did not paint a clear or full picture." He vowed, "Our
state's curriculum will not downplay the role of slavery in American history."[91]

But in some places that is exactly what is happening. In forty-eight states
(all but Delaware and Massachusetts), local, state, or federal actors have proposed or enacted through "legislation, letters, statements, executive directives,
resolutions, or regulations," rules restricting the teaching of "critical race
theory," according to the UCLA School of Law's CRT Forward Tracking
Project.[92] Many of the new rules are vague or tough to parse, leaving local
administrators to insert their own jittery judgments. In many cases, teachers
now avoid talking about things they think could get them fired.[93]

In Florida, Governor Ron DeSantis solved the problem by telling teachers what to teach. Since taking office in 2019, he has pressed for legislation
to limit what teachers could discuss, to have the state "identify errors and
inaccuracies in state-adopted materials"—what he termed as taking the
"woke" out of textbooks—and to rewrite civics standards.[94] The new standards minimize slavery, elevate Christian values, and center patriotism as
a value.[95] They swap open-ended student exploration for the inculcation of
conservative principles. Seventh-graders no longer analyze qualifications of
candidates, hold mock elections, or simulate jury trials. Rather than "compare
different forms of government," students now "analyze the advantages of the
United States' constitutional republic over other forms of government in
safeguarding liberty, freedom and a representative government." One draft
standard (since removed) required students to "recognize the influence of
the Ten Commandments on establishing the rule of law in America." (US
law is not based on the Ten Commandments).[96]

The new standards were not an accident. In fact, the 2019 Florida law
calling for the revamp stipulated that certain organizations be consulted
on school curriculums; organizations named included the Bill of Rights

Institute (founded by the Charles G. Koch Foundation in 1999) and Hillsdale College.[97] As the education historian Diane Ravitch put it in her blog, "Old-style Republicans believed in leaving teachers alone and letting them [do] their job. The new-style, Trumpist Republicans believe that they must tell teachers what to teach." She went on to quip, "DeSantis is a busy guy, so he has outsourced the Florida civics curriculum to Hillsdale College, the go-to evangelical college that tells conservative leaders what to think and converts it into a school curriculum."[98]

Teachers were not happy. After teacher trainings for the new civics standards were held in June and July of 2022, news reports found teachers alarmed by the rewrite. One social studies teacher saw "this Christian nationalism philosophy that was just baked into everything that was there." Facilitators reportedly focused on how many people were born into slavery, rather than brought on ships, which one teacher saw as trying to make America seem "less bad." A Fort Lauderdale government teacher saw irony in the situation: As educators, they are constantly being falsely accused of "indoctrinating" students. "But that is nothing compared to what the state just threw in new civic educators' faces. That's straight-up indoctrination."[99]

With "CRT," far-right activists discovered that they could take something that people did not really understand and use its acronym as a tool to wield power. It left teachers across the country afraid of talking about race in class. In Kingsport, Tennessee, when I attended a forum organized by the local education association, I asked the president if anti-CRT laws were affecting teachers. She did not pause. "They are terrified," she said. Certainly, every teacher gathered in the Kingsport Civic Auditorium knew what had happened to Matthew Hawn. Of course, race was not the only thing that made the far-right uncomfortable. By August 2022, Christopher Rufo, a senior fellow at the conservative Manhattan Institute and key DeSantis advisor, had sounded a fresh alarm, describing a new threat in America's schools: "Radical gender theory."[100]

CHAPTER 5

DECENCY AND DEFENDING LGBTQ+ STUDENTS

W HEN FLORIDA GOVERNOR Ron DeSantis signed the "Parents Rights in Education" law on March 28, 2022, the official press release proclaimed, "Parents' rights have been increasingly under assault around the nation, but in Florida, we stand up for the rights of parents and the fundamental role they play in the education of their children."[1]

The law included a ban on discussion of gay and transgender issues in grades K–3, gave parents the ability to sue school districts over teaching they didn't like (and have districts pay for it), and require schools to notify parents if students received mental health services.[2]

It didn't take long for HB 1557 to be known as the "Don't Say 'Gay'" law—and for legislators elsewhere to begin crafting versions of their own, some even more restrictive. The law's most powerful effect, however, was not explicitly spelled out in the legal language.

Rather it was implicit, emboldening far-right activists to publicly attack LGBTQ+ youth. Such attacks had been on the rise, but the Florida law institutionalized them. The "parents" mentioned in the law's text were a particular set of people who suddenly found their hatred recast as righteous protection of far-right Christian values. Their "attacks" became a "defense" of children. (In March 2023, DeSantis doubled down, expanding the law to all grades, K–12.)[3]

Far-right anti-LGBTQ+ activism has shown up in local communities as book bans and pressure to frame support for LGBTQ+ students as "political" rather than as the same protection or treatment that would be accorded any student in the district. It happened quickly. In Pennsylvania, even before the state legislature voted on its own version of the Florida law, local school boards—some newly stacked with far-right majorities—began putting anti-LGBTQ+ dictums into district policy.

The Pennridge (Pennsylvania) School Board, on September 27, 2022, found the matter so urgent that it fast-tracked a new policy—policy changes ordinarily require two readings at consecutive meetings—to bar teachers from "advocacy" in school. The following day, the district sent staff instructions to remove "all advocacy-related materials" by the following week; these included LGBTQ+ pride materials, religious symbols, abortion-rights and anti-abortion materials, and political party symbols or "geopolitical" materials, including Ukrainian flags.[4]

The policy grouped symbols of support for LGBTQ+ students with controversial political issues such as abortion. Pennridge was not the first or only school district to do this. The venture capitalist Paul Martino, who is listed on the Federalist Society's website as a "contributor" and who has spoken or otherwise participated in society events or publications, spent $500,000 on school board races, including in the Central Bucks School District. The Central Bucks School District, where contentious school board races in the fall of 2021 ended with a 6–3 far-right majority, took similar action as Pennridge. A few months later, a spate of policy changes, directives, and building-level instructions to teachers set up a charged and hostile climate.[5]

The series of actions by district-level leaders and some building principals in the Central Bucks district's twenty-three schools came in rapid succession. Teachers were ordered to remove pride flags from classrooms. The board voted to change the school district's library policy, allowing community members to challenge books "on the basis of appropriateness," a thinly veiled attack on books with LGBTQ+ themes. The policy detailed "sexualized content" that was newly prohibited at the elementary, middle, and high school levels. The board also passed a policy censoring such content in textbooks and classroom materials. For example, parental consent became required for elementary students to be exposed to "depictions of nudity or implied nudity," including those "relating to classical works of art." The district also put online a human development course that separated students by sex for instruction, after a transgender student requested to join the class of their preferred gender identity. The board turned down funding for teachers to attend workshops around support for LGBTQ+ students.

Then, administrators at two schools, Lenape Middle School and Central Bucks West High School, barred teachers from using students' preferred names and pronouns without parent approval. At the high school, staff were informed of this "gender identification procedure" a few days into the new 2022–2023 school year.

David Klein, a social studies teacher at Central Bucks West who was beginning his thirtieth year of teaching, wasn't having it. Klein was revved up when he strode into the sports bar where we met near the train depot in Doylestown, a charming city of stick-style brick Victorians with gingerbread flourishes and broad porches.

"They tried to fire me today," he said, sliding onto a stool. He quickly launched into an analysis of the power of identity in shaping people's embrace of rigid beliefs. Klein projected the intellectual intensity of someone who has spent decades with primary source historical documents and high-schoolers. He didn't get to the story of what happened that afternoon until he shared his educational philosophy: "To me, the worst things are grades," he said, adding that he was more interested in "What did you learn? What can you do? . . . I am indoctrinating them to be knowledgeable, self-aware thinkers."[6]

As a father of three, including a daughter who is a member of the LGBTQ+ community who was relentlessly bullied in school, opposing the new directive was not difficult. Klein understood how critical it was for there to be signals of protection and for his daughter to have allies among the staff. He was grateful for "how those teachers protected her and offered her a safe space." (Klein's children attended school in a different district.) In Central Bucks, "Over the past five years I can count twenty kids who committed suicide or were lost or almost lost."

To Klein, this was not about politics. It was about protecting students, the young people to whom Klein and others like him devote their attention and care each day. When the policy forbidding the use of preferred pronouns was announced, Klein spoke up, telling local reporters that he would not comply. Most teachers kept mum.[7] "I am one of only two teachers out of one hundred some odd in our building who have publicly said anything," Klein said. "They are all afraid."

And for good reason. The previous school year a middle school social studies teacher, Andrew Burgess, who was seen as an ally to the LGBTQ+ community, was suddenly placed on administrative leave by the Lenape Middle School. Parents and students believe the action was taken because he provided a student who had been bullied with contact information for the US Department of Education's Office of Civil Rights. Students organized a multiday walkout at Lenape. In a move that angered the principal, students who accepted a flyer supporting Burgess were given free pizza delivered by a high school student. The principal took to the loudspeaker with an angry rant that was recorded by students and posted online.[8] She also called the police.[9]

At a school board meeting, the superintendent, Abe Lucabaugh, denied that Burgess faced retaliation for helping a student. "There is a narrative out there that the district has punished an employee for being a supporter of LGBTQ+ students. That narrative is offensive and false," he said. He refused to provide information on the suspension.[10] (The teacher was on the teaching staff list at a different middle school in the district for the 2022–2023 school year.)

Shortly before I met with Klein, he had been called into a meeting with his principal. School leaders had seen his comments in the newspaper. He brought a union representative with him. Klein told me that he had been asked, "What are your intentions regarding this procedure?" referring to the gender identification procedure. He refused to answer, claiming that it was a hypothetical scenario as he wasn't aware of having any such students in class currently.

But Klein made it very clear: "I will never hurt a child. I will never intentionally harm a child."[11]

"EVERY SINGLE DAY MY FRIENDS AND I HAVE SLURS SHOUTED AT US IN THE HALLWAYS"

For LGBTQ+ students, the explosion of school board policies and building-level decisions were one part of the problem. The other—like the Florida law—was the tone and messaging such policies set for the treatment of LGBTQ+ students.

Or, as Alexandra Coffey, a high school junior with a broad, generous face and shimmery pink lip gloss, put it to me, "People in general have been getting more brazen. They are not as uncomfortable about sharing hateful opinions." There exists a climate in which "people are now more open about their homophobia and transphobia."[12]

And it wasn't just the high school, said Rowan Hopwood, an eighth-grader at Lenape Middle School, who radiated both generosity ("Can I get you a water?") and spunk, with a swirl of magenta in his hair, a prominent curled nose ring, and headphones nestled around his neck. Hopwood has been on the receiving end of open animosity in school.

"As a queer student, literally, like every single day my friends and I have slurs shouted at us in the hallways," he said. And while school leaders outwardly "urge us to come to them when there is any kind of bullying happening," when the students do that, "they don't do anything."

The problem is that it "triggers all the bad stuff," he said. "As a trans person, I already don't feel comfortable with how I am and how other people see me." The slurs reinforce that internal discomfort and fuel stress around his safety, he said. "Even though I am trans, I still go by my birth name, but I know people who have very unsafe transphobic environments. School was a special place where they used to be able to be called what they wanted to be called. Now they either have to come out to their parents or they have to be deadnamed or misgendered."

I met with Coffey, Hopwood, and Zandi Hall, a senior at Central Bucks West, at Jules Thin Crust in downtown Doylestown on a warm September day after school. It is a favorite teen hangout, where the pizza comes as a long strip of dough and toppings for sharing, delivered to wood tables with fire-engine red seating. Hall also works at Jules—she instinctively grabbed a spray bottle and towel to wipe down our table when we finished.

It was Hall who had delivered the donated pizza to the Lenape Middle School protestors the previous spring. Although she had never had so much as a detention during her entire school career, after the protest she found herself suspended from school for ten days (she served seven). Hall said she was not told why she was suspended but can't think of any other reason besides her protest participation.

To all three, actions in the district have felt like a kind of attack on LGBTQ+ students, making it difficult for teachers to overtly show support for students. Coffey recalled that when teachers were ordered to remove pride flags, one hung up solid pieces of construction paper in the colors of the rainbow. "It was sweet," she said. Hall said students noticed on a trip when a teacher, in the heat, pulled out a rainbow fan to cool herself. The students said that their peers appreciated the support. But, said Coffey, they also can tell that "teachers are scared."

The situation did not escape the notice of the American Civil Liberties Union of Pennsylvania, which on October 6, 2022, filed a seventy-one-page complaint with the US Department of Justice and with the US Department of Education's Office for Civil Rights, alleging that the Central Bucks School District violated the rights of LGBTQ+ students under Title IX and under the Equal Protection Clause of the Fourteenth Amendment. Not only did the district fail to address "persistent and severe bullying and harassment of LGBTQ+ students," the complaint charged, but "a school board majority elected in November 2021, joined by complicit upper-level administrators, have exacerbated the hostile environment by making homophobic and transphobic statements, enacting blatantly discriminatory practices and policies targeting LGBTQ+ students, and retaliating against teachers and staff who support LGBTQ+ students."

The complaint detailed actions that included "intimidating teachers into removing LGBTQ+ themed resource materials from their classrooms," and supporting a culture so hostile to LGBTQ+ students that many feared eating lunch in the cafeteria. "One student for the 2022–2023 school year had been eating lunch in the bathroom to avoid bullying, until staff caught them and ordered them to a remote hallway location," the complaint said. It further stated that this environment "can and already has had tragic consequences" with "multiple serious incidents of student self-harm, including one trans student attempting to take his life in school in 2019." The complaint included twenty-six pages of testimony from seven students that had been gathered over five months (students' names were redacted in the document).[13] The school district responded to a query from the *Philadelphia Inquirer*, saying that it would not comment on legal matters but that "we believe it is paramount that all students and teachers are cared for and respected as members of our learning and teaching community."[14]

Less than two months earlier, at their August 26, 2022, meeting, the Central Bucks School Board had voted to spend $180,000 a year plus expenses to hire a public relations firm to improve the school district's image.[15]

WHY "BELONGING" IS MORE THAN A FUZZY FEELING

As a parent and a former teacher, Kristen Bruck noticed when buzz arose over a poster that had hung in a teacher's classroom at Southern Lehigh High School in Pennsylvania for several years. The poster was hand-painted in red, orange, green, blue, and purple—basically, a rainbow. It read, "Women's

Rights Are Human Rights," "Kindness Is Everything," "Climate Change Is Real," "Celebrate Diversity," and "Love Is Love."

Suddenly, now, it was controversial. Photos surfaced on social media.[16] Then, at parent meetings, Bruck heard complaints about rules that let transgender students use the bathroom of their gender identity, in line with federal regulations under Title IX.[17] In March 2022, sarcastic posts popped up in local Facebook groups such as "Dear Fellow Community Members, Please Take Time to Answer This Question. What is a Girl?" Before long, another urged parents to "guard your children from radical gender ideology." "The radicals [want to] affirm their own twisted world view while exploiting children. They are child abusers."[18]

The far-right crusade, with its hyped-up language about "radical gender theory" and "gender ideologies" and attacks on LGBTQ+ students, had arrived in Bruck's suburban community in Pennsylvania's Lehigh Valley. Like a kind of infection, such attacks have spread and flared in school districts around the country, including with some force in eastern Pennsylvania. It would soon drive Bruck to found and lead a nonprofit to oppose such attacks.

As the mother of two high-schoolers, Bruck knew that students had taken to watching school meetings on Zoom "to hear what parents are saying." Bruck, who left teaching a few months before we first spoke in September 2022, said, "They all know what is going on."[19] Specifically, she understood that this could affect students: "I had multiple trans kids in every class that I taught." Her school was also racially diverse: a school profile says 40 percent of students represent "diverse backgrounds."[20]

"I was concerned about kids and mental health," said Bruck. "I have been in education for twenty years, and messages of belonging are important for everyone, and especially for kids who are being marginalized."

She wasn't wrong to be thinking about this. Research on the power and importance of student "belonging" in school and its link to academic performance is robust. Geoffrey Cohen, a professor of education and psychology at Stanford University, has studied it for years and, with his team, developed interventions. In 2022, he published *Belonging: The Science of Creating Connection and Bridging Divides.* He and other researchers have shown that how students conceive their abilities in relation to a task can shape its outcome.

"Much of intellectual performance is more malleable than we thought," Cohen told me in 2013 when I interviewed him for a story about the impact of seemingly slippery qualities like "grit" on school success. Cohen's point is that belonging—"the sense that you are accepted and respected in a domain"—affects how students tackle schoolwork.[21]

To demonstrate this, he and colleagues conducted a randomized study in which two groups of seventh-graders were given a structured writing assignment at four stress points during the year—at the beginning of school and on three days when tests were scheduled. Half selected core values from a list and reflected on how the values mattered to them and helped in their lives. Other students wrote about the values but as unconnected to themselves.

The results were striking. Black students in the first group earned higher grade-point averages than their same-race peers in the control group. The effect persisted through middle school. It may look like magic, but removing a barrier to success by cueing students to their strengths in a setting where they feel unsure of themselves "sets the tone and changes their trajectory," Cohen explained to me.

He cautioned that the intervention works in part because performance traits don't exist in isolation but in relation to a specific situation: "When we are often at our best, it doesn't depend just on what's inside of us but on being in the right circumstance with people we trust." More recently he observed, "If you feel like your belonging's on trial, and you're wondering if this is a place where you're regarded favorably . . . it takes up working memory." Which is "mental energy taken away from learning, focusing, performing, growing."[22]

As researchers like Cohen have demonstrated the sturdy power of psychological and emotional engagement to school success, it has become a tool not to replace content such as math, but to make it more likely that students will acquire the math skills being taught.[23] Helping students to feel comfortable, capable, and welcome primes them to learn. A poster that signals "you belong" may not alone do the trick, but it can help. This is what the far right labels as "woke."

A FIGHT OVER SIGNS

Bruck believed she needed to respond to the negative energy. "I was upset about how these parents were talking about these children," she said. She and friend Krissy Laverty, who has a background in art, designed a simple lawn sign, "YOU BELONG. YOU MATTER. WE ARE ALL SOUTHERN LEHIGH." The letters were in rainbow colors, plus brown and black.

Bruck went to her local print shop and ordered fifty. She stuck one in her front yard, near the street at the end of her sloped driveway, then placed a few in visible public spaces. "I put some in intersections around the schools," she said. Her goal: Let kids know that they were OK, that they belonged. People noticed the signs immediately.

"The teachers started talking about it," said Alexandra Cooperman, a music teacher at the intermediate school, which serves students in grades four to six. "I said, 'Does anyone know who is making these signs? Because I want one.'"[24]

Cooperman, who is married to a high school teacher in the district, is now a mother of two. She spoke to me one afternoon during her maternity leave as her three-month-old son gazed up from an infant lounger. She sat at her dining-room table and had set out fresh veggies, hummus, and water as a snack. Cooperman said she has always sought to be the teacher that students could talk to.

In her classroom, she has a box labeled "I wish Mrs. Cooperman knew." Students put notes in the box, anonymously or including their name, in which case Cooperman responds. There are months with few or no messages. But in September 2021, a student wrote, "Is it OK to like girls if I am a girl?" She signed her name.

Cooperman consulted the guidance counselor, who told her that she should go ahead and talk with the student. "She didn't tell me what to say," Cooperman said. Then, at an opportune moment, she and the student strolled school hallways and talked. "We had an absolutely amazing conversation," recalled Cooperman, who told the student that her feelings were "absolutely okay." The student said she had not before shared her feelings but wanted to tell her parents—and soon did—yet seemingly first wanted to speak with a trusted adult.

That role of being available for students to process personal concerns does not show up as a school metric. It is why some who believe that school should be strictly academic object to such conversations. Yet school *is* social. Students *do come to trust* teachers and *do choose* to lean on them emotionally. Following their conversation, Cooperman saw the student feel at ease, happily asking, "Did you know we are going on the field trip on the first day of pride month?"

When Cooperman spotted Bruck's signs, she asked around to find out who was making them, then bought one for $10. As did another teacher. Bruck delivered a sign to Cooperman and asked if she wouldn't mind bringing the other one to her colleague. The next day, Cooperman brought in the two signs. The other teacher was out, so, she said, "I just put it behind her desk."

What happened next set off a controversy in the district. A parent visiting the school spotted the sign and complained. Some days later, on March 11—a date Cooperman recalls because it was "pajama day" and she was wearing pajamas and was "very pregnant"—her principal told her to remove the sign, which was "right on my white board." The parent, she was told, "had said it was political." Cooperman reached out to a union representative and learned that as a teacher, she said, "you don't have the right to free speech." A few days later, however, she put the sign back up. "If I am ever going to get fired as a teacher, it would be for protecting a student," she told me. If losing her job "came down to me sticking up for a student for the color of their skin or who they love, then fine, I won't be a teacher anymore. Because it's messed up." Yet, she was also nervous. "I don't want to walk on eggshells but at the same time, I have to because I have to keep my job. That is where I am stuck in this very bad place."[25] Word quickly traveled, and soon there was coverage in local news outlets.

By the time the Southern Lehigh School District met on March 28, 2022, the room was charged. The board was to consider a hastily drafted policy to restrict what teachers could post on their walls (it was not adopted). But two-thirds of the almost three-hour meeting was devoted to public comments and discussion about what signs and decorations could hang in teachers' classrooms. Essentially, the speakers were second-guessing teachers' judgment.

Board members and people in the audience generally agreed that classrooms should be politically neutral. But there was disagreement about what that looked like. To several board members, the signs were a problem. "Just like obscenity," said one board member, "you know a political message when you see it." And, he said, "Some of these signs that we have discussed are political and are meant to be political."[26]

Another countered that a message of inclusion, given the history of where power resides in schools and curricula, was welcoming and valid. Yet another argued that the phrase "Women's Rights Are Human Rights," in the original hand-painted poster that was first posted on social media but not included on Bruck's signs, was actually an abortion rights message and therefore had no place in the classroom. (There was some confusion among board members as to which sign was the source of the controversy.)

Demand for Bruck's signs exploded. She printed fifty more, then another fifty, then yet another fifty. At the same time, the hostile posts on social media continued. Then a second issue erupted. Some white middle-school students were using avatars in Google Classroom of Black faces with caricatured features. Bethlehem NAACP held a press conference at the middle school calling for their removal, and they were removed.[27]

The climate in the district, "started to get very hot and heated," said Andrea Lycette, a mom of four and a pediatric therapist. The angry responses to the signs with their message of inclusivity "was enough for me to say 'enough.'" By May 2022 Lycette had rented two electronic billboards—one on Route 378 as you left the school district and one on Route 309 as you entered it—and posted the message "YOU BELONG, YOU MATTER," using Bruck's design.[28]

Lycette intentionally did not put the billboards near schools nor include the district's name. She wanted to simply share the positive message. "There needs to be some calm in this storm," she said. On a sunny September morning, as Lycette sat in her kitchen with its sweeping view of the Lehigh Valley, she said that things were not as outwardly tense as before.

But the division remains. The mom of her twin daughters' close friend, who is now a school board member, no longer talks to her. "She can't speak to me in the bleachers," said Lycette, whose daughters play lacrosse.

"This is breaking down some of the most essential, some of our most basic needs of interaction—and I am speaking as a therapist. You cannot have a happy life if you are afraid to go to Giant and buy a gallon of milk because you might see somebody and get anxious. And that is what I see around us in the community."

As tensions have risen, demand for Bruck's signs has grown in other communities, probably for the same reasons that people in her community wanted them. "It never occurred to me that we would make signs in any other district," she said. Yet at the print shop one day, a woman said, "Gee, we would really like to do this for East Penn." Bruck also made T-shirts, magnets, and stickers (her kids report that even "the conservative kids" put them on their water bottles). The signs have spread to nearby districts, and farther afield, including in Illinois and Oregon, and in Arizona they appear on car magnets.

When I stopped by Bruck's home on a late September afternoon, she had just picked up more signs. A Southern Lehigh stack sat in the garage. The back of her maroon Honda Odyssey held boxes of generic signs reading simply

"YOU BELONG, YOU MATTER" (with no district), plus an order for a new community, Saucon Valley. Someone from another district had just called.

Bruck was also in the process of turning her You Belong campaign on Facebook into a 501(c)(3) nonprofit, the YouBelongCampaign. She is clear about the role the organization should play: "We are not going to create a PAC" or be involved in elections. The only goal is to be supportive of students: "I want these signs to be just what they are." By spring 2023, Bruck's organization's website was up and running; the group announced its monthly selection for its new book club, held in-person "in various locations throughout the United States." The book, *This Is How It Always Is*, by Laurie Frankel, is about a family grappling with the "secret" that begins when one of the family's sons, Claude, "puts on a dress and refuses to take it off."[29]

QUIET, POWERFUL INFLUENCE: 7M CHRISTIAN NATIONALISM

Tension in the Southern Lehigh School District, as elsewhere, stems from the fact that those on the far-right view messages of support for LGBTQ+ students as political statements, rather than signals of safety or welcome. As a result, some far-right majority boards are trying to effectively cleanse schools of acknowledgment of or support for LGBTQ+ students.

These actions align with a Christian nationalist quest embraced by far-right politicians like Senator Ted Cruz to make the United States into a Christian nation. A national poll by *Politico* and the University of Maryland in May 2022 found that 61 percent of Republicans favor declaring the US a Christian nation. Of course, not all Christians welcome this extremism, and many are energetically fighting it.[30]

What Christian nationalists mean by a "Christian nation" is not just a throwback to more conservative God-fearing times, but a specific doctrine known as "dominionism." Since the early twenty-first century this extreme ideology has quietly gained support with conservative politicians. As one religion writer put it, "Dominionism is the idea that conservative Christians have the right—and the responsibility—to take dominion over all aspects of life, including the government."[31]

The movement is commonly traced to 1950s-era teachings of R. J. Rushdoony, an activist and founder of the Christian think tank the Chalcedon Foundation. But it was in the mid-1970s that three religious leaders—Bill Bright of Campus Crusade for Christ, Loren Cunningham of Youth with a Mission, and Francis Schaeffer of L'Abri—"each independently reported

God-given revelatory instructions to his people to focus on seven areas" that, if they gained control of them, would allow Christians to achieve a state of dominion.

These areas, known as the Seven Mountains, or 7M, are business, government, media, arts and entertainment, education, the family, and religion. The Seven Mountain Mandate, which places the law of God above secular law, shows up in politicians' calls for severe reductions in government regulations, even abolishing government agencies and supports such as social programs and education. Betsy DeVos, a former secretary of education, had declared at the Moms for Liberty National Summit, "I personally do not think the Department of Education should exist." The goal of the 7M movement, one religion journalist explained, is that the "federal government would no longer be responsible for laws that govern public safety, social programs (including public schools and welfare), or just about anything else."[32]

For Christian extremists, LGBTQ+ individuals, and especially transgender students, are a deviation from "God's design" and a clear "problem" in the extremists' quest for a Christian society. To Christian extremists one's biological birth sex is the only acceptable gender identity. The insistence that there are only biological males and females surfaces in attacks on transgender students. In the Southern Lehigh School District, a parent ranted on Facebook about "this whole Transgender/Identity issue that currently plagues our country." The parent said, "Since NO one can change their gender, there is no such thing as Transgender."[33]

The refusal to acknowledge gender as a crucial social expression, rather than a biological fact, is driving far-right school board members to regulate what they can't control. Three months after the Patriot Mobile Action PAC "flipped" the Grapevine-Colleyville ISD school board in Texas, trustees passed restrictive policies limiting how teachers could discuss race, gender, and sexuality and directed which bathrooms transgender students could use. The board also voted to give itself control over which books are available in schools. The new rules were passed by a close vote at a contentious meeting on a Monday evening.

Students at Grapevine High School reacted immediately. On Friday, more than one hundred students walked out of class, chanting, "Protect our rights" and "Protect trans kids," according to a news report. "We are here to show that the school board cannot get away with treating our education, our lives, as a playground for politics," Marceline Temple, one of the organizers, said in remarks directed at school board members. "We will not let this school board treat the existence of minorities as a controversy."[34]

A CHANGING SCHOOL POPULATION

Since the time when today's parents were students themselves, the nation's public schools have grown dramatically more diverse. In 1986, 70.4 percent of US public school students were white. By 1995 that percentage had dropped to 64.8 percent and by 2020, whites were 46 percent, less than half of the public school population. The white population is projected to fall further, to 43 percent, by 2030, according to the National Center for Education Statistics.[35]

This affects (or should) how schools operate, from what is taught to norms that shape the culture. Consider that schools long operated on the assumption that children had mothers at home who could serve them lunch, so school would break at midday. That seems absurdly out of touch now. Some places are adjusting to the changes. In 2020, Connecticut became the first state to require that every high school offer courses on African American, Black, Puerto Rican, and Latino studies. In 2022, the Connecticut legislature mandated that Asian and Pacific Islander history be taught in grades K–12 in the state beginning in the 2025–2026 school year.[36]

Ironically, the refusal to acknowledge the needs of LGBTQ+ students in schools comes as more young adults and teens identify as gay, bisexual, nonbinary, or transgender. An analysis of federal health data found that between 2017 and 2020, 1.4 percent of thirteen-to-seventeen-year-olds and 1.3 percent of eighteen-to-twenty-four-year-olds identified as transgender. In contrast, just 0.5 percent of adults did. The report got a lot of attention because since 2017 data showed that the percentage of transgender youth had nearly doubled. That surprised people. At the same time, other data show that from 2015 to 2019, the prevalence of fifteen-to-seventeen-year-olds who describe themselves as "non-heterosexual" rose from 8.3 to 11.7 percent. Clearly, the landscape of gender identity among young people is shifting.[37]

What does this mean? Angela Goepferd, who is nonbinary and the medical director of the Gender Health Program at Children's Minnesota hospital, observed that not every transgender teen will seek medical treatment, which is a chief far-right concern. Today, she said, "it's developmentally appropriate for teenagers to explore all facets of their identity," including their gender identity.[38]

It may not have happened as much in the past, Goepferd said, but "generationally, gender has become a part of someone's identity that is more socially acceptable to explore." As a result, people "just need to lean into the fact that there is gender diversity among us" and that "as a society we need to make space for that."

When far-right activists seek to halt that acceptance, it offers tacit permission to harass members of the LGBTQ+ community. And when school leaders are themselves not accepting, it creates a threatening climate.

That is what students from Carroll High School in Southlake, Texas, have experienced for years. When members of the Gay Straight Alliance put up posters, they would be ripped down, said Aaliya Mithwani, who had just graduated a few weeks before we spoke in June 2022. I met with Mithwani and Marissa Vazhappilly, a 2020 graduate, in the business center of a hotel in Southlake Town Square, an upscale shopping area with a Tesla dealership tucked amid suburban staples like Oakley, Sephora, Free People, Vineyard Vines, and Vera Bradley.

Mithwani and Vazhappilly were members of the Southlake Anti-Racism Coalition, a student and alumni justice group formed in the summer of 2020. Verbal slurs and attacks on students of color and those who identified as LGBTQ+ were not new, the two students said. Mithwani, who appeared fashionably put together in a Def Leppard T-shirt, a lime-green scarf tied at the waist, clear-rimmed glasses, and riveting red lipstick, said you could never feel at ease because school leaders didn't hold aggressors accountable.

Hostile students would joke about attending Gay Straight Alliance meetings, said Mithwani, "'to find out who the queers are.'" She continued, "And that is a direct quote that stuck because a lot of [queer] students would be scared to come to meetings or skip them or wait until all the hallways were clear before they would come to the meetings."[39]

A HOSTILE CLIMATE

It is not by accident that Carroll ISD has felt unwelcoming to LGBTQ+ and students of color. Not only is Southlake a few short miles from the Grapevine, Texas, headquarters of Patriot Mobile, the conservative Christian cell-phone carrier that formed the influential Patriot Mobile Action PAC. It is also where Glenn Story, the company's cofounder, and Leigh Wambsganns, executive director of the PAC, live. In fact, Wambsganns's husband has even served as mayor.

Students in the district have organized and pushed back. But their battle reveals how tough it can be to dislodge an entrenched far-right culture, and to survive when you are not supported. According to students, classmates could use the N-word or F-slurs in hallways and class and teachers would ignore it.

It was in this climate that the videos of white students using the N-word went viral, leading to creation of the District Diversity Council and the drafting of the thirty-four-page five-year Cultural Competency Action Plan (CCAP). The plan called for the sort of training that has become standard in schools and workplaces around the country. It also called for changes to discipline policies to address what students of color said was an openly racist environment.[40]

The CCAP was expected to be adopted by the Carroll ISD school board on August 3, 2020, but that didn't happen. How did the far-right shut down what looked like a surefire and needed measure? And how did students stand up?

It started in the summer of 2020, racially charged with the murder of George Floyd and protests around the country. In Southlake, much to the consternation of local leaders—including the mayor, who warned on Facebook that she could not guarantee people's safety—members of Carroll High School's Progressive Activism Club organized a Black Lives Matter protest. More than one thousand people attended. It was entirely peaceful. A few weeks later, the group held an event they called a "BLM + Pride Celebration." On Twitter, they urged attendees to wear masks. The poster said it would be "family friendly" with "activities and speakers!"[41]

The success of these gatherings emboldened activist students, including Anya Kushwaha, a 2016 graduate of the high school who was home after graduation from college, and felt compelled to get involved. She cofounded the Southlake Anti-Racism Coalition, known locally as "SARC," and still helps to lead it. The protesting students came together with Kushwaha and proceeded to compose a list of demands directed toward the school board.[42] The SARC demands went viral on local social media and were met with vitriol by community leaders, including a former mayor. SARC quickly sought testimony from students who had faced discrimination and received over six hundred submissions on a Google doc. Kushwaha was not surprised. For years, Kushwaha and other LGBTQ+ and students of color had faced treatment that was so damaging that "we had to learn to psychologically tune it out or we would not have survived."[43]

Kushwaha described a fifth-grade teacher who idolized Robert E. Lee and hung Confederate flags in his classroom. Another teacher broke the class in two sections and had students argue about slavery pro and con. "People of color had to argue for slavery," she said. As a biracial student whose father is Indian, Kushwaha's skin tone confused people. She was asked if she was adopted and, she said, faced beliefs that she was a terrorist: a classmate once said, "You might watch out, Anya might drop a bomb." Students of color felt like second-class citizens. "Everyone knew that Southlake was richer and whiter and better than you."[44]

The actions that followed reveal the far right's determination to maintain control over public schools. As students organized their group, Wambsganns organized the Southlake Families PAC ahead of the August 3 Carroll ISD board meeting. At the meeting, some one hundred speakers signed up to make public comments. Some spoke in favor of the CCAP, while others argued that it promoted reverse racism and countered efforts to teach conservative Christian values at home.

In a strange move, the board voted to receive the plan—literally, to take it in, in a confusing, awkward, and ultimately meaningless action—but not adopt it. It was a victory for Southlake Families PAC, which on its website had cast the plan as "bad for students" and claimed that the plan would "potentially impact the right to freedom of religion" and "be used for shaming and discipline." The Southlake Families PAC identified and backed school board candidates; by November 2021 the effort had produced a board with a majority who opposed the diversity plan.

As if that were not enough to secure their influence, the Southlake Families PAC supported a parent who filed a civil suit against the school board charging that text exchanges made by some board members ahead of the August 3 meeting had violated the Texas Open Meeting Act. In December 2020, a Tarrant County judge ordered a temporary restraining order, and by spring, a grand jury had indicted the Carroll ISD School Board president and vice president on charges that they had violated the open meetings law. When the case was settled in January 2022, the agreement settlement resulted in shelving the CCAP for good.[45]

Then, in a further action that branded Carroll ISD as a far-right Christian district, Patriot Mobile on August 15, 2022, presented the school board with framed blue posters with the words "In God We Trust" above the image of an American flag. The state legislature had passed a law in 2021 requiring schools to display a "durable poster or framed copy of the national motto" with an American flag and the state flag centered below it—if they were donated or purchased with donated funds. The Carroll ISD board eagerly accepted the posters.[46]

Two weeks later, on August 29, another group arrived at the Carroll School Board meeting with posters to donate. They bore the same motto, "In God We Trust," with the American flag and Texas state flag below. But the words sat on a rainbow-hued background. A second version included the motto in Arabic. The signs, designed with help from the Southlake Anti-Racism Coalition, were rejected. The board said it already had posters for each school.[47]

THE POLITICS OF "PARENTAL RIGHTS"

The push to control culture and limit curriculum, books, and materials in public schools has been cast by the far right as an emergency. The alarmist message to parents is that their children are in danger, that they are being "indoctrinated" with "woke racial and gender ideologies" that threaten their well-being. One solution, they are told, is to secure "parental rights" to oversee as many elements as possible of what their child experiences in school.

The problem is that this message is emotionally charged and manipulative. It taps into a parent's basic instinct to protect their child from harm. It also tampers with the task of helping a child navigate adolescence and reach independence. Parenting is messy and not always linear. Children under eighteen may be the legal subjects of their parents, but the reality is that children have interior lives and access to people and ideas far outside of school. Successful parenting is less about exerting control than knowing a child deeply enough to guide them meaningfully.

Yet, in the name of "parental rights," there has been a surge of proposals to shut down diverse views and halt support for racial and gender minority students in favor of centering extremist Christian values. This comes despite the fact that parents *already* had many rights over their child's education and, more broadly, over their child's health and religious upbringing. Parents may not dictate curricula or what books are included in school library collections. But there are long-standing procedures to challenge books. Parents can bar their child from accessing certain books. And they may opt their child out of some lessons and activities, including sex education. Parents are encouraged to visit schools and to communicate with their child's teacher.

Yet parental rights legislation has surfaced as if these measures were not already in place. What's happened is that in the name of "parental rights" a group of extremists has sought control not over just their own child's experience but over everyone else's, too. Some proposals seem Orwellian, like a Florida bill calling for video cameras in classrooms and microphones on teachers (it didn't pass). "Parental rights" are not about parenting, but about politics. They allow those on the far right to claim they are "protecting children" while actually doing harm.[48]

Virginia's Governor Glenn Youngkin may be the poster child for exploiting parental rights for political gain. It carried him into office in 2021, which he reprised a year later.[49] In September 2022, he reminded his base of his commitment when the state Department of Education issued *2022 Model Policies on the Privacy, Dignity, and Respect for All Students and Parents in Virginia's Public Schools* to replace 2021's *Model Policies for the Treatment of Transgender Students in Virginia's Public Schools*. The new policy document states that the old policies "promoted a specific viewpoint aimed at achieving cultural and social transformation in schools" and "disregarded the rights of parents."[50]

The new rules announced new parental control over students, including being able to decide "what names, nicknames and/or pronouns, if any, shall be used for their child by teacher and school staff while their child is at school." It let parents decide if a child may engage in "any counseling or social transition at school" different than their birth sex. And it demanded that schools "keep parents fully informed . . . [on] matters related to their child's health, and social and psychological development"—or, as several news outlets put it, that they "out" transgender students to their parents.

For many LGBTQ+ students, parents are powerful allies. But for some, coming out involves very real risks, including emotional rejection, loss of financial support—even a place to live. This is why schools have mechanisms for students to access counselors, and why they offer students a choice as to whether to include parents in the communication.

The American Civil Liberties Union, among several civil rights groups, opposed the new policies in Virginia, saying that they would "inflict serious harm on transgender and non-binary students." On September 27, 2022, thousands of students in more than ninety public schools in Virginia seemed to agree, walking out of class in a massive protest. The far right has painted teachers as "indoctrinating" students into "gender ideologies," but a student at McLean High School told a television reporter that's just not accurate. "I had

had teachers who would actively acknowledge queer history, queer problems and queer existence," said Casey Calabia. "It was life-changing. That's not what made me queer; that's what made me feel safe and happy to be queer."[51]

PHYSICAL AND PSYCHOLOGICAL EFFECTS OF STRESS

The attacks on LGBTQ+ students, particularly transgender students, may be political in intent, but research shows they have real and serious consequences for the students themselves; transgender and nonbinary youth especially suffer from direct stressors—discrimination, victimization, rejection, nonaffirmation—as well as from the fallout from expected rejection, concealing their identity, and internalizing transphobia.

Mollie T. McQuillan, assistant professor in the Department of Educational Leadership and Policy Analysis at the University of Wisconsin, Madison has stated, "It is well-established that there are mental health disparities among LGBTQ+ youth. Some of the stress is getting under their skin," leading to high rates of depression, anxiety, and suicidality. McQuillan studies stress effects on LGBTQ+ youths, including in schools.[52]

Research by McQuillan and others has found that these stressors have physical effects. Studies show that transgender and nonbinary (also "gender expansive") students experience heightened systemic inflammation, the body's response to physical and psychological threats. Researchers link inflammation to documented health disparities. These young people also have higher rates of substance abuse and self-harm.

But research also shows that these negative health consequences can be avoided. Socially transitioned transgender children who are supported "have developmentally normative levels of depression and only minimal elevations in anxiety, suggesting that psychopathology is not inevitable within this group," according to a study at the University of Washington. Other research finds positive effects of support on physical health.

The big problem, said McQuillan, is that in a politically charged environment, many schools have become threatening places for transgender and nonbinary youth. Federal and state law may protect them, but in this environment, "Trans kids in particular have been targeted and used as political pawns" by the far right. This creates "misalignment" among public institutions that students interact with, exacerbating stressors. It is one reason why her recent research with Cris Mayo—a gender studies scholar, professor, and director of the Interdisciplinary Studies Program in the University of

Vermont's Department of Education—found that "even in states with policy protections, principals and superintendents are confused about what they should be doing."

Far-right groups have exploited this confusion. McQuillan found school leaders, "folding to real or perceived pressure from parents who feel really very uncomfortable with gender non-conformity." More troubling, she found that leaders "are contributing to the bullying" of transgender students by not educating their staff or themselves about some of the risks queer and trans students are facing in schools. "Some [superintendents and principals] don't see it as their role to interrupt bullying. Some see it as their role, but they are excluding trans kids from their conceptualization of what they include as bullying."

CHAPTER 6

THE NEW PARENT INVOLVEMENT

ABOUT A MONTH before the 2022 midterm elections, a mom I had met the previous June in Texas texted me the image of a poster invitation that had all the energy of a public school parent gathering—only it was about voting. "This is how I'm fighting back!" texted the mom, Laura Leeman. "I've put four months of work into this. We finally launched tonight." It was the start of yet another parent group, SPENT—Saving Public Education in North Texas—with a private Facebook page and over 250 members. The evening event, "Public Education Get Out the Vote & Craft Beer!," with a QR code to use for registration, featured a lineup of seven speakers, several of whom I had come to know as stars of the progressive or simply the non-far-right North Texas education universe.

They included Chris Tackett, a campaign finance expert who was a must-follow on Twitter; Colleyville Heritage High School's Dr. James Whit-field[1]; the Reverend Dr. Katie Hays, pastor of the LGBTQ+-friendly Galileo Christian Church in Fort Worth; and candidates for state senate, county judge, and county district attorney.

Another speaker was Tracy Fisher, a former lifelong Republican from a military family who was running for the state board of education. In December 2021, she had switched political parties. When we spoke in June 2022, she said that the far-right swerve by the Republican Party she had belonged to for forty years had made it clear that "this is not my party anymore." Like Nancy Garrett in Williamson County, Tennessee, Fisher believed that serving, in her case on the state board of education, "should not be political." Yet the world was making it so. She changed parties because being labeled a RINO (Republican in Name Only) would hurt her candidacy more than being a Democrat. She would still lose. But the day after the election, she took to Twitter to remind people of her principles, urging followers, "Vote in your local [school board] elections. Keep them non-partisan at all costs. Partisanship divides households and communities. Our children deserve better."[2]

Despite the drawing power of craft beer, the event was hardly a PTA social. Yes, it was about supporting schools, but—in a measure of a changed world—"support" no longer meant buying tissues, markers, and other classroom supplies. Rather, Leeman was among the parents around the country who found themselves pulled into a fight they never expected to have and did not know was a possibility in a nice, otherwise functional suburban community—until far-right attacks on the schools started to unfold.

So now, instead of gathering to hear about the special class project near Thanksgiving and who would organize the snacks, parents needed to hear why their vote mattered in November or May or whenever was next. And why they needed to show up at school board meetings and pay attention to what those in power were saying and doing. They needed to know what to watch out for. Because over the past two years, these active parents had learned the hard way that what had happened in Carroll ISD would come to Grapevine-Colleyville ISD, to Mansfield ISD, to Richardson ISD, to Keller ISD, and Frisco ISD, and other school districts. Even in Pennsylvania, parents were watching Texas. "The hope is that we can connect like-minded public ed supporters across N TX and learn how to save our school districts from extremists; essentially save Pub Ed as America has known it!" Leeman wrote in an email. In recent months, she and other parents had reached across school district boundaries and connected over Facebook Messenger. So when the craft beer gathering happened, some two dozen parent leaders came to rally support, network, and share information. To be sure, "parent involvement" had changed.[3]

And it needed to. After all, Patriot Mobile Action PAC and the 1776 Project PAC and others like them were not going to stop finding and funding far-right school board candidates who would, like those in Central Bucks School District in Pennsylvania, pass policies that attacked children, teachers, and public schools themselves. Parents like Leeman needed to build coalitions and play the long game.

POLITICS, NOT PLAYDATES

The rise of parent activism has put the inner workings of public schools into the national spotlight. Who knew the power of public comments at school board meetings or cared about the contents of classroom libraries? It has also raised the profile of what moms can do.

Classrooms are expected to be politically neutral spaces. But outside of them, seemingly everything else about education has become partisan. How did this happen? Covid restrictions and calls to reflect the history of systemic racism in school curricula spurred parents to form new alliances, based not on a kid's favored playdate friends—but on politics. In this new environment, everything had a side: masks, books, pride flags, pronouns, history lessons. At the same time, the partisan political universe decided that public schools were not a neutral educational space, but valuable cultural real estate. School boards—long overlooked and, frankly, boring administrators of bus routes, calendars, and budgets—became high-profile and influential bodies.

In a short period of time, this changed how moms—those practiced school volunteers—applied their expertise and offered their time. It may have surprised some to see the shift from wrapping-paper fundraisers to political organizing, but it is more natural than you'd think. That is because mothers' labor has long been an undervalued force. Moms were already expert in assembling networks, organizing volunteer labor, and considering how best to respond to policies impacting children's experiences. Now, they simply applied those skills in a new setting.

The reality was that moms were tapping abilities that few gave them credit for having. An important lesson from this moment is the degree to which society has failed to acknowledge the detailed work of motherhood. Research shows that college-educated women begin their careers earning the same as male peers, but by age forty-five, men earn 55 percent more. According to Sari Kerr, an economist who leads the Women in the Workplace Initiative at the Wellesley Centers for Women, there are several reasons for this, but having children is a key contributor; notably the wage gap narrows for women after age fifty, when children are no longer at home. Lower wages and slowed career advancement are often described as the "motherhood penalty."[4]

The assumption is that mothering is "time off," a blank space on a résumé when nothing is happening—at least nothing that affects the public sphere outside the home. In fact, though, the child-raising years are a potent time of skill acquisition. This is when you become a masterful multitasker, manager, project planner, and negotiator. The experiences translate in a strikingly direct manner to managing people in the workplace, completing projects under pressure, dealing with conflicts, and devising novel solutions in messy situations. Mothers are required to be creative problem solvers. The failure to acknowledge the skills moms gain and practice reveals a cultural gender bias in our conception of work.

So one should not be surprised at the professional-level organizing going on in grassroots public education groups. Nor at the capacities of the moms leading them.

FROM ADVOCACY TO LEADERSHIP

In some ways, Leeman's path to public school activism is not uncommon. Although she has a master's degree in intergenerational studies from Wheelock College in Boston and previously worked in the insurance rating industry, her involvement with schools began when she became the mother of a child with special needs.

"Everything for me started with my older son and disability advocacy," she said. We spoke in the family room of her home in a development of well-kept brick houses with tidy landscaping. Mylar balloons floated in the corner of the room. Leeman's eldest son, Vic, who required "total care" as a medically complex and disabled child, had turned seventeen just days earlier. The family of four moved from Seattle to Colleyville, Texas, in 2015 specifically for the schools, Leeman told me. She had investigated states and districts to find the right fit for her eldest, and while delighted by the special education available to Vic, she was surprised and then disturbed by unusually sharp attacks around something that she was initially less focused on: school board elections.[5]

She had joined a "mom's group," where conversation centered on medical and school issues relating to children with special needs. When debates on health care escalated in Texas and nationally, including threats to the Affordable Care Act, she got more involved. She brought Vic to a rally at the state capitol and met with legislators. Soon, she was asked to speak at rallies. In 2017, Representative Beto O'Rourke visited with her and her son at their home.

At the same time, Leeman noticed far-right activists exerting power and getting little pushback. As the parent of a child who "needs real representation!" she grew concerned about local extremists. "I very quickly learned about local and Texas politics when I wasn't even looking for it," she wrote me in an email. A friend started a Protect GCISD Facebook group to write postcards supporting moderate school board candidates. Leeman joined, and is now one of the administrators of the group. In her mind, she linked growing extremism with the district's increasing racial diversity. In fact, the percentage of white students had been shrinking for years as the share of students of color, including Hispanic and Southeast Asian students, rose. In 1987, the district was 93 percent white; in 2006 it was 75 percent white; in 2021 it was just under 52 percent white.[6]

In August 2021, however, Leeman was propelled to a new level of involvement. During the public comment period at a July 26 school board meeting, a man in jeans and a white buttoned-down shirt named Stetson Clark, a former school board candidate, had taken to the podium to accuse James Whitfield, the Black principal of Colleyville Heritage High School, of "the implementation of Critical Race Theory." He claimed that a letter Whitfield had penned nearly a year earlier following the murder of George Floyd included "extreme views on race" and revealed that he "promotes the conspiracy theory of systemic racism.

"He is encouraging the disruption and destruction of our district," Clark charged, and asked that Whitfield's "contract be terminated, effective immediately." While Clark was speaking—which he did despite admonitions against discussing a district employee by name—an audience member shouted, "How 'bout you fire him!" When Clark stepped away from the microphone, a group of audience members clapped and cheered.[7]

At his home, Whitfield had been watching the live stream and never expected to hear his name, let alone be verbally ambushed. He had received little response to his original letter prompted by the George Floyd killing. "I was watching sitting right here and my phone started blowing up," he said, as we sat at the dining-room table in his family room. Before him was a stack of books, including *Courageous Conversations About Race*, *The Art of Coaching: Effective Strategies for School Transformation*, and a spiral-bound notebook, pages curled with writing. He wore an orange T-shirt and shorts and seemed still stunned at all that had unfolded—and what it meant.[8]

Leeman needed no translation. She was outraged. A few days after the school board meeting, she started a petition, #IStandWithDrWhitfield. In a little over a week, she had some 2,273 signatures.[9] For Leeman, the attacks on "our beloved Dr. James Whitfield" were an early sign of trouble. She *had* to organize. She *needed* to connect with other parents angered by far-right activists and apply her energy and expertise to supporting public schools.

THE MESS IN TEXAS

Leeman was not the only one to notice the rise of extremism in her local school district. The same thing was happening in nearby communities, spurring groups to organize on Facebook. By the time I found my way to Graduate Coffee in Southlake, Texas, I had heard Jennifer Hough's name more than a few times.

The coffee shop was spacious and quiet with an industrial vibe, tucked into a strip mall–style building off a multilane road that happened to pass the main campus of Carroll Senior High School. The sign in front of the school boasted of the state championships won by the sports teams. If parents here could agree on one thing, it was a kind of Southlake exceptionalism—that somehow everything in Southlake was a little better, the kids were built to succeed.

The school mascot, the dragon, seemed to surface everywhere. It was echoed in the serpentine-styled logo on banners and street signs, the result of a design team hired in 2008 to create way-finding signage to enhance "the existing brand of this city," which Forbes had that year named as most affluent neighborhood in the US.[10] But truly one of the most striking signals of local allegiance through identification with the school mascot came during the public comments sections of school board meetings: Regardless of what side they were on, as parents took to the podium—before launching into statements that invariably were emotionally charged—they introduced themselves as "I am the parent of a dragon," or "I have three dragons." The common identity was second nature. To an outsider it was odd to have parents in perturbed tones introducing themselves as parents of dragons. Yet it underscored how much they shared, and what was being lost in this divisive moment.

Inside Graduate Coffee, Hough, a mom with shoulder-length blond hair, no makeup, wearing comfy clothes, a small cross-body Gucci bag, and black-framed glasses, paused to order a London Fog on ice. Then she strode back to a more private lounge area with two sofas and a coffee table. It was a quintessential suburban mom meeting room. It was also occupied.

Two women in their late forties or early fifties, stylishly but comfortably dressed, were knitting. One was clicking away on a blue and white afghan. The other had just been taught how to knit. As we entered, they broke out into chatter about children and goings-on. Hough turned to me, saying, "These are friendlies." Within moments, as if understanding the need for a quiet spot where conversation could not be overheard, they started packing up their knitting. "We were just leaving," said the afghan knitter, gathering a blue ball of yarn to tuck into a clear plastic bag.

Hough, like many moms and dads, found herself pulled into public school activism in ways she could have never imagined when she and her family moved to Southlake in 2011. She would become infamous and would be attacked verbally in parking lots and supermarkets and targeted in a printed circular that arrived in local mailboxes, ironically enough, on Easter weekend, 2021.

The headline of the full-page graphic in the circular trumpeted to readers in white lettering on a dragon green backdrop "THE 'WOKE' LEFT'S WAR ON SOUTHLAKE." The subtitle: "How the Progressive, Liberal Machine is Organizing an Attack on Southlake Values." The page featured a list of the names of the apparently offending organizations printed in red ink, including the Southlake Anti-Racism Coalition. It also vilified "Media & Solicited Outside Forces (DOJ/DOE/NAACP)"—actually, governmental and legal entities looking into possible civil rights violations.

The circular also listed eighteen individuals and used arrows to indicate relationships among them and to the groups. Hough was one, identified as connected to the Southlake Anti-Racism Coalition (SARC), another group, and "Laura Durant's Treasurer." Durant was also singled out, as a "current school board candidate." Like Hough, Durant wanted to address something that felt out of balance. For them and others, the 2018 video of students using racial slurs had been consequential. Although Southlake appeared to be an ideal affluent suburban community, Hough said the video revealed a world that had been invisible to her.

"You listen to all your neighbors of color up there talking, telling about their experiences that you don't see or hear because you are a white, Christian woman in this community," she said. When the community advisory committee was formed to work on what would become the controversial Cultural Competency Action Plan (CCAP), Hough recalled, "Nobody paid attention, cared if you were a Republican, if you were a Democrat. All they cared about is if you wanted to come in and make this a better place for everybody in our community."

Two years later, that sentiment had evaporated.

Hough got involved. So did Durant, who decided to run for school board in the May 7, 2022, election. She soon became a target. Durant, who said she was "raised Christian in Texas," started a Facebook group, Love Every Dragon, to support LGBTQ+ students. I met her on a sweltering summer day when air conditioning barely registered against triple-digit temperatures. She wore a pink blouse and had smartly styled hair and makeup. In other words, she was the very picture of a suburban Texas mother, a married, stay-at-home mom. And that is what she was. Durant said she stepped forward because, "I am white, and I am rich, and I can."[11]

The school board campaign was tough. She was harassed in parking lots. "I went from being a Girl Scout cookies mom to being notorious. It was ridiculous. I was accused of 'grooming' children," she said. One morning, driving with her two children, she found her most visible campaign sign ("it was the length of my Tahoe" and cost $600) ripped in half and impaled on a stake in a field. A nearby sign was untouched. She kept her composure in front of her children but after she pulled into her garage and they had gone inside, she broke down. "I felt very threatened," she said.

But the next day, she put up another sign "because they win if I don't do that." Durant knew she was unlikely to win the election, but she felt it was important to show LGBTQ+ students that adults were willing to stand with them. "I was tired of them getting vilified for standing up for themselves and living in the upside-down world here where right is wrong and wrong is right," Durant said. Her opponent, Alex Sexton, was backed by the far-right Patriot Mobile Action PAC, one of the "11 out of 11" victories touted. He was also supported by the Southlake Families PAC. Durant got 2,045 votes to Sexton's 5,098.[12]

Ahead of the May election, the *Dallas Morning News* published an editorial declining to endorse any school board candidates, including Durant or Stephanie Williams, a prodigious volunteer, teacher, and "Dragon mom of four." In it doubts were expressed that either could "marshal the broad coalition of voters needed" to address serious problems of diversity and inclusion in the community, including coming up with an alternative to the Cultural Competency Action Plan. One reason: Both Durant and Williams had signed the controversial SARC demand letter created by students, which called for defunding school resource officers. The editorial board said the letter's "didactic tone did not help" to bridge the divide.[13]

Yet, the editorial said, "the real issue here is not a student letter. It's Southlake's addiction to its Dragon Nation mythos," one focused on protecting "the tradition" rather than facing and addressing racial problems. It charged, "The Southlake Families PAC has exploited that sense of shared community" and the "PAC's dominance of local politics makes it untenable for the school board to speak openly about addressing racism or promoting diversity and inclusion for fear of sparking another backlash about critical race theory and indoctrination."[14]

For Durant and Hough, it was important to confront extremism, but it exacted a personal price. Hough talked of moving away from "the Texas crazy" once her son graduated from high school. She also described a deep and strangely fractured landscape in which politics have filtered down to which parents help with which clubs. Hough heads hospitality for the water polo team, on which her son plays, but steers clear of others. "So, I do food for the meets," she said, "but I can't get on the theater booster board because conservatives run that. I can't get on the choir booster board because conservatives run that."

Six weeks after the Southlake Families PAC and Patriot Mobile "flipped" the Carroll ISD board, Hough could not imagine what the future held. How could they combat the far-right turn of the school board? How would they find a candidate willing to run? "Laura Durant was called a 'groomer,'" she said. "Who will subject themselves to that?"

What is the response when far-right candidates control school boards and use them to make schools reflect Christian nationalist values? "What do we do? Do we continue to try to fight?" she asked. "Or do we focus our efforts on, 'How can we build a community that might be able to work together on something to make some progress to protect some of these kids?'"

MARSHALLING A DEMOGRAPHIC

If extremism is not in your community now, "what we say is that it is coming or coming somewhere close soon," said Katie Paris, who lives in Cleveland, Ohio. After years of compiling an impressive résumé as a progressive political operative in Washington, DC—former CEO of Shareblue Media (now the

American Independent); senior vice president of Media Matters; former vice president of Faith in Public Life—Paris moved to suburban Cleveland in 2012 and became a mom. A decade later, she found herself drawn into the battle against political extremism, founding the group Red Wine & Blue, which has national reach. I spoke with Paris on Zoom, late in the day, both of us still wearing morning workout clothes. One of her sons zipped into view. Where were his soccer cleats? "Try the soccer bag," she said reflexively.

In hindsight, the creation of Red Wine & Blue made sense. Moms and dads had seen crazy PAC money and big endorsements being funneled into local school board races, pride flags vanishing, and books being pulled off library shelves. Alarmed, they found one another in supermarkets and on the sidelines of soccer games. They started groups. Some groups—especially in places like North Texas—found one another.

They chatted about what they were seeing and compared notes. In North Texas where districts faced early and strident far-right activism, parents like Leeman and Hough and their parent groups formed a communication chain to share experiences and strategy. T. J. Callaway, a dad with a child in the Richardson ISD in Texas was drawn into activism when his son entered first grade. An accomplished sound designer, Callaway is also neck-deep in political organizing around schools. In Richardson ISD, the superintendent was pushed out in December 2021, but the district staved off a far-right school board candidate in May 2022. In October 2022, he told me in an email that Round Rock ISD is "going through a similar election," writing, "I've chatted with them about how we ran our campaigns here and offered that as advice." He added, "School board races become very personal," and every community is different.[15] Callaway was also part of SPENT. (The Round Rock parent organizers, Access Education Round Rock ISD, put forth five candidates who all won over far-right candidates and let parent groups elsewhere know they were there to help.)[16]

What Paris was able to see because of her professional background was an even larger landscape. From years of working on campaigns or following them, Paris knew that suburban moms were a powerful and sought-after demographic in electoral politics. Sure, the labels shifted—from "soccer moms" to "security moms" to "new security moms"—but they referred to the same people: college-educated, affluent, often but not only white women with children. Since 1980, according to Census data, women have registered and turned out to vote at higher rates than men, even in non-presidential election years. Analyses of the 2020 election showed women and suburban voters were key to President Joe Biden's victory.[17] And, during his reelection campaign, former President Donald Trump begged, "Suburban women, will you please like me?," at times adding, "Please, please." He also called them "housewives," which Paris noted.[18]

Paris couldn't ignore the signals from her politically experienced eye. Yes, she said, "I was looking forward to raising my family in an interesting purple state, being exposed to a diversity of ideas." But a few months after her second son was born, she awoke the morning after the 2018 midterms and despite Democratic advances around the country, saw little changed in Ohio. Although a Democrat, Sherrod Brown, had won a Senate victory, elsewhere Republicans dominated. Of sixteen House seats, twelve went Republican. In the Ohio legislature, ten Republicans and seven Democrats won Senate seats; sixty-one Republicans and thirty-eight Democrats won in the House. To be fair, voters had favored incumbents, but in a year of flipped seats, that was Paris's point.[19]

And then there was this: after years of political awareness of suburban moms as a coveted demographic, she said, "I had become a suburban mom." Paris saw opportunity. She met with women around Ohio, including candidates who had barely won or barely lost. She had conversations, often over a glass of wine. What emerged were facts that anyone who has been a suburban mom understands: you are taken for granted as volunteer labor, you have more skills and intelligence than you will ever be recognized for, and you are busy. So busy as to have no time to do anything with your energy, your skills, your intelligence. Except that Paris knew how to knit this together. She understood that the women she met "were so smart, so creative," and wanted to have impact, but "had no idea each other existed."

SUBURBAN "HOUSEWIVES" REVOLT

Drawing these women together into an organization was the foundation for Red Wine & Blue. In January 2020 it was registered as a not-for-profit and by fall 2022 had about a dozen paid staff in each of four swing states—Ohio, Pennsylvania, Michigan, and North Carolina—and had drawn more than four hundred thousand women to online trainings, events, and private Facebook groups and into their social media circles. The tagline "Channeling the

Power of Suburban Women" reflected the goal of helping women transform personal relationships into a political force, rather than sit back and wait to be courted by operatives at desks in Washington, DC.

Paris called it "relational organizing." "They have these networks that no one else can tap into but them," she said of suburban women. "I wanted to create a community that felt the way these women felt when they got together in their living rooms." Early on one person she connected with was Julie Womack, a suburban mom in Mason, Ohio, outside Cincinnati, with a law degree who had joined a Facebook group for progressives commiserating after the 2016 election about "feeling alone in this red area." That group grew in to a local Democratic club. Womack also became the chief organizing officer of Red Wine & Blue. She is often the face of online public events, Zooming in from what she calls "my pretty room," a sitting area with a stylish gray sofa.

When we spoke on Zoom, she was working from one of her kids' bedrooms and sipping on a Kroger brand flavored seltzer to avoid drinking Diet Coke, an admitted weakness. What's key about the suburban woman demographic, said Womack, is that their networks are "not really polarized. So many people who have been activists for a long time, you know, your friends are just other activists. In the suburbs, my friends are my friends because I met them through my kids' sports or we were on the PTO together or they live in my neighborhood. We didn't come together because of politics."[20]

They are also busy and may not be fully aware of political happenings. "Women in the suburbs have a lot on their plate," said Womack. Whether they work outside of the home or not, "You have a lot going on with your family." People want to be informed, but that's difficult with the dearth of local news and wan local reporting on extremism, she said.

There is a lot to keep track of in Ohio. The state's "heartbeat law," that led to a ten-year-old rape victim's traveling to Indiana to get an abortion, did make national news in July 2022.[21] But the legislature also took up anti-trans bills (one had a provision for genital inspections in disputes about transgender athletes) and a ban on teaching "divisive concepts" in which a sponsoring legislator reportedly suggested students consider the Holocaust "from the perspective of a German soldier." In March 2022 the legislature passed, and Governor Mike DeWine signed into law, legislation permitting anyone twenty-one or over to carry a concealed firearm without training or a permit and another that allowed teachers to carry guns after just twenty-four hours of training.[22]

"I bet you if I went out with my girlfriends for happy hour they would have no idea" about some of the laws, said Womack. "Not because they don't care but it's not on their radar." In this environment, she believed in "making sure people are aware of who they are voting for and what they stand for. When you make them aware, they will vote against extremism. But there is a need to raise awareness."

If you are not tracking what's unfolding, said Paris, phrases like "'parental rights' sound nice," but mask moves to censor what teachers can say and what books are available in libraries. "I believe in my right to know what's going on in my child's classroom. But I've always had that right," she said. "This is all about extremism. If you are attacking reproductive rights or trans kids who just want to fit in schools or pulling books about kids of color, that is causing chaos in our communities. We are moms. We do not like chaos."

Given moms' busy-ness, communication is best done with fizzle and froth. A key factor in Red Wine & Blue's success is the group's sassy, pissed-off sisterhood vibe. "Wine" in the name "is more of a metaphor than a ticket for admission," said Paris. But, sure, there is wine. No shame. After all, organizing is most effective when it's social. "People engage because they care about something as a human being," said Paris. "Too often we treat them like warm bodies."

The tongue-in-cheek tone is also a jab at Trump's "housewives" characterization.[23] That's why you get the send-up of 1950s-era tropes and images of women in kitchens, wearing aprons and red lipstick and sometimes curlers and holding cocktails—and a heavy serving of sarcasm. The group's podcast is *The Suburban Women Problem.* Voter guides and how-to political tips are delivered in a tone that feels like girlfriend advice on managing menstrual cramps or making better brownies. *The Parent Playbook: A Step-By-Step Guide for Mainstream Moms Who've Had Enough BS,* tells how to organize a local group, optimize social media, speak at school board meetings, and run for school board "(Yes, you!)"[24]

Because it began during the pandemic, Red Wine & Blue depended on online gatherings. Some forty people joined the first "Troublemaker Training." Sessions have featured women sharing experiences and tactics like using jazz hands to show support for speakers at school board meetings when clapping isn't allowed. The events have drawn celebrities and politicians like Soledad O'Brien, Tammy Duckworth, Elizabeth Banks, Cory Booker, and Sherrod

Brown. Some seven thousand joined a session with Heather Cox Richardson, the author of the wildly popular *Letters from an American* on Substack.

Ahead of the 2022 midterms, comedian Amy Schumer hosted a "Rally Your Squad" event around voter turnout. "The plan for the night," Red Wine & Blue offered, is that "we'll get started with a super inspiring (and maybe a little bit swear-y) pep talk from Amy. Then we'll pull out our phones and pick at least ten friends to reach out to about what's at stake this election. It's so easy! We'll give you everything you need to get started: tips, talking points, and voting guides to share. You'll even be able to look up who of your friends has already voted and who needs a little extra nudge."[25]

In a morning-after-the-midterm email, Paris celebrated that "contrary to conventional wisdom that women would forget about overturning Roe come November, women soundly rejected Republican extremism." She ticked off victories in Michigan, North Carolina, Ohio, and Pennsylvania that she said were driven by suburban women. In Ohio, she said, "We were able to kick two extremists off the state Board of Education and replace them with common sense folks." These wins, she said, grew out of hard work from "our amazing community of badass troublemakers!" Yet, there was more to do. "A lot of it. But we're not going anywhere."[26]

"I AM A STRAIGHT, WHITE, CHRISTIAN, MARRIED SUBURBAN MOM"

Michigan State Senator Mallory McMorrow has been a guest on Red Wine & Blue online gatherings several times. McMorrow became a political celebrity after she took to her state senate podium on April 19, 2022, to repudiate a far-right lie with bracing clarity. The speech was her response to a Republican colleague, State Senator Lana Theis, who sent out a fundraising email accusing McMorrow of wanting to "groom and sexualize" children. McMorrow was "livid."[27]

McMorrow stood up to correct the record and explain who she *actually* was: "a straight, white, Christian, married, suburban mom"—exactly the kind of person *who would stand up* and counter untruths and defend children who were LGBTQ+ and students of color. Claims that learning about slavery or redlining mean that "children are being taught to feel bad or hate themselves because they are white is absolute nonsense," she said. McMorrow wanted "every child in this state to feel seen, heard and supported, not marginalized and targeted because they are not straight, white and Christian."

Her words riveted parents and politicians exhausted by the same far-right attacks. She deftly demonstrated that pushing back mattered. "I know that hate will only win if people like me stand by and let it happen," she said. "And I want to be very clear right now: Call me whatever you want. I know who I am. I know what faith and service mean, and what it calls for in this moment. We will not let hate win."[28]

By the time McMorrow arrived online to the Red Wine & Blue "Great Troublemaker Turnout" on June 6, 2022, at 8 p.m. EST, she was a major celebrity.[29] Nearly 1,500 people had signed on to hear her tell how she had never intended to run for office. Yet a few days after the 2016 election Mc-Morrow saw a viral video of middle school students chanting at a Latina student "Build a wall!" She was horrified.

"That video took place at Royal Oak Middle School, which was my polling place in 2016," McMorrow told the group. Days earlier she had stood in line there to vote. The students on the video, she noted, "were kids. These were kids that learned it either from their parents who were mimicking what Donald Trump said or they heard it from TV." She was upset at how the election had "somehow made this targeting of somebody who was different acceptable." And she decided, "That's not who we are. That's not who my community is. I know that, and I have to do something." It was a turning point. "So," McMorrow quipped, "like any professional, I googled 'How to run for office.'" She ended up discovering that she liked being out and talking with voters. She unseated a Republican to win in 2018. In 2022, she trounced her Republican opponent, 76,899 votes to 24,388.[30]

As McMorrow spoke, the chat exploded with messages like "Mallory: you are an inspiration!!" and with moms eager to share their presence and connect. Some messages: "Hey Alabama folks, let's find each other on Twitter. Post with #RedWineBlueAlabama," "Hello from Boise Idaho!," "Another Florida mom here who wants to push back." Greetings came from Georgia, Massachusetts, Ohio, Indiana, Wisconsin, Nueva Mexico, Pennsylvania, North Carolina, and South Florida, among others. People were notably jazzed about being in the same virtual space with other moms—including McMorrow—who were facing the same hard battles.

The session also addressed a perennial worry that was a central theme at the Moms for Liberty summit in Tampa in July 2022: that politics was not for women. Yes, McMorrow said, of course she hears from women who worry that politics is "really nasty, I'd rather stay out of it." But as women "We are the majority. We are the most powerful voting bloc in the entire country and if we mobilize and we get active and we get out there, we have the loudest voice," she told the online gathering. What's frustrating is "that we have been ingrained with this idea that we shouldn't use it. That it's not polite."

A HISTORY OF MOTHER-ACTIVISTS

The question of where power resides and how it can be expressed is meaningful, especially lately. The rise of identity politics makes who you are and what you represent a key electoral consideration. McMorrow addressed this in her speech, ingeniously recasting her identity not as one that excludes her from debates around race and LGBTQ+ issues, but precisely as one that empowers you to support those who do not share her identity.

Several months later, in October 2022, she was a guest at Vanderbilt University, invited by the LGBTQ+ Policy Lab and the Divinity School. While there, McMorrow made the point that even though she identified herself as "a straight, white, Christian, suburban mom," several times in her speech, that description did not mean she had to align with a stereotype.

"It just felt so important for me to reclaim my own identity and to use it to signal to other people like me, that it is on us to fight back so these identities are not taken away from us and they're not used against us," she told the crowd. She also said that people were surprised that she even responded to the smears against her. Several cited former first lady Michelle Obama's mantra "When they go low, we go high." The phrase, she told the group, didn't mean people should not push back against "hateful" language. "That just means we don't lie. We don't cheat," she said. "I think we can be strong and kind simultaneously."[31]

McMorrow's framing was a reminder that identities are powerful, but incomplete at revealing people's views. Part of her appeal, no doubt, was that she looks like a buttoned-up mom who knows her manners and says her prayers (she is a graduate of the University of Notre Dame). With her pulled-up hair crowned by a navy-blue headband, which matched her clerk-collared top, she evoked a certain conservative image. Yet her message challenged that image. It was an important lesson, particularly at a moment when identities are "read" quickly.

Women have for years felt or faced ambivalence around the exercise of political power because of their maternal identity. After all, like sports, politics has historically been gendered as "male" and a bellicose pursuit. Yet women have also smartly used their expertise with children to gain political standing. Women asserted authority from the very beginnings of public education, in part by framing schools as an extension of the home, a realm they governed without dispute.

Even before women gained the right to vote in 1920, as early as the 1850s, according to one scholarly account, women sought (and in some cases won) "school suffrage," the right to vote and/or run for school offices, which were locally determined. The piecemeal nature of these rights—only in some communities for some positions—annoyed woman suffrage leaders, who saw limited rights as distracting from the quest for national universal suffrage.[32]

Yet even outside of the suffrage question, public schools offered women caught in a culture of rigid gender roles a socially acceptable way to exert political influence. As the education scholar William J. Reese put it in a paper on this history written in 1978, for activist women, "Theirs was not a vision of the school as a factory, turning out finished products like an assembly line, but of the school as a center of everyday neighborhood activities, reflecting the congenial atmosphere of their own well-furnished homes." These mother-activists sought to make the neighborhood school more "homelike," and, in the process, bring it into their domain.[33]

Rather than object to their "place" as being in the home, women extended the home's reach to the school. "The environment of every woman is the home, wherever she goes she carries this with her," the president of the Wisconsin Federation of Women's Clubs wrote in 1900. "The time has come, however, when it is not enough that woman should alone be a home-maker, she must make the world itself a larger home." (That also became more possible with the introduction of labor-saving devices and a decline in family size.)[34]

As another scholar, Marilyn Schultz Blackwell, framed it, by casting themselves as "republican mothers"—literally raising virtuous citizens for the republic—women could underscore their attention to moral matters while seeking social change. This was a useful claim to make as the nation moved from an agrarian to an industrialized society. The problems that came with this transition—urbanization, poverty, hunger, the need for training and schooling, stresses on shifting family structures and the changing nature of work—were problems that women, even if they could not solve, could credibly engage with.[35]

Early women's circles and parent-teacher groups studied the state of child welfare outside of the home in ways that were important and revealing. When the National Congress of Mothers and Parent-Teacher Associations—founded by Alice McLellan Birney and Phoebe Apperson Hearst (yes, of the Hearst family, which provided financial support)—began its work in 1897, according to one scholarly account in 1916, "Children were in prisons and jails in every state, associated with confirmed criminals in all court procedures before and after trial." And the state of Michigan, the writer noted, was the only state, that "had assumed the responsibility of providing adequately for its dependent or orphan children."[36]

The National Congress of Mothers and Parent-Teacher Associations had national reach, held conventions, and published the *Child-Welfare Magazine* (cost: "$1.00 a year"). From the start, the organization encouraged women across the country to form chapters, spurring a child welfare movement.

Local groups sprang up all over, some affiliated with the National Congress and some not. But the emphasis on child well-being surfaced in reports from its state chapters, including efforts to help with food and clothing. A report from Delaware after the 1922 convention in Tacoma, Washington, stated that after finding "many children suffering from malnutrition," one parent-teacher association raised money and "thousands of gallons of milk are distributed each day."

The same chapter reported, "hundreds of dollars have been spent in 'scholarship' funds to keep in school the thousand or more children who would otherwise stay away for lack of proper clothing." Their standing as mothers also enabled women to advocate for social issues like school nutrition and immunizations. At a time when school attendance could be casual (to put it mildly), women pressed for passage of child labor laws and for mandatory school attendance, lest youths with idle hands and barred from factory jobs would cause trouble.[37]

These concerns were a far cry from the parent-teacher tasks of modern times. But the structure and intent of the organizations—and their rapid growth in the opening years of the twentieth century—unfolded in a country still trying to sort out its educational responsibility. Several chapters worked for "larger national recognition and support" from Washington, DC. While control of education belonged to the states, and largely still does, advocates wanted the value and practice of educating America's youth elevated to national attention, "just as agriculture has growth in the support that it receives from the Federal Government."[38]

Yet even as these groups attacked social problems, they breezily ignored the harms of racial segregation. A Kentucky chapter president, in one of the few reports to even mention race, noted that the "one colored county council" had a "splendid working body, eager to accomplish great things for their race." It failed to acknowledge the effect of laws and practices that left schools attended by Black children with scant public funding. This made the work of the National Congress of Colored Parents and Teachers particularly critical.

When Selena Sloan Butler, a Spelman College graduate who started the first kindergarten in Georgia, organized the National Congress of Colored Parents and Teachers in May 1926 with 4,500 members in 300 chapters, it focused on cooperation between schools and parents. Butler, a prominent figure in Atlanta community work, spoke at a committee meeting ahead of an invitation to a White House conference whose theme was "Child Health and Protection." She emphasized that "educators as well as parents have learned that a school can put over a better and bigger program when parents and teachers are organized so they can co-operate in attacking the problems so vital in developing the physical, mental, moral and social sides of the child."[39]

Butler pointed out that the work was "both educational and constructive." And she also meant "constructive" literally: they took on tasks related to building and equipping schools. Educational programs were wide-ranging, from physical education and preschool circles to "music, thrift, social standards, home economics." But the "constructive" aspect underscored the unequal support enjoyed by Black and white students.

That work included purchasing land to build schools, "beautifying school grounds and buildings," and equipping them with items, from pianos and phonographs to outfitting cafeterias. Notably, the National Congress also stated as a goal "contributing to the Rosenwald school fund." Rosenwald schools were built by Booker T. Washington and Julius Rosenwald, a philanthropist who was the president of Sears Roebuck, specifically to educate Black children; by 1928 they served about one-third of Black children in the rural South.[40]

Brown v. Board of Education would make such schools obsolete. Yet, in a testament to persistent racial divisions in education, it wasn't until 1970, after five years of negotiation, that the National Congress of Mothers and

Parent-Teacher Associations and the National Congress of Colored Parents and Teachers merged to become the National Parent Teacher Association. Butler had died several years prior, but is named as a founder of the National PTA.[41]

SOCIALIZING, MOTHERHOOD, AND EXPERTISE

Parent-teacher organizations not only tackled societal problems and supported schools—sometimes overbearingly so—but also offered social connection. Reese, the education scholar, described these clubs as "community meeting places" where "old friendships were retained or renewed," and where "solitary individuals gained a sense of belonging."[42]

The dull routine of household chores could be forgotten when women could meet and "gossip about trivial matters as well as unite in support of a new school program or activity." Reese cited a report by a woman in Des Moines, Iowa, who, burdened with doing family wash eight times a week, saved her pennies to send it out one day so she could attend a mothers' meeting. Although not "a club woman," the woman was "so tired I don't know how to keep my patience with the kids if I don't come to the mothers' meeting and get rested."[43]

In its report of the 1922 National Congress of Mothers convention in Tacoma, *Child-Welfare Magazine* included a detailed accounting not just of business but also of social opportunities. Mary L. Langworthy chronicled "the glad hours" that were "the leaven in our serious week of business and education." She described receiving "a nosegay of that flower of Tacoma, the rhododendron" with her convention badge, gushed over the opening banquet, "the Blue Bird Luncheon," dancing, a tea, and "Stadium Day with its Pageant of Schools," featuring seventeen thousand schoolchildren and sixty thousand attendees. Langworthy also shared the "National Anthem of the Convention," with the song's final lines: "I shall never forget the good times I've had here (you bet) / Oh dear! I want to stay here; / I don't want to go home."[44]

There was a fine line between social connection and frivolity. The clubby vibe could feel overbearing, a surfeit of white, middle class "expertise." Social service endeavors were valuable but fit a particular convention. With the era's passion for efficiency and regard for science, there seemed a "right" way to do everything. Social ills were often assumed to be the result of poor parenting rather than a more complex array of socioeconomic forces. This offered a pretext for providing child-rearing advice, which parent groups embraced.

Many such groups, like the Boston Parents' Council, a short-lived orga-nization that existed from 1930 to 1938 (whose papers are at the Schlesinger Library at the Radcliffe Institute for Advanced Study), seemed to have a passion for lectures and luncheons.[45] The council even entertained a re-quest from Filene's, a Boston department store, to collaborate in hosting a conference offering lectures and luncheons, until it became plain that the retailer wanted to peddle children's clothes and toys. The conference, "Parents and their Children," was held May 13–18, 1935, without council involvement. Lecture topics included "Toys for All Ages," "The Effect of Clothes on Personality," and "The Normal Desires of the Adolescent." A few months later, Jordan Marsh, another Boston department store, sought the Boston Parents' Council's help to create a "Family Consultation Center [for parents] who wish advice or direction in connection with the problems arising in bringing up their children." It's unclear whether Jordan Marsh officials knew of the Filene's discussion, but in describing the request in a letter, the Jordan Marsh executive said its effort "will be on a high educa-tional non-commercial level."[46]

Who knows why Jordan Marsh wanted to place a parenting help center in their store. It certainly looks more like a ploy to draw shoppers than the Filene's effort. Regardless, it is noteworthy to see big retailers viewing a role in parent education as a route to the pocketbook. If tapping home life was an effective tool to gain an audience, many were in on it. Just as these retailers extended their reach into parenting, women's clubs, under the umbrella of the General Federation of Women's Clubs, sought to reframe mothers' homemaking skills—and apply them more broadly to engage in "municipal housekeeping." According to Paige Meltzer, who has written and taught on gender and politics of twentieth-century social movements, club women aimed to "clean up politics [and] cities, and see after the health and wellbeing of their neighbors. Donning the mantle of motherhood, female activists methodically investigated their community's needs and used their 'maternal' expertise to lobby, create and secure a place for themselves in an emerging state welfare bureaucracy."

Interestingly, Meltzer observes that the "maternalist politics that defied easy left-right distinctions and brought women together" initially saw ten-sions arise as early as the late 1920s. "Many clubwomen became increasingly uncomfortable with the surrogate parenting of the new welfare state." Some conservative women "became vocal opponents to anything that resembled communism, including the [General Federation of Women's Clubs'] support of progressive legislation."[47]

History is not a blueprint for the present, but we are seeing a replay of this similar tension around the exercise of parental control. How far should parent "expertise"—which necessarily includes one's beliefs and preferences—extend into the professional realm of schooling? Is it enough to give parents individual rights to opt their children out of lessons and experiences they disagree with—rights they have always had—or do they have the right to decide what is appropriate material for all children?

That question is at the heart of the controversy over curriculum and, especially, library books. Ironically, the early strategy by women to expand the reach of the home to have authority in schools has a new twist, as far-right parents press for schools to mirror their Christian home values. In some cases, it has transformed parents from supporters to opponents seeking authority over how schools operate. This strategy is being touted as "parental rights."

BATTLING BOOK BANS

This quest for authority has been particularly vivid in face-offs around school libraries. As we've seen, far-right parents and far-right school board members, even pastors, have employed the inflammatory charge of "pornography" to challenge or censor which books are available in schools. This is not a new issue, but recently, across the country, book bans and challenges have exploded. They most often target books authored by LGBTQ+ or people of color or that included them as characters. Pen America counted 1,145 book titles banned across eighty-six school districts in twenty-six states in a nine-month period, from July 1, 2021, to March 31, 2022. And the American Library Association reported in September 2022 that the number of book challenges was on pace to exceed the prior year.[48]

Professional school librarians follow strict guidelines in selecting titles. One requirement is that a school library's holdings reflect the community it serves, which means libraries have different collections; books are also chosen for the specific ages of the children who will have access to them. Are mistakes made? Of course. But there is a process for challenging books, which has been used for years. What we have seen more recently is a crusade to take power from professionals and use books as a political tool.

That is what happened in Central Bucks School District in Pennsylvania after the far-right majority school board in July 2022 passed a "library materials policy" that put new restrictions on "sexualized content" of any kind (including nudity in classical works of art) and allowed any community member to challenge books. Although some members of the school board insisted it was "not a ban," many parents saw it otherwise. This was why, on the first chilly night of fall of that year, I found myself in Doylestown at an in-person outdoor Red Wine & Blue event attended by about fifty people ahead of National Banned Books Week, an awareness effort started in 1982.

I mounted steep outdoor wooden steps onto a deck overlooking a bar and outdoor space strung with patio lights. There was a charity event on the lower level with a jazzy, bass-heavy band and a row of auction-worthy baskets encased in cellophane. Parents made their way up to the banned books event carrying pitchers of beer past posters that read "Ban Guns, Not Books" and "Hate Has No Home in CBSD." There was a table of banned books, clipboards of information, and postcards to fill out supporting librarians at the district's twenty-three schools.

Amy McGahran, Red Wine & Blue's event organizer, sported a bright red sweatshirt with the group's logo. She was eager to host "a nice community evening because we have been going through some rough stuff with our school board," she said. Although the purpose of the get-together was social, moms I chatted with—including two raised in Westchester County, New York—were there because they were alarmed at recent developments. As well they should be, one invited speaker, Kristen Mae Chase, an author, parenting commentator, and single mother of four, told the crowd.

"A very small group of people" is attempting to override decisions about books and materials that "were picked by experts, yes, librarians," she said. These librarians, Chase said, need public support. "Let's remember, it's not really about the books. If we think it is just about the books, we are not looking at what is coming next. We don't want to be a theocracy. We want to make sure our children who are in public education are being exposed to different people. All the differences, that is part of public education."

People shivered in the wind but stayed attentive. There was information to be shared. The mayor had come. So had a state representative, a former school board member—and even Michigan State Senator Mallory McMorrow's mom, Kathleen Cranmer. (She told me that she worried for her daughter's safety and also had police stationed outside her home for several days after her daughter's controversial speech because she had been doxxed.)

A representative from a local PAC, Neighbors United for Central Bucks School Board, announced that she was seeking candidates to run for school board a year out; she had flyers with a QR code for more information. "We are actively creating a list and actively recruiting," she said. Kate Nazemi, a mother of two students in the district who had organized a banned books parade for the following afternoon, pitched a new local group of which she is the director, Advocates for Inclusive Education, formed by parents, teachers, students, and community members concerned by the far-right turn of the school board. The website had all the background and detailed analyses of policies and issues plus details on how to get involved and when to show up at school board meetings.

"We need an informed electorate," Nazemi pressed. "If we can't flip the board in '23, we will have the same stuff, but worse." A day earlier, when I interviewed Nazemi at the Native Café on South Main Street, both of us sitting on squeaky wicker furniture, she said something I have thought about a lot. We were talking about the library materials policy and the debate over whether it was or was not a ban and how it would be implemented.

It almost doesn't matter, she said. "What I have learned now, in late September, is that you don't need to have a policy of censorship to have censorship. It's almost unnecessary. You just need to have the idea that it's there, with maybe some instruction coming—or not. And have it vague enough that you freeze, you paralyze your teachers and librarians. Not only from materials, but of discussions of topics."[49]

Nazemi was right; it was already happening. At the Red Wine & Blue event, when Marlene Pray, a parent who started Little Free Libraries in the community and helped to run an LGBTQ+ youth center, stepped up to speak next, the tone of her voice was urgent. Pray wore a rainbow bracelet and a black T-shirt. She apologized for being late. Pray had just come from back-to-school night at Lenape Middle School. Yes, she reported, the rumors were true. Some teachers had removed their classroom libraries—books teachers have available in their classrooms for students to read if they finish an assignment before peers or to supplement what they are studying in class.

"That is a new phenomenon," Pray warned. She called on people to fill out postcards on the back table with messages of support to librarians. "We will be mailing all of those in the next few days," she said. "They need to know that we are with them, and we have their backs."

ACTIVISM IS POLITICAL–AND PERSONAL

For parents who expected their child's public school experience to be what it was for them, a place of connection forged around drop-offs and pick-ups, homework and science projects demanding a bit too much adult input, this is a new world. Especially in fast-growing suburbs, the rise of remote work and the influx of new people from all over has disrupted demographics and values. This clash of parents eager for a community that reflects what they see as neutral, progressive values with extremists who view them as a grave threat has turned idyllic suburbs into battlegrounds.

It is challenging parents to step into a fray many never saw coming. They never planned to become experts on policy, school board governance, or American Library Association standards or on investigating the use of dark money in down-ballot political campaigns. Yet that is where they have landed, deploying every ounce of time, attention, and expertise they can spare.

Laney Hawes, a mom of four in Keller ISD in Texas, has spent hours sifting through campaign finance reports, connecting parents (she is part of SPENT), and poring over voter turnout data. Hawes met her husband at Brigham Young University; both were "raised as conservative Mormon Republicans." At BYU Hawes was president of her college Republican club.

The family lived in different places, including Buffalo, New York, and came to Keller, Texas, seeking a "family-friendly" community with neighborhood schools. Hawes, who does permissions and copyright work, said that through her children's attending city schools, "we learned, we grew, we saw experiences very different from our own." Her allegiances changed. "I'm not sure if our politics shifted or the Republican Party shifted and pushed us out," she said when we met in her home near Fort Worth.

Like many who did not intend to become activists, Hawes was pulled in after attending school board meetings. She started tweeting about what she saw—for instance, a speaker with Bible in hand calling on the board and audience to "repent." Attending another meeting prompted her to tweet, "Extremists are showing up to these meetings in full force. They will take over our schools. And they're doing it in the name of God. Book banning is in full force in TX." At another, she live-tweeted that people were "quoting scriptures" and "screaming about school libraries full of pornography." Less than a month later she served on a committee that reviewed a book being challenged, *Anne Frank's Diary: A Graphic Adaptation*. "Everything but the illustrations come from her diary," Hawes tweeted. "We voted unanimously to keep it on the library shelves."[50]

For Hawes, as for many of her peers, involvement is political but also personal. Even as she presses for the schools she wants for her children, she also wants them to feel free to just be kids. "I try not to let it affect my children, but they know that I'm involved," she said. A school board member unfriended her on Facebook, "but our sons are friends."

At home they talk "about racism, white privilege, queerness." She wants her children "to have principles." One son was handed in school a white card that looked like a credit or membership card but had printed on it "White Privilege Card" and "Trumps Everything." On the back it stated, "This card grants its bearer happiness and success because of the color of your skin and not the choices you make that determine your abilities to be successful."

Hawes wants her children to object when people use the N-word or "gay" as a slur. But she knows they live in a charged world and must navigate the social world of adolescence. "I have to raise four children in this," she said.

Hawes was not the only parent I interviewed who sought to protect their children from their activism even as their work was animated by the desire to make schools better for them.

One mother of an LGBTQ+ child got involved because she saw, firsthand, policies that would hurt her child. "I always cared about the issue, but it became incredibly personal," she said. When calls to ban books surfaced, she mobilized parents to respond but said, "I also felt I had to be very careful. I felt like I would be outing my child."

The tragedy is that schools have become so politically charged, and with them, so has parental involvement. For parents, and especially moms, whose intense volunteerism has long been foundational to how local communities function, this is changing lives and even friendships. It is not always about who is on which side, but who is stepping up to the plate to get involved.

Hawes is upset by low voter turnouts in her local school board elections. "We are still trying to find that magic trick of trying to get people to care who don't, who aren't aware. And that is really frustrating," she said. What can one do "to get non-extremists to vote?" she asked.

One challenge facing the parents who have stepped to the front lines is the struggle to understand those who don't grasp the threat to public schools. Nazemi, for one, said it has impacted her relationships. "I'll tell you something I didn't expect," she said—that it would be tough to stay connected to friends "who are allies but don't do the work." And it goes both ways. "I noticed they have backed off from me, too, and I think that is because they are probably afraid that all I will do is talk about this stuff," she said. Those who "can't handle it" are drifting away. "I'm not even doing social stuff with them anymore."

The political and cultural battles may be nationally engineered, and even funded. But when they are fought at the most local level, in our public schools, when they activate and enlist parents as warriors, there are likely to be consequences that we may not see or understand for years. We have counted on communities to be places where everyone could belong and where the public schools were the recipients of mass support, regardless of party or politics. That is no longer true. And we are the worse for it.

HOW TO FIGHT FOR
SCHOOL COMMUNITIES

TOM MOORE BROUGHT GIFTS to his final meeting as a member of the Croydon (New Hampshire) School Board. He had carved pens from exotic wood and used a laser to personalize them for his two fellow board members, Aaron McKeon and the chair, Jody Underwood.

Admittedly, the two sometimes "drove me nuts," said Moore, a lumberjack of a man with a gray and ginger beard who taught high school woodworking and electrical engineering in nearby Lebanon. But he had worked at the relationships. Together they had crafted a $1.7 million school budget for fiscal year 2022–2023, which they unanimously recommended to Town Meeting for approval.[1]

Moore had chosen not to run again but felt good as the board prepared to present the budget at Town Meeting on Saturday, March 12, 2022. He expected that there would be nitpicking—there was always some—but that the budget would pass. So when snow began falling on Saturday, he told his wife to stay and play in the snow with the kids. He would go to Town Meeting by himself.

As the snow picked up, others stayed home. The town hall was what you might expect in a community of eight hundred: a white Colonial-style New England structure with a great room, a sober space with a proscenium stage and hardwood floors. The floors warranted an orange sign, "Floor Care," taped to a wall with instructions that included a prohibition on using soap and hot water to clean. "Use a damp mop with a little vinegar and cool water only."

The meeting was sparsely attended. After Moore gave McKeon and Underwood the pens he had carved for them, then hugs, they presented the budget. Initially Moore was unsurprised when questions arose about the purchase of violins and snowshoes. The district received a grant to buy them—a distinction "that just falls on deaf ears."

But soon the atmosphere grew "a little contentious." People were "getting fired up about the snowshoes and violins." Then, Ian Underwood, Jody Underwood's husband, who was a town selectman, called for slashing the budget to $800,000. Cutting it by over half.

It was a stunning move.

Underwood later stated, "I stood up and said, 'What we are being presented by the school board is a ransom,'" when he described the scene on *Free State Live*, a weekly podcast "featuring the leaders, activists, movers and shakers of the Free State Project."[2] New Hampshire's state motto is "Live Free or Die."

The Underwoods are Free Staters, a group of libertarians seeking to draw twenty thousand like-minded people to New Hampshire to take over communities and cut taxes and regulations. The couple, who moved from Pennsylvania in 2007, do not have children. McKeon has said he is not a Free Stater, but "does agree with some of the things they try to do."[3]

Then, in what some described as a quick, bewildering series of motions and amendments, Underwood's call to cut the budget went to a vote. It passed, 20–14. Moore was shocked. "I came home and poured a big fat glass of whiskey," he recalled. "I said, 'School's done.'"

DEMOCRACY DEMANDS PARTICIPATION

As I visited communities and met with those countering far-right attacks on public schools, I was struck by how much extremist maneuvering was in plain sight. Yes, there might be labyrinthine networks for funding and strategy, but the attack on schools was not a secret operation.

To those paying attention in Croydon, Underwood had broadcast his plans. The day before Town Meeting, he wrote of his intentions on the Granite Grok, a far-right New Hampshire political website. In a post titled "Budget or Ransom?" he wrote, "What we are being asked to vote on is a *ransom*." He advocated a call to "amend the amount in Article 2 to reflect a *budget*—that is, the amount that the voters in the district want to pay—rather than a *ransom*—that is, the amount that district officials feel like demanding."[4]

Underwood passed out a pamphlet at Town Meeting with the same information. In it he impugned the premise of public schooling, asking, "Why are we doing this in the first place?" He said public tax dollars should only pay for education to participate "intelligently in the political, economic, and social systems of a free government." That did not include learning to "speak a foreign language, play a sport or a musical instrument, calculate a derivative, weld two pieces of metal together, or set up a spreadsheet"—some activities that, a *New York Times* story observed, he had enjoyed himself as a public school student.[5]

Town Meeting is a participatory form of local government, the rugby of municipal proceedings that relies on residents to press their causes in person. But like voting in local elections, it may feel like something that can be left to others. Yet the Croydon experience—like school board races in Texas with low voter turnouts—reveals how much showing up matters.

Angi Beaulieu, who took the Town Meeting minutes on March 12, said people "were clearly confused." Some who voted to cut the budget later claimed that they "just didn't understand what it would mean for the kids of our community."

What *did* it mean? Because Croydon is small, it does not have its own high school. Children attend the village school (called Little Red) for kindergarten through fourth grade, then attend other area district schools, including certain nearby private schools. The district covers tuition for students in grades five to twelve for these enrollments. The budget for tuition alone was over $950,000 a year, said Moore.

The new budget would effectively end traditional in-person schooling at Little Red—some voters proposed an online curriculum with a coached "micro school." Families of older children would have to pay thousands themselves to cover gaps in tuition. But most critically, the slashed budget would turn public schooling from a community enterprise to a budget item that offered some funding but left families to figure out how to make it work.

"A BLACK EYE AND A BRUISE ON THE ASS"

Amanda Leslie, a high school teacher with two teens in a nearby district, ran for Moore's seat but lost, by nine votes. As she listened to Ian Underwood on March 12, she texted her husband, a lineman repairing downed wires in the snow. "I said, 'You need to get down here,'" she said. "He did. But by the time he got here, it was done."[6]

After the vote Leslie found Kathy Ivey, a grandmotherly figure who was at the PTO table selling brownies, cookies, cupcakes, and bottled water. Ivey, a speech pathologist, had retired to Croydon in 2016 but was soon working at the school. On a day I visited, she unlocked the door to Little Red. We walked through the tiny schoolhouse and nearby portable (I saw snowshoes). The school was located on a two-lane road just down from Coniston General Store, where public notices were posted, and two doors from the town hall.

You could miss it if you blinked, but it was an emotional center. When Town Meeting ended, Leslie approached her with "a look of distress," Ivey told me. "I assume I have the same look."[7] News spread in a frenetic volley of texts and emails. Leslie tapped education contacts around the state. Chris Prost, a father of two who with his wife had moved to town to start a brewery in his barn, said, "I kept thinking, 'There has to be some way to figure this out.'"[8] He went deep into state statutes accessible on websites. He also emailed Granite State Progress.

Granite State Progress is a progressive group and "communications hub" that tracks far-right activity in the state. While not specifically a school advocacy group, they had noticed conflicts at school board meetings around the country, said Zandra Rice Hawkins, the executive director, and "realized pretty early on that this was going to be an issue in our state."

When far-right extremists, including white supremacists and militia groups, including the Proud Boys, showed up at New Hampshire school board meetings in the summer of 2021, said Hawkins, "We saw it as part of a far-right template to try to sow division within schools and attack public educators as a way to undermine public education."[9]

Because of that insight, the group researched over three hundred school board races and focused on key contests in fourteen districts. They organized support for thirty-four candidates whom they classified as "pro–public education"—regardless of political party. Granite State Progress helped with strategy, campaign mailers, outreach via texts, and phone-banking. The effort paid off. Every candidate they supported in March 2022 won.

In Croydon, after the March 12 vote, Granite State Progress provided school funding and town meeting experts to the Croydon neighbors; they also compiled voter lists and set up phone banks and canvasses. Hawkins said the Croydon group largely organized themselves. It was the "the only time we have ever watched a small group of organized neighbors reach so deeply and bring everyone together in such a short time," she said.[10]

The Croydon group quickly created a Facebook page, We Stand Up for Croydon Students (now Stand Up for Croydon) and found a path to reverse the budget. It required getting 50 percent of the town's 565 registered voters to show up and cast ballots at a special meeting. This was no small feat, given that only 6 percent of voters had been present at the original meeting. The Croydon group gathered needed signatures on a petition to ask for the special meeting, which Beaulieu presented to the school board on March 21. The select board agreed to the re-vote, which was set for May 7.[11]

That gave organizers less than seven weeks. They printed "We Stand Up for Croydon Students" yard signs, made phone calls, and tracked every voter. They also went door to door. Beaulieu and her sister visited one neighbor who was mowing his lawn. He wasn't inclined to restore the budget. She and her sister talked to him for forty-five minutes.

"She just got really personal," said Beaulieu, who grew up in Croydon. Her sister explained that for her son to finish high school it would cost $8,000 to $10,000. "She said, 'How am I going to afford to pay that?' He shrugged his shoulders." As they left, the two felt the conversation had gone well, but were not hopeful. Yet on May 7, the man and his wife turned up and voted to restore the budget. "He said, 'We are here because of you, because of your story,'" said Beaulieu.[12]

Stories like this turned the grassroots effort into a compelling national story. From beginning to end there was drama. Two days after the budget slashing, a school board meeting was scheduled to figure out how to operate on $800,000 (Jody Underwood called it "an opportunity").[13]

The room pulsed with disbelief and anger. Residents lined up to speak. A woman in a green sweater berated the board, saying it was "supposed to be representing the best interests of the school" and that their job was "to make it better, not to throw it away."[14]

Edward Spiker, a painting contractor and father of two, approached the mic. The vote, he complained, was "a black eye and a bruise on the ass." Spiker said it was "one thing to maybe alter the budget. It is a whole different thing to decimate it completely." He had expected the civic machinery to work and for things to go on as they had been. Spiker, like many of those who were upset, had missed Town Meeting and had not been present for the vote. But times have changed. He would not make that mistake again.

SHOWING UP

The thing about community is that we are supposed to be able to lean on others, and they on us. This is fine if we all want approximately the same things. In Croydon—and around the country—school communities have long trudged on. There are new ideas, new people, new efforts, pendulums swing one way and then the other, but the community still works.

This is not to celebrate mediocrity, but to recognize that eager as we are to measure end points, success is often about the process. What's troubling now is that the process, the arrangement, the unspoken agreements we have with one another, are broken. We cannot trust. And so we must show up and make clear what we want and expect.

What I appreciated about the neighbors in Croydon is that they got it. They immediately understood what was required and acted. And this is New Hampshire, where "Live Free or Die" is not just a license plate motto. This is a state in which you aren't required to wear seatbelts and you can carry a gun without a permit. Individualism reigns.

When I visited in June 2022, the neighbors were animated by their victory. On May 7, the re-vote, held at the YMCA Camp Coniston drew 379, all but two of whom voted to restore the budget. It was 66 percent of registered voters, well over the 50 percent required.[15]

The story could have ended there, but democracy needs tending. The Croydon group saw that they could not leave governance to others. I gathered hours of recordings and notes and came away with a sense that residents genuinely enjoyed working for a common cause—across political leanings, ages, and economic and life situations.

Prost, the brewer who wore a Muddy Waters T-shirt and showed off baby photos, emphasized that this was about more than one vote. "The short story is this happened, and people banded together and democracy worked," he said. But it's not over. You can't leave the work to others. Especially when Free Staters "are trying to dismantle our town."[16]

In recent years, Free Staters had run for posts, and won, sometimes in uncontested races. The Croydon neighbors were now paying attention. A few months after the budget debacle, Ian Underwood quietly resigned from the select board. Angi Beaulieu's sister, Amie Freak, was appointed to fill the seat.[17] Beaulieu herself decided to run against Jody Underwood for school board in a March 14, 2023, contest; Beaulieu beat Underwood, 229 votes to 36.[18] Leslie told me she may run in 2024, when Aaron McKeon is up for reelection.

Another Croydon group member, Hope Damon, a dietician and avid gardener with a knack for canning, decided to get *much* more involved. She ran for the state House of Representatives with the slogan "Hope for New Hampshire" in fall 2022—and won. She was assigned to the education committee. In January 2023, she was urging people to attend a hearing to overturn the state's "banned concepts" legislation, prohibiting certain discussions in classrooms.[19]

Croydon residents recognized that they needed to be informed. One person making sure of that was Spiker, a bear of a man who boasts Pittsburgh Steelers tattoos and works three jobs. Given his work schedule—which includes helping a quadriplegic man with his evening routine—you could forgive him for missing the March 12 vote. But Spiker seems not to have forgiven himself.

Shortly after that meeting, he began recording (often live-streaming) school board meetings, including strategic planning and policy committee meetings. Then he added planning, zoning, and select board meetings. He posted it all to his YouTube channel. On the Stand Up for Croydon Facebook page, it was often Spiker who reminded residents of meetings, like a January 3, 2023, select board meeting at 7 p.m. where members would be working on the budget. "Hope to see you there!" he urged.[20]

We traded Facebook Messenger texts one evening in early 2023 right after Spiker returned from a select board meeting. He was planning a warrant for Town Meeting to require meetings be accessible remotely, for instance, by Zoom. "A lot of folks simply don't have time to attend numerous board meetings multiple times a week," he wrote. (Damon also planned to introduce a bill in the New Hampshire House to require communities to live-stream and record meetings. "We'll see if it gets traction," she wrote in an email.[21])

When I first met Spiker with other Croydon neighbors at Damon's home on a summer evening on her deck overlooking an orderly garden, he presented me with a jar of homemade strawberry peach jam. I appreciated the gesture, for I grew up being sent to take to the neighbors fresh eggs and jelly made from grapes that grew wild on our road.

Spiker is not easy to pin down politically. He eagerly shares his passion for firearms and the Second Amendment. As our gathering ended, he lifted the bottom of his T-shirt to reveal a gun at his waist. "Conceal carry?" I asked, wanting to know if he had such a permit. I was in New Hampshire, however. Spiker corrected me: "Constitutional carry."[22]

One striking thing about the Croydon neighbors was that they were not trying to win a political battle. This is a small town. A few months after the vote, the group organized a cookout and posted photos on Facebook. Everyone, no matter how or if they voted on the budget, was invited.

The goal was not to win, or gain power. It was about making sure that everyone was OK. The public schools, even if the Croydon part was only K–4, mattered deeply to those who lived here. I asked Spiker if he was running for select board, as he had previously hinted. He was thinking about it, he said, but only if he could get all the meetings he was attending now live-streamed. At the end of the day, he texted, "I just want to be able to say that I'm doing something positive for my community." A few weeks later, he decided to run and messaged me just after he turned in his papers to be on the ballot in March: "I won't pretend to have answers to every problem that may arise," he wrote. "But I can give my word to do my best for this town if or when I'm elected." On March 14, he won a one-year seat, beating two opponents, Ryan Ball and Ryan Shackett, by 142 votes to 64 and 46, respectively.[23] Spiker told me that the school board budget situation had activated community members to run for office at all levels of local government. "To say that public awareness and participation is up would be an understatement. If anything positive came out of last year's schoolhouse scare, it's the reawakening of people wanting to be involved."[24]

When it came time for Town Meeting, a local news report observed that "voters here turned out in relatively large numbers" for the March 18, 2023, community vote on the school budget. Ironically, Ian Underwood—who had the previous year called for slashing the budget by over half—proposed a $700,000 increase to hire ten full-time reading specialists in a bid to improve scores on the statewide assessment. Leslie, who was a key force in restoring the previous year's budget, wasn't having it. "I think everyone here remembers what happens with Ian's ideas," she told a local reporter. Leslie urged voters to reject his plan and "proceed with a rational conversation about the budget proposal from the School Board."[25]

GETTING TO PROBLEM-SOLVE

While reporting for this book, I realized I was running down many things that had little to do with what actually happens in school. I met interesting and passionate people—parents, educators, students, school board members, and others—and I poured over reports, articles, and documents. But I was not doing what I often did: sit in an actual classroom.

So, while in Pennsylvania, I found my way to a tiny chair in Matthew Weimann's third-grade classroom. The place looked like Mrs. Frizzle had rushed through and left a load of educational debris in her wake: waves of construction paper, anchors colored with crayons, a treasure chest tucked behind some books, and a blue paper fish dangling from the ceiling.[26]

I saw immediately that Weimann—wearing black-framed glasses, his head shaved, with an expressive voice—had a way of making ordinary instructions like "Don't touch the fish tank" into a curious conversation about how fish might communicate and what they might be thinking.

He cast his students as the "polite pirates" and at the same time taught them what a fancy word like "irony" meant, setting up a climate in which learning and playfulness were cleaved together. Even preparation for a science activity involving magnets reflected this goal. As he went over instructions it became a game. Some students who had already done a magnet lab helped the newbies. Students were to pretend this was an old-fashioned schoolhouse, so they were to stand at attention behind their chairs and ask permission to respond to his queries. It was a barrel of fun.

He reminded those who had already done the lab that they would be "facilitators." He paused. "That is a *really* good word, 'facilitators.'" He said that the facilitators would guide and answer questions from their classmates. "I don't want you to boss them around," he said to the facilitators. Then he suggested, "Maybe you will see something new when you do it again."

For Weimann, a painter whose fine interior work is in high demand, teaching is a second career (one that pays less than painting). He is a creative thinker whose high pulse rate comes across in his tweets, blogs, and posts. He has even written about teaching controversy—not controversial subjects, but the idea of controversy, guiding children in "pitting equally potent concepts against one another during a normal educational lesson."[27]

What he is up to is amazing teaching.

"My agenda, personally, is to help my third-graders—my polite pirates—fall in love with learning, make habits of learning and enjoying math, and feel they can do any of the things I give them to try," he said when we found a table in the hall outside his classroom. "I try to get them to enjoy the idea of being challenged. I always say, 'Ooooooooooh we have a *challenge!!!*,'" Problems, he tells his students, are opportunities. "Because then we get to problem-solve!"

There are many problems in public education. For one, there are not enough Matthew Weimanns in classrooms. But visiting his classroom reminded me of what is at stake and why this battle matters. We need people like him to be able to teach. And to *want* to teach.

We need to object when politicians and far-right extremists outside of schools who do not know or appreciate the sizzling moments of exchange that set off classroom fireworks, giggles, or jokes and instead use their power to direct what can be discussed or hung on walls.

It matters to be unequivocal about support for teachers, students, and public schooling. This does not mean we should not call out and tackle educational shortcomings. But that is not the conversation we are having now. Rather, we now need to defend public schooling as an institution.

In writing this book, I have been heartened to see attacks by far-right extremists countered by ordinary people, often parents, who decided to show up and speak out. I have appreciated school leaders who stood firm in the face of florid claims of "pornographic books" and objected to library book bans, who were clear about seeing and including all students. I have admired the superintendents who resolutely stood behind their principals, teachers, and librarians.

Support for public schools—like the attacks on them—doesn't happen by accident. We have decisions to make individually and collectively. Mark Sirota, a veteran school board member in the Upper Dublin School District in Pennsylvania, told me that his board specifically "draws a pretty hard and fast line between governance and management," meaning that they hire the administrators "so we'd better trust them" to do their jobs, he said.[28]

Unlike some districts in, say, Texas that are now reviewing and approving library book purchases, his board has specifically steered clear of taking on more authority over the workings of classrooms. "We hear about all the stuff going on elsewhere," he said when we sat down on a Saturday at a booth in a strip-mall Panera. "We do defend against it happening here. We have concerns that it could happen here because it's happening all around us. So, we organize to minimize the opportunity. For example," Sirota said, "our school board does not really get involved in curriculum. At all."

Lately, he noticed, "People think that school boards are really all about the curriculum." But by law in Pennsylvania, the only thing school boards approve are textbooks. "Actual textbooks," he said—not any videos, handouts, or other materials a teacher may use. And unlike in previous eras, he said, textbooks are not something students work through, page by page.

"They are reference resources," he said. This move—putting more power in the hands of professional educators and less in the hands of elected board members—makes it less likely that matters become political. As a result, "We get to focus on all the stuff we want to focus on," and not have meetings hijacked by angry culture-war rants.

Of course, politicians and state legislatures are now getting involved in dictating what can happen in classrooms. And that is a problem. It is often fed by attacks on public schools by leaders who *seem* to address concerns we all have, like about performance. But they often make wrong assumptions or call for vague remedies, such as urging schools to "get back to basics." These repeatedly miss the point that education involves not just facts and content but engaging young people in their own growth. You cannot shovel "basics" at students who are often motivated to come to school not because they are starved for facts, but because they want to participate in the life of the school, see friends, and reach toward a future aim.

The better question is: How can we use this social, human institution to ignite in children the ability and desire to know and do more? How can we use the opportunity that all these young people from different backgrounds come together willing to be guided by adults?

If there is one thing that thirty years of education reporting has taught me it is that schools are very, very different from one another. And yet, the magic is that when we say "public school" everyone knows what that means. Everyone understands that it is a gift from a community to its young people and a foundation of our democracy. We need to make sure that remains true.

ACKNOWLEDGMENTS

J UST AS WE DON'T ATTEND school or learn in classrooms by ourselves, I
have benefitted from a community's worth of help in writing this book.
I am, first, grateful to my editor, Rachael Marks, who immediately saw the
value in writing about what was unfolding in public schools—and the worth
of bringing context and connections to the headlines. And then, of course,
for giving me a crazy tight deadline to get it done.

She was correct. And it launched me into reporting mode, which meant
traveling and meeting people, who then introduced me to other people.
Gratitude to the real life "school moms" who not only met with me but
contacted others, also in other states, and then stayed in touch, forwarding
videos and links and giving me a heads-up about what was on the agenda at
the next school board meeting that I should tune into. They were essential
to this project.

I appreciated how willing so many—including teachers, students, librarians, education leaders, school board members, candidates, advocates, organizers, professors, and scholars—were to meet and talk about public school.
I interviewed some seventy-five people in six months, many in person and
on short notice. To all of you, thank you for speaking and for connecting me
to others. Conversations beget conversations. All the hours of talk, even if
the words don't directly appear in print, were valuable in crafting this story.
Meeting with so many who are so passionate about public schools also reminded me—over and over—why this book needed to be written.

I also could not have done this book if I had not been writing about education for more than thirty years. I knew where to look and what the issues
were. For that I thank my editors, who are also dear friends, especially Lawrie
Mifflin of the *Hechinger Report* and Jane Karr, former education life editor at

the *New York Times*, with whom I worked for nineteen years. For years, Nancy Walser at the *Harvard Education Letter* also pressed me to dig into learning and pedagogy and explore granular questions about how schools worked.

While writing for the *Boston Globe* I tracked the advent of Social Emotional Learning, now a bugaboo of the far right, and the sex-ed battles in Newton, Massachusetts. It was interesting but not surprising to discover that the vocal leader who in the 1990s opposed a pilot sex education program is now busy leading a national anti-LGBTQ+ group, working to ban books in school and public libraries across the country.

And as a reporter for the *Patriot Ledger* in Quincy, Massachusetts, I was drawn to education reporting just as the heavy reliance on property taxes became a contentious determinant of school funding. I saw which communities could pass Proposition 2½ overrides and which slashed budgets and cut special subjects like art. Interestingly, some school moms stepped in to teach art classes. Yet even as I covered education reform in the 1990s and 2000s, including what was taught and how to measure student learning, I noticed that even sharp debates, such as how charter schools should be funded, were philosophical, not political. That has changed.

I have also benefitted in my understanding of school from volunteering to run a journalism program for students in grades three to eight in New Haven, Connecticut. For the past decade—and before Covid (when we met on Zoom)—I spent time every week inside a public school, working with Yale student mentors and with students, sometimes as many as fifty-two young reporters. They gave me a direct line into what mattered to young people. For instance, they wrote about TikTok before any adult had even heard of it. They told me what things in school captured their concern, such as that recycling wasn't *really* happening; and why was Spanish the only foreign language offered, when so many already knew it? I am grateful to these students; to the school moms at East Rock Community & Cultural Magnet School, whom I have come to know; and to Claudia Merson at the Yale Office of New Haven Affairs, who has enabled this. But most especially, to the principal, Sabrina Breland, who is one of the most authentic and warm school leaders I have ever met.

Keeping up with what was happening in school districts around the country would not have been possible without relying heavily on local journalists who do what I once did: cover education in their communities. Local and regional journalism matters, and there are really excellent people bringing insight and great reporting to their work. Among them are Melanie Balakit of *The Tennessean* (now at the *Baltimore Sun*), Emily Donaldson and Talia Richman of the *Dallas Morning News*, Ana Ceballos and Sommer Brugal of the *Miami Herald*, Emily Rizzo of WHYY radio, Maddie Hanna and Oona Goodin-Smith of the *Philadelphia Inquirer*, multiple reporters at the *Morning Call*, Elizabeth Campbell of the *Fort Worth Star-Telegram*, Sandra Sadek, formerly of *Community Impact* and now a Report for America Corps member, Megan Mangrum of *The Tennessean* (now at the *Dallas Morning News*), Alex Hanson and Darren Marcy of the *Valley News* in New Hampshire, Brian Lopez and others at the *Texas Tribune*, Tori Keafer at the *Williamson Herald*, and not-so-local journalists Mike Hixenbaugh and Antonia Hylton, whose *Southlake* podcast and continued reporting and tweeting in Texas are an invaluable source of information for me and for others.

This book also required a lot of research, from digging into news and library archives to collecting social media posts before they vanished. Luckily I tapped into the talents of four Wellesley College students through the college's summer Hive Internship Project program. Aidan Reid, Laila Brustin, Sunny Lu, and Catherine Sneed spent hours poring over school board campaign finance reports, demographic data, local election results, social media accounts, newspaper stories, and historical documents. Laila met me in Williamson County, Tennessee, and interviewed voters as they left the polls while I interviewed candidates. The students' observations about what they found were key in shaping my own reporting and thinking.

Ever since I was a visiting scholar at the Radcliffe Institute for Advanced Study decades ago, I have appreciated the Schlesinger Library's holdings, which cover many aspects of women's lives. I was able to make two trips to Cambridge and spend several days there and at the Gutman Library at the Harvard Graduate School of Education. Given the tight deadline for this project, I could not have navigated the holdings without the expertise of Carla Lillvik, special collections and research librarian at the Gutman library. Her knowledge of what was contained where and her proficiency in tracking down materials was a marvel. I am utterly and completely indebted to Carla.

It is one thing to gather research, and another to turn it into a compelling story. From the start, my son, Donovan Lynch, heartily agreed to help. He is an obsessive reader and fluid writer unafraid to critique his mom. (He once told me, after reading a draft, that I needed to "just start over." He was right.) This time after reading the first draft of the first chapter, he asserted that I "was prancing" (that is family-speak for not getting down to it). Soon, I got on track and he encouraged me to "keep letting it rip." I really, really valued his early feedback.

Fortunately for everyone, the prancing chapter was cut, thanks to my dear friend Maria Trumpler, who while teaching at Yale and helping to lead the Dudley Farm museum in Guilford, Connecticut, read, critiqued, and reorganized the manuscript. She has been a critical thought partner from the very first day that I told her I was thinking of writing this book. It is always great to have a professor on your team. Especially one tuned to scholarship and culture.

One of my oldest and most trusted friends, Mandy Bass—who has been through this read-your-friend's-book drill before—has been an invaluable eye, catching things that would have been embarrassing had she not pointed them out. But like the great friend she is, I am trusting she will keep mum about what those things are.

I also must thank all the unsuspecting people who have been subjected to my banter about my latest breathless findings, interviews, observations, and arguments. It is so helpful to test things out before you actually put them on the page. To members of my Central Park Tennis Club teams in Kirkland, Washington, my New Haven Lawn Club tennis friends, my non-tennis-playing dinner-party-debate friends, my inquiring Yale Field Hockey teammates, curious people I met, and the whole gang of parents at Madzy Bessalear's pickleball birthday party, thank you.

My family (in addition to Donovan) has been on this journey from the start. I talked over the plan as I hiked with my daughter (now Dr.) Olivia Lynch in Zion National Park and then Bryce Canyon National Park; months later we tossed around title ideas as we drove over the Northern Cascades. My daughter Molly Lynch, now a principal in Texas, was my go-to for questions like "What does Social Emotional Learning *actually* look like in the classroom?" and a critical eye on how classrooms and schools really work. Sam Eppler sent me stories and alerted me to things I should look at from the moment he heard about this project.

And, of course, I could not do this or probably anything without the tremendous love and support from my incredible life partner, my husband,

Tom Lynch. As soon as he gets behind something, there is no amount of enthusiasm he doesn't bring. Some of the eagerness can be a challenge ("This book should come out *now!*" Note: Beyond my control). But he let me know early on that he believed in this project: he had made a folder. Which, apparently, he does not do lightly. I am flattered, though I have no idea what is actually in said folder. I will let you know when I find out.

NOTES

PREFACE

1. Dewey quoted in Tracy L. Steffes, *School, Society & State: A New Education to Govern Modern America, 1890–1940* (Chicago: University of Chicago Press, 2012), 169–71.

2. Steffes, *School, Society & State*, 95.

3. US Department of Education, "The Department's History," Sept. 2010, https://www2.ed.gov/about/overview/focus/what.html, accessed Dec. 7, 2022.

4. Lyndon B. Johnson, "Excerpts from President's Special Message to Congress on Health and Education," *New York Times*, Mar. 1, 1967, 26, https://www.nytimes.com/1967/03/01/archives/excerpts-from-presidents-special-message-to-congress-on-health-and.html.

5. National Center for Education Statistics, "Public School Revenue Sources," chapter 2 in *Report on the Condition of Education 2022*, NCES 2022–44 (Washington, DC: US Department of Education, May 2022), https://nces.ed.gov/programs/coe/indicator/cma, accessed Dec. 7, 2022.

6. US Department of Education, "U.S. Department of Education Confirms Title IX Protects Students from Discrimination Based on Sexual Orientation and Gender Identity," press release, June 16, 2021, https://www.ed.gov/news/press-releases/us-department-education-confirms-title-ix-protects-students-discrimination-based-sexual-orientation-and-gender-identity, accessed Dec. 7, 2022.

7. Catherine E. Lhamon, *Safeguarding Students' Civil Rights, Promoting Educational Excellence: Report to the President and Secretary of Education* (Washington, DC: US Department of Education Office for Civil Rights, July 2022), 41, https://www2.ed.gov/about/reports/annual/ocr/report-to-president-and-secretary-of-education-2021.pdf, accessed Dec. 12, 2022.

8. Joshua Q. Nelson, "Arizona Pushes Most Expansive Education Savings Account Program in the U.S.," Fox News, June 24, 2022, https://www.foxnews.com/media/arizona-education-savings-account-program; on legislatures taking up ESAs and voucher expansion, see Bella DiMarco, "Legislative Tracker: 2023 State Bills on Public Support of Private Schooling," FutureEd, https://www.future-ed.org/legislative-tracker-2023-state-bills-on-public-support-of-private-schooling, accessed Mar. 13, 2023.

9. Wayne Carter, "Charity Has Difficulty Donating Dictionaries to Students Due to New Board Book Policy," NBCDFW, updated Dec. 9, 2022, https://www.nbcdfw.com/news/local/carter-in-the-classroom/charity-has-difficulty-donating-dictionaries-to-students-due-to-new-board-book-policy/3144962.

CHAPTER 1: WHAT THE "WAR MOMS" WANT

1. Tim Craig, "Moms for Liberty Has Turned 'Parents Rights' into a Rallying Cry for Conservative Parents," *Washington Post*, Oct. 15, 2021, https://www.washingtonpost.com/national/moms-for-liberty-parents-rights/2021/10/14/bf3d9ccc-286a-11ec-8831-a31e7b3de188_story.html; Tiffany Justice and Tina Descovich, "What 'School Board Moms' Really Want—And Why Candidates Ignore Us at Their Peril," Opinion, *Washington Post*, Nov. 8, 2021, https://www.washingtonpost.com/opinions/2021/11/08/moms-for-liberty-education-elections; Moms for Liberty at Division of Corporations, https://search.sunbiz.org/Inquiry/corporationsearch/SearchResultDetail?inquirytype=EntityName&directionType=Initial&searchNameOrder=MOMSFORLIBERTY%20, accessed Oct. 6, 2022.

2. Alessandro Marazzi Sassoon, "Jennifer Jenkins Beats Tina Descovich in Big Upset: Politics or Pandemic?" *Florida Today*, Aug. 19, 2020, https://www.floridatoday.com/story/news/2020/08/19/mail-voting-covid-19-and-brevard-politics-why-did-jenkins-beat-descovich/3399851001.

3. State of Florida, Department of Education, DOE Order No. 2020-EO-06, https://www.fldoe.org/core/fileparse.php/19861/urlt/DOE-2020-EO-06.pdf.

4. Owen Dyer, "Covid-19: Fired Florida Statistician Says Police Raid Aimed to Identify Her Government Contacts," *BMJ* 371 (Dec. 2020), https://doi.org/10.1136/bmj.m4781.

5. Florida Education Association, *FEA's Safe Schools Report 2020–21*, https://feaweb.org/covid19/fea-safe-schools-report; Victor Chernozhukov, Hiroyuki Kasahara, and Paul Schrimpf, "The Association of Opening of K–12 Schools with the Spread of Covid-19 in the United States: County-Level Data Analysis," *PNAS* 118, no. 42 (Aug. 2021): 3, https://doi.org/10.1073/pnas.2103420118.

6. Kim Hough (candidate for Brevard County School Board District 5 and cofounder of Parents for Safe Schools) and Michelle Barrineau (vice president, Parents for Safe Schools), author interview, Melbourne, Florida, July 14, 2022.

7. Heather Beal (treasurer, Parents for Safe Schools), author interview, via Zoom, July 18, 2022.

8. My account of the Moms for Liberty conference is based on my notes as an attendee, including my recordings of the event. There are also selected videos of the event on the Moms for Liberty website, including speeches by Governor Ron DeSantis ("FL Gov. Ron DeSantis Stands Up for Parental Rights," https://www.momsforliberty.org/news/ron-desantis-parental-rights/); Dr. James Lindsay ("Dr. James Lindsay—Education Not Indoctrination," https://www.momsforliberty.org/news/dr-james-lindsey/); Ben Carson ("Dr. Ben Carson and the American Dream," https://www.momsforliberty.org/news/dr-ben-carson/); and Betsy DeVos "'End the US Department of Education' Betsy DeVos Sits Down with Moms for Liberty," https://www.momsforliberty.org/news/betsy-devos/).

9. Laura Pappano, "Class Confessional: When Kids Open Up," *Boston Globe*, Jan. 7, 1991, 30.

10. Peter Salovey and John D. Mayer, "Emotional Intelligence," *Imagination, Cognition and Personality* 9, no. 3 (2016), https://journals.sagepub.com/doi/10.2190/DUGG-P24E-52WK-6CDG.

11. James P. Comer, "Educating Poor Minority Children: Schools Must Win the Support of Parents and Learn to Respond Flexibly and Creatively to Students' Needs," *Scientific American*, Nov. 1, 1988; James P. Comer, "Child and Adolescent Development: The Critical Missing Focus in School Reform," *Phi Delta Kappan* 86, no. 10 (2005): 757–63, http://www.jstor.org/stable/20441901. For an overview, see Diane Curtis, "Core Classes: Social Development in Action: New Haven Public Schools Emphasize Socialization on Par with Academics," *Edutopia*, Feb. 21, 2001; Martin R. West, Libby Pier, Hans Fricke, Heather Hough, Susanna Loeb, Robert H. Meyer, and Andrew B. Rice, "Trends in Student Social-Emotional Learning: Evidence from the First Large-Scale Panel Student Survey," *Educational Evaluation and Policy Analysis* 42, no. 2 (June 2020): 279–303, https://doi.org/10.3102/0162373720912236. For the original paper on emotional intelligence see Peter Salovey and John D. Mayer, "Emotional Intelligence," *Imagination, Cognition and Personality* 9, no. 3 (Mar. 1990): 185–211, https://doi.org/10.2190/DUGG-P24E-52WK-6CDG.

12. Abby (Los Angeles kindergarten teacher), author interview, via Zoom, July 24, 2022. Last name withheld to maintain privacy.

13. Stuart J. Foster, "Red Alert! The National Education Association Confronts the 'Red Scare' in American Public Schools, 1947–1954," *Education and Culture* 14, no. 2 (Fall 1997): 1–3.

14. Robert A. Skaife, "Right-Wing 'Front' Organizations: They Sow Distrust," *Education Digest* 16, no. 8 (Apr. 1951).

15. George Gallup, "Majority Found to Favor Ban on Communist Party," *Boston Globe*, Apr. 19, 1947, 3.

16. "President's Order on Loyalty Hailed," *New York Times*, Mar. 23, 1947, 48, https://www.nytimes.com/1947/03/23/archives/presidents-order-on-loyalty-hailed-but-congressmen-warn-that.html.

17. Newspaper archives of this period are replete with articles in which Republican candidates for a variety of offices charge that Democratic opponents are "soft on communism." See, for example, "Rivals Too Soft, Hanley Declares: Democrats' Record Toward Communists 'Appalling' He Tells Bronx Audience," *New York Times*, Oct. 22, 1950, 59, https://www.nytimes.com/1950/10/22/archives/rivals-too-soft-hanley-declares-democrats-record-toward-communism.html.

18. "'Barefaced Lies' Hensel Declares: Top Defense Aide Challenges McCarthy to Repeat Charge Without Senate Immunity," *New York Times*, Apr. 21, 1954, 1, 16, https://www.nytimes.com/1954/04/21/archives/barefaced-lies-hensel-declares-top-defense-aide-challenges-mccarthy.html; "Flanders Expects a Vote of Censure: Confident Senate Will Rebuke McCarthy in Showdown Vote Scheduled for Tuesday," *New York Times*, July 18, 1954, 31, https://www.nytimes.com/1954/10/17/archives/flanders-approves-censure-vote-delay.html.

19. Dugan Arnett, Hannah Krueger, and Brendan McCarthy, "Like a Plot from 'The Americans': An Alleged Russian Smuggling Ring Found in N.H. Town,"

Boston Globe, Dec. 13, 2022, https://www.bostonglobe.com/2022/12/13/metro/spies-microchips-night-lights-story-an-alleged-russian-weapons-smuggler-small-town-nh.

20. Beverly Gage, "Hooverism," *G-Man: J. Edgar Hoover and the Making of the American Century* (New York: Viking, 2022), 386.

21. C. P. Trussell, "New Inquiry Seeks Reds in Education," *New York Times*, Feb. 12, 1953, 16.

22. "Somerville Teacher Suspended as Result of Red Probe Here," *Boston Globe*, Mar. 31, 1953, 1.

23. "N.Y. Court Upholds Firing or Suspension of Six Teachers," *Boston Globe*, Apr. 18, 1953, 4; "2d Red Teacher Suspect Faces School Board Today: 'Mr. X. Called to Explain His Status,'" *Boston Globe*, Apr. 18, 1953, 1; *Harvard Crimson*, n.d., in Foster, "Red Alert!," 3.

24. This has become an issue in K–12 and higher education, where simply teaching about racial justice has also become grounds for dismissal in some settings. See Jon Skolnik, "Fired over CRT: Missouri High School Teacher Accused of Teaching 'Critical Race Theory' Loses Job, *Salon*, Apr. 13, 2022, https://www.salon.com/2022/04/13/fired-over-crt-missouri-high-school-teacher-accused-of-teaching-critical-race-theory-loses-job; Jared Gans, "Florida English Professor Fired After Parent Complaint About Social Justice Lessons," *The Hill*, Mar. 17, 2023, https://thehill.com/homenews/state-watch/3905677-florida-english-professor-fired-after-parent-complaint-over-racial-justice-lessons; see also chapter 4 of this volume.

25. James H. Hammond, "Wayland Ousts Teacher, Ex-Red: Board Chief Quits After 2–1 Vote," *Boston Globe*, July 8, 1954, 1.

26. Anne Hale Jr., "Teacher's Statement," *Boston Globe*, July 8, 1954, 6.

27. Robert E. Mainer, "The Red Scare in Wayland," contribution to the Wayland Historical Society, 2003, https://www.uuwayland.org/wp-content/uploads/2015/05/Red-Scare-by-Bob-Mainer.pdf.

28. Foster, "Red Alert!," 1.

29. Patricia Mazzei, "Most of the School Board Candidates DeSantis Backed in Florida Won," *New York Times*, Aug. 24, 2022, https://www.nytimes.com/2022/08/24/us/politics/ron-desantis-florida-school-board.html; Ron DeSantis (@RonDeSantisFL), "Today is Election Day for crucial school board races across our state. Florida has led with purpose and conviction that our school system is about education, not indoctrination," Twitter, Aug. 23, 2022, 10:19 a.m., https://twitter.com/RonDeSantisFL/status/1562127282398969858.

30. Although George Zimmerman, in his trial for the fatal shooting of Trayvon Martin, did not invoke Florida's "Stand Your Ground" law, the jury did receive information about the law. In the decade following Martin's killing, similar laws have proliferated in states around the country. See Hannah Knowles and Emmanuel Felton, "'Stand Your Ground' Laws Spread—and Grow More Extreme—10 Years After Trayvon Martin's Death," *Washington Post*, Feb. 25, 2022, https://www.washingtonpost.com/nation/2022/02/25/stand-your-ground-trayvon-martin.

31. Leadership Institute, "The Leadership Institute's Finance Page," link to Form 990 for 2021, https://www.leadershipinstitute.org/aboutus/Finance.cfm,

Schedule A, p. 2; Leadership Institute, "Staff Directory, Bridget Ziegler," https://leadershipinstitute.org/contactUS/staff/?staff=7000711.

32. Citizens for Renewing America, "Toolkit: Combatting Critical Race Theory in Your Community," June 8, 2021, https://citizensrenewingamerica.com/issues/combatting-critical-race-theory-in-your-community, 9.

CHAPTER 2: HOW SCHOOLS ARE BECOMING PARTISAN AND POLITICAL

1. "97 Tennesseans Including Cyrus to Carry the Torch," *The Tennessean*, Feb. 16, 1996, 20; "Those Chosen to Run with the Flame," *The Tennessean*, Feb. 16, 1996, 20; Nancy Garrett, author interviews, Franklin, Tennessee, Aug. 5 and 6, 2022.

2. Nancy Garrett (@NancyGarrettD12), "That Teacher Was My Dad," Twitter, July 1, 2022, 8:20 a.m., https://twitter.com/NancyGarrettD12/status/1542848060757352449?s=20&t=ftolmxMxPwN-5h3j7yHNrw.

3. Zach Harmuth, "New Williamson County School Board Member Appointed," *Williamson Source*, Nov. 15, 2016, https://williamsonsource.com/new-williamson-county-school-board-member-appointed; Tori Keafer, "WCS School Board Appoints Nancy Garrett Chair, KC Haugh Vice Chair," *Williamson Herald*, Sept. 21, 2020, https://www.williamsonherald.com/news/wcs-school-board-appoints-nancy-garrett-chair-kc-haugh-vice-chair/article_f7a89d94-fc76-11ea-9a8d-4ba2893410f3.html.

4. Meghan Mangrum, "Gov. Bill Lee Signs Bill Greenlighting Partisan School Board Elections in Tennessee," *The Tennessean*, Nov. 12, 2021, https://www.tennessean.com/story/news/education/2021/11/12/tennessee-gov-bill-lee-greenlights-partisan-school-board-elections/6284601001.

5. Brian Stetler, "This Infamous Steve Bannon Quote Is Key to Understanding America's Crazy Politics," *CNN Business*, Nov. 16, 2021, https://www.cnn.com/2021/11/16/media/steve-bannon-reliable-sources/index.html.

6. Patriot Mobile Action, "Announcing: Patriot Mobile Action," May 16, 2022, https://www.patriotmobileaction.com/announcing-patriot-mobile-action.

7. Glenn Story and Leigh Wambsganns, interviewed by Steve Bannon, *"Overturned over 4 School Boards": Glenn Story Explains the Steps to Taking Back America's Education*, Bannon's War Room, Aug. 8, 2022, Rumble video, https://rumble.com/v1ezwa3-overturned-over-4-school-boards-glenn-story-explains-the-steps-to-taking-ba.html; Patriot Mobile Action, "Flipped Four School Boards—Taking Back America," Aug. 8, 2022, https://www.patriotmobileaction.com/in-the-news.

8. Matthew C. Moen, "From Revolution to Evolution: The Changing Nature of the Christian Right," *Sociology of Religion* 55, no. 3 (Autumn 1994): 346–48, https://www.jstor.org/stable/3712058.

9. Harry Covert, "Ministers Shocked: Carter Says He Will Veto Bill to Restore Prayer in Public Schools," *Moral Majority Report* (Mar. 14, 1980): 3.

10. Charles E. Judd, "What Was Wrong Is Now Right," *Liberty Report* (Jan. 1987): 2.

11. "Pat Robertson Group Says It's Disbanding," *New York Times*, Sept. 9, 1986, https://www.nytimes.com/1986/09/27/us/pat-robertson-group-says-it-s-disbanding.html.

12. Moen, "From Revolution to Evolution," 348.

13. E. J. Dionne Jr., "Dole Wins in Iowa with Robertson Next," *New York Times*, Feb. 9, 1988, https://www.nytimes.com/1988/02/09/us/dole-wins-in-iowa-with-robertson-next.html.

14. Steve Bruce, "Modernity and Fundamentalism: The New Christian Right in America," *British Journal of Sociology* 41, no. 4 (Dec. 1990): 484.

15. Wayne King, "Pat Robertson: A Candidate of Contradictions," *New York Times*, Feb. 27, 1988: 1, https://www.nytimes.com/1988/02/27/us/pat-robertson-a-candidate-of-contradictions.html; Lisa Myers, NBC *Nightly News*, Dec. 21, 1987, *NBC News on Pat Robertson's 1988 Presidential Bid*, YouTube video, https://www.youtube.com/watch?v=zJsgAEQAvis.

16. Ruth Walker, "'Stealth' Candidates in American Politics," *Christian Science Monitor*, Dec. 2, 1992, https://www.csmonitor.com/1992/1202/02192.html.

17. Laurel Shaper Walters, "Religious Right Win Seats on School Boards Across the U.S.," *Christian Science Monitor*, Aug. 9, 1993, https://www.csmonitor.com/1993/0809/09011.html; Liz Galst, "The Right Fight," *Mother Jones*, Mar.–Apr. 1994, https://www.motherjones.com/politics/1994/03/right-fight.

18. League of Women Voters, "'What If' Tips for League Candidate Forums-Debates," https://my.lwv.org/sites/default/files/empty_chair_debate_tips_1_.pdf, accessed Mar. 18, 2023.

19. Walters, "Religious Right Win Seats on School Boards Across the U.S."

20. Laura Pappano, "Newton to Try Sex Education in 9th Grade," *Boston Globe*, May 11, 1993: 21, 23; Laura Pappano, "A Fundamental Issue in Newton? Sex Ed Supporters Say Religion Spurs Its Foes," *Boston Globe*, May 10, 1993, 17.

21. Laura Pappano, "Newton Vote Sends Message on Sex Education," *Boston Globe*, Nov. 4, 1993, 39; Laura Pappano, "Quietly, Newton Sex Ed Is OK'd," *Boston Globe*, Dec. 19, 1993: 37.

22. Laura Pappano, "Sex Education Advocates Unite," *Boston Globe*, Feb. 6, 1994, 35; Jenna Fisher, "Waltham Anti-LGBTQ Organization Listed as Hate Group," *The Patch*, Feb. 9, 2021, https://patch.com/massachusetts/waltham/waltham-anti-lgtbq-group-listed-hate-group-splc.

23. American Presidency Project, "Voter Turnout in Presidential Elections," UC Santa Barbara, https://www.presidency.ucsb.edu/statistics/data/voter-turnout-in-presidential-elections; Jacob Fabine, "Despite Pandemic Challenges, 2020 Election Had Largest Increase in Voting Between Presidential Elections on Record," US Census, Apr. 29, 2021, https://www.census.gov/library/stories/2021/04/record-high-turnout-in-2020-general-election.html; Who Votes for Mayor? "Too Few People Choose Our Elected Leaders," http://whovotesformayor.org; National School Board Association, "The Public's Voice," Apr. 1, 2020, https://www.nsba.org/ASBJ/2020/April/the-publics-voice.

24. Frisco ISD, "Board of Trustees: Board Election Notices and Results," see "2022 Official Results," https://www.friscoisd.org/about/board-of-trustees/board-elections/results; on Frisco general election 2021 turnout, see Frisco, "Voter Participation," https://www.friscotexas.gov/1671/Voter-Participation; on Denton County turnout for Frisco ISD race, see Denton County, TX, "2022 Joint, General, and Special Election, May 7, 2022," https://results.enr.clarityelections.com/TX/Denton/112974/web.285569/#/summary?category=C_2&subcategory=C_2_7; on Collin County, see "Summary and Results Report, General and Special

Election, May 7, 2022," https://www.collincountytx.gov/elections/election_results
/Archive/2022/05072022/May%207,%202022%20Combined%20Election%20
Day%20and%20Early%20Ballots%20-%20Accumulated%20Totals.pdf.

25. Natalie Hebert, author interview, Frisco, Texas, June 15, 2022.

26. Rich Lowry, "How Southlake, Texas, Won Its Battle Against Critical
Race Theory. And the Lessons for Everyone Else," *National Review*, June 23, 2021,
https://www.nationalreview.com/2021/06/how-southlake-texas-won-its-battle
-against-critical-race-theory.

27. Elizabeth Campbell, "Tarrant County Judge Candidate Says 'Critical Race
Theory Is Now Dead' In Carroll ISD," *Fort Worth Star-Telegram*, Dec. 14, 2021,
https://www.star-telegram.com/news/local/education/article256592651.html.

28. Transparency USA, "Southlake Families PAC, Texas Committee, Contributions," https://www.transparencyusa.org/tx/committee/southlake-families-pac
-00084934-gpac/contributions?cycle=2020-election-cycle&page=8, accessed Mar.
19, 2023.

29. Sandra Sadek, "Carroll ISD Halts Work on Cultural Competence Action
Plan Following Court's Temporary Restraining Order," Community Impact, Dec.
3, 2020, https://communityimpact.com/dallas-fort-worth/grapevine-colleyville
-southlake/education/2020/12/03/carroll-isd-halts-work-on-cultural-competence
-action-plan-following-courts-temporary-restraining-order; William Joy, "Carroll
ISD Rejects Long-Debated Diversity Plan in New Lawsuit Settlement," WFAA,
Dec. 21, 2021, https://www.wfaa.com/article/news/education/schools/southlake
-carroll-isd-rejects-long-debated-diversity-plan-in-new-lawsuit-settlement/287
-c36a4bc6-b6ee-4097-a7dc-9db62ea5bf4c.

30. Abby Church, "Southlake Carroll Schools Face More Civil Rights Investigations from Education Department," *Fort Worth Star-Telegram*, Feb. 9, 2023,
https://www.star-telegram.com/news/local/education/article272340083.html.

31. Transparency USA, "Southlake Families PAC, Texas Committee, Pay-
ments," https://www.transparencyusa.org/tx/pac/southlake-families-pac-00084934
-gpac/payments, accessed Aug. 18, 2022; Axiom Strategies, https://axiomstrategies
.com/about; Vanguard Field Strategies, https://www.vanguardfieldstrategies.com
/about-us1.

32. "Active Campaign Filer Lists," Political Committee with Treasurer Ap-
pointment, Texas Ethics Commission, included in downloadable Excel file, "Start
Date: 7/26/21," "Treasurer Name: Janagarajan, Muniraj," https://www.ethics.state
.tx.us/search/cf, accessed Mar. 19, 2023.

33. Morgan O'Hanlon, "Gov. Greg Abbott's Two Most Vocal GOP Challeng-
ers Have Long Sought to Push Their Party to the Right," *Texas Tribune*, Feb. 23,
2033, https://www.texastribune.org/2022/02/23/texas-primary-governor-don
-huffines-allen-west-greg-abbott; Matthew Rosenberg and Maggie Haberman,
"The Republican Embrace of QAnon Goes Far Beyond Trump," *New York Times*,
Aug. 20, 2020, updated Aug. 22, 2020, https://www.nytimes.com/2020/08/20/us
/politics/qanon-trump-republicans.html; *"We Are the Storm Rally," with Texas Republican Party Chairman Allen West—August 4, 2020*, YouTube video, https://www
.youtube.com/watch?v=EelBqXocW9w, at 42:35.

34. Lowry, "How Southlake, Texas, Won Its Battle Against Critical Race
Theory. And the Lessons for Everyone Else."

35. Talia Richman and Corbett Smith, "Bolstered by CRT, Book Fights, Conservative PACs Aim to 'Take Back' Texas School Boards," *Dallas Morning News,* Mar. 3, 2022, https://www.dallasnews.com/news/education/2022/03/03/bolstered-by-crt-book-fights-conservative-pacs-aim-to-take-back-texas-school-boards.

36. "Approved Budget Includes Pay Raises, Additional Staff," *Frisco ISD eNewsletter,* June 22, 2022, https://www.friscoisd.org/news/district-headlines/2022/06/22/fisd-enews.

37. Frisco Economic Development Corporation, "Companies in Frisco," https://friscoedc.com/companies-in-frisco.

38. Former member of Families 4 Frisco, author interview, via telephone, Aug. 24, 2022. Legal release signed, but identity withheld for interviewee's personal safety.

39. Tracy Gamble, author interview, via Zoom, June 20, 2022.

40. Emily Donaldson, "Frisco Schools Leader Rebukes GOP Lawmaker on 'Sexually Inappropriate' Library Book Claims," *Dallas Morning News,* May 20, 2022, https://www.dallasnews.com/news/education/2022/05/20/frisco-schools-leader-rebukes-gop-lawmaker-on-sexually-inappropriate-library-book-claims.

41. "Attention Frisco Residents: Your Schools Are in Trouble," editorial, *Dallas Morning News,* May 21, 2022, https://www.dallasnews.com/opinion/editorials/2022/05/21/attention-frisco-residents-your-schools-are-in-trouble.

42. For campaign finance reports for all candidates see Frisco, "Board of Trustees, Board Elections Notices and Results," https://www.friscoisd.org/about/board-of-trustees/board-elections/results.

43. Stephanie Elad, *A Movement Just Beginning in Frisco, Texas; Interview with Bannon's War Room,* May 9, 2022, video at https://stephanie4fisd.com/a-movement-just-beginning-in-frisco-texas; Francesca D'Annunzio, "'This Is Just the Beginning,' New Frisco School Board Trustee Says on Steve Bannon Show," *Dallas Morning News,* May 11, 2022, https://www.dallasnews.com/news/politics/2022/05/11/this-is-just-the-beginning-new-frisco-school-board-trustee-says-on-steve-bannon-show.

44. Maurice T. Cunningham, *Dark Money and the Politics of School Privatization* (Cham, Switzerland: Palgrave MacMillan, 2021), 8–9.

45. Jeffrey R. Henig, Rebecca Jacobsen, and Sarah Reckhow, *Outside Money in School Board Elections: The Nationalization of Education Politics* (Cambridge, MA: Harvard Education Press, 2019), 181.

46. Jane Mayer, "State Legislatures Are Torching Democracy," *New Yorker,* Aug. 15, 2022, https://www.newyorker.com/magazine/2022/08/15/state-legislatures-are-torching-democracy; David Pepper, *Laboratories of Autocracy: A Wake-Up Call from Behind the Lines* (Cincinnati: St. Helena Press, 2021).

47. Jacob M. Grumbach, *Laboratories Against Democracy: How National Parties Transformed State Politics* (Princeton, NJ: Princeton University Press, 2022), xx.

48. Grumbach, *Laboratories Against Democracy: How National Parties Transformed State Politics,* 172, 195, 198.

49. National School Boards Association, "Today's School Boards & Their Priorities for Tomorrow," 2018 K–12 national survey, https://cdn-files.nsba.org/s3fs-public/reports/K12_National_Survey.pdf; Ballotpedia, "Understanding the Nation's More than 82,000 School Board Members," *Hall Pass* (newsletter), Aug. 24, 2022, https://ballotpedia.org/Hall_Pass_-_August_24,_2022.

50. Ballotpedia, "School Board Elections 2021," see "Historical Election Data," https://ballotpedia.org/School_board_elections,_2021.

51. Ballotpedia, "Conflicts in School Board Elections 2021–2022," https://ballot pedia.org/Conflicts_in_school_board_elections,_2021–2022.

52. The 9-12 Project Tennessee was led by J. Lee Douglas, who was quoted in local news reports as working to support far-right candidates: "Seeing what took place last election, those people that opposed my viewpoints—they're going to be out." Melanie Balakit, "Despite Politics, Williamson Schools See Little Change," *The Tennessean*, Dec. 18, 2015. Douglas also sought the ouster of the superintendent at a school board meeting Jan. 20, 2015. See *Williamson County School Board Meeting, Jan. 20th, 2015*, YouTube video, https://www.youtube.com/watch?v=3PlS1D4jigM at 9:06; Melanie Balakit, "Brentwood Resident Files PAC Complaint Against Project 912," *The Tennessean*, July 14, 2015, https://www.tennessean.com/story/news/local /williamson/2015/07/13/brentwood-resident-files-pac-complaint-project/30116037. As of August 2022, the organization's website and Twitter account appear to be inactive.

53. Joey Garrison and Maria Giordano, "Koch Brothers Group Vows More Spending on Fight," *The Tennessean*, Aug. 14, 2014, https://www.tennessean.com /story/news/education/2014/08/13/koch-brothers-group-vows-anti-common-core -spending-tennessee/14012641.

54. Garrison and Giordano, "Koch Brothers Group Vows More Spending on Fight."

55. "Americans for Prosperity Action, Outside Spending," Open Secrets, https://www.opensecrets.org/outsidespending/detail.php?cmte=C00687103&cycle =2020. Americans for Prosperity Action became a super PAC in 2018 and spent $47.7 million in the 2020 election cycle.

56. Esan Swan, "Williamson Passes Resolution Addressing Common Core," *The Tennessean*, Oct. 21, 2014, https://www.tennessean.com/story/news/local /williamson/schools/2014/10/20/williamson-school-board-passes-resolution-opposing -common-core/17646619.

57. Balakit, "Despite Politics, Williamson Schools See Little Change."

58. *Williamson County School Board meeting, Jan. 20th, 2015*, at 15:12.

59. Steve Cavendish, "Judge: Williamson Strong Is Not a PAC," *Nashville Scene*, Mar. 30, 2017, https://www.nashvillescene.com/news/pithinthewind/judge -williamson-strong-is-not-a-pac/article_1a79d73d-2a55–54a7–9f11–3d5e61915229 .html.

60. Williamson Secrets (four parts), *Medium*, July 2014, https://medium.com /@WilliamsonSecrets.

61. Dearestwcs, Instagram, 468 posts, July 2–17, 2020, https://www.instagram .com/dearestwcs, accessed Aug. 23, 2022; Anika Exum, "New Parent Group One WillCo Seeks to Address Racism in Williamson Schools," *The Tennessean*, Mar. 24, 2021, https://www.tennessean.com/story/news/local/williamson/2021/03/24 /williamson-county-schools-one-willco-addresses-racism/6851551002; Fostering Healthy Solutions, *Catalogue Final Report Prepared for Williamson County Public Schools*, Aug. 2021, https://bloximages.newyork1.vip.townnews.com/williamson herald.com/content/tncms/assets/v3/editorial/8/29/8299d9ba-012e-11ec-b01f -cbcd29dfb4cf/611ec341b55bf.pdf; Anika Exum, "Diversity, Inclusion and Student Safety Efforts at WCS Have Come Far, What's Next?" *The Tennessean*, Apr. 4,

2022, https://www.tennessean.com/story/news/local/williamson/2022/04/02 /diversity-inclusion-and-safety-efforts-williamson-schdiversity-inclusiools-have -come-far-whats-next/7154624001.

62. Natalie Allison, "Tennessee Bans Schools from Teaching Critical Race Theory amid National Debate," *The Tennessean*, May 6, 2021, https://www .tennessean.com/story/news/politics/2021/05/05/tennessee-bans-critical-race -theory-schools-withhold-funding/4948306001; Meghan Mangrum, "TN Schools Chief Faces Pressure over Curriculum as Group File First Complaint Under New Critical Race Theory Law," *The Tennessean*, July 5, 2021, https://www.tennessean .com/story/news/education/2021/07/06/tennessee-penny-schwinn-pressure-over -curriculum-critical-race-theory-law/7837346002.

63. Nancy Garrett, author interview, Franklin, Tennessee, Aug. 4, 2022.

64. *Williamson County Board of Education Meeting, August 10, 2021*, YouTube video, https://www.youtube.com/watch?v=kbWVNlhlmME, accessed Mar. 20, 2023; *"President Biden Reacts to Williamson County School Board Meeting,"* WKRN News 2, YouTube video, https://www.youtube.com/watch?v=a1nNLnlTrV8, accessed Mar. 20, 2023.

65. *"'We Will Find You!' Parents Threaten Mask Supporters at Tennessee School Board Meeting,"* YouTube video, https://www.youtube.com/watch?v=fAcpKEPmwTA, accessed Aug. 24, 2022.

66. Josh Vardaman, "School Board Candidates Meet on Zoom for Forum," *Williamson Herald*, June 29, 2022, https://www.williamsonherald.com/news/local _news/school-board-candidates-meet-on-zoom-for-forum/article_dd8530d0-f7dd -11ec-ac93-b7ef267eea8b.html.

67. Matt Masters, "WCS Board Candidate 'Doc' Holladay Says Lessons from Troubled Past Make Him Right Choice for Voters," *Brentwood Home Page* (online newspaper), Aug. 5, 2022, https://www.thenewstn.com/brentwood/wcs-board -candidate-doc-holladay-says-lessons-from-troubled-past-make-him-the-right -choice/article_f6d378cc-122b-11ed-9476-63c60f9871f8.html; William Holladay, "Liberalism Is the Real Pandemic," Facebook post, July 22, 2022, https://www .facebook.com/williamdocholladay.

CHAPTER 3: WHEN LIBRARIANS COME UNDER ATTACK

1. Lindsey Kimery, author interview, via Zoom, July 25, 2022; Tennessee State Assembly, "House Criminal Justice Committee," Mar. 2, 2022, https://tnga .granicus.com/MediaPlayer.php?view_id=610&clip_id=26352, testimony of Representative Scott Cepicky at 14:16, Andrew Maraniss at 1:39:04, and Lindsey Kimery at 1:40:43; Senator Joey Hensley, Tennessee General Assembly, Senate Judiciary Committee, SB 1944, Apr. 6, 2022, https://wapp.capitol.tn.gov/apps /BillInfo/Default.aspx?BillNumber=SB1944&GA=112, at 49:45.

2. New International Version of the Bible, "Two Adulterous Sisters," Ezekiel 23:20–21, https://www.biblegateway.com/passage/?search=Ezekiel%2023%3A20 &version=NIV.

3. Board of Education, Island Trees Union Free School District No. 26, et al., Petitioners, v. Steven A. Pico, by His Next Friend, Frances Pico, et al. (1982); available at Cornell Law School, Legal Information Institute, https://www.law .cornell.edu/supremecourt/text/457/853.

4. Blythe Bernhard and Jane Henderson, "School Librarians in Missouri Pull Books as New Law Allows Charges for 'Explicit' Material," *St. Louis Post-Dispatch*, Aug. 12, 2022, https://www.stltoday.com/news/local/education/school-librarians -in-missouri-pull-books-as-new-law-allows-charges-for-explicit-material/article _eb7ed4ba-e6a3-5f83-bf10-223d27e6b081.html.

5. Marta W. Aldrich, "'Age-Appropriate' School Library Bill Heads to Governor's Desk," *The Tennessean*, Mar. 15, 2022, https://www.tennessean.com/story /news/education/2022/03/15/tennessee-age-appropriate-school-library-bill-heads -gov-bill-lee-desk/7049218001; Natalie Allison, "Tennessee Bans Public Schools from Teaching Critical Race Theory amid National Debate," *The Tennessean*, May 21, 2021, https://www.tennessean.com/story/news/politics/2021/05/05/tennessee -bans-critical-race-theory-schools-withhold-funding/4948306001; "Summary of New K–12 Laws Approved by the Tennessee General Assembly in 2022," staff report, *Rogersville Review*, May 13, 2022, https://www.therogersvillereview.com /rogersville/article_c0ac8548-a769-5911-a542-b642d929ff7b.html.

6. Office of Governor Ron DeSantis, "Governor Ron DeSantis Signs Bill That Requires Curriculum Transparency," news release, Mar. 25, 2022, https://www .flgov.com/2022/03/25/governor-ron-desantis-signs-bill-that-requires-curriculum -transparency; for the text of the bill, see Florida House of Representatives, "Enrolled-CS/HB147 Enrolled, 2022 Legislature," https://www.flsenate.gov/Session /Bill/2022/1467/BillText/er/PDF; Judd Legum, "Florida Teachers Told to Remove Books from Classroom Libraries or Risk Felony Prosecution," *Popular Information*, Jan. 2023, https://popular.info/p/florida-teachers-told-to-remove-books; Eesha Pendharkar, "New Training Tells Florida School Librarians Which Books Are Off-Limits," *Education Week*, Jan. 18, 2023, https://www.edweek.org/leadership /new-training-tells-florida-school-librarians-which-books-are-off-limits/2023/01.

7. Matt Krause, chairman, Committee on General Investigating, Texas House of Representatives, letter to Lily Vaux, deputy commissioner, school programs, Oct. 25, 2021, https://static.texastribune.org/media/files/965725d7f01b8a25ca44b 6fde2f5519b/krauseletter.pdf; Bill Chappell, "A Texas Lawmaker Is Targeting 850 Books That He Said Could Make Students Feel Uneasy," Oct. 28, 2022, National Public Radio, https://www.npr.org/2021/10/28/1050013664/texas-lawmaker-matt -krause-launches-inquiry-into-850-books.

8. Mary Woodard, author interview, via Zoom, June 13, 2022. Woodard's term as president of the Texas Library Association ended in April 2023.

9. Ballotpedia, "Matt Krause," https://ballotpedia.org/Matt_Krause. After leaving office, Krause joined the Texas Public Policy Foundation, a conservative think tank, as senior fellow. See Texas Public Policy Foundation, "Matt Krause Joins TPPF," press release, Jan. 17, 2023, https://www.texaspolicy.com/press/matt-krause -joins-tppf.

10. Cassandra Pollock and Jolie McCullough, "Gov. Greg Abbott Calls for Criminal Investigation into Availability of 'Pornographic Books' in Public Schools," *Texas Tribune*, Nov. 10, 2021, https://www.texastribune.org/2021/11/10 /abbott-pornography-texas-school-books; Nicole Chavez, "A Texas Lawmaker Is Investigating 850 Books on Race and Gender That Could Cause 'Discomfort' to Students," CNN, Oct. 29, 2021, https://www.cnn.com/2021/10/28/us/texas-school -books-race-gender-investigation/index.html.

11. Andrew Solomon, "My Book Was Censored in China. Now It's Black-listed—in Texas," Nov. 23, 2021, https://www.nytimes.com/2021/11/23/books/review/far-from-the-tree-matt-krause-texas-book-blacklist-ban.html.

12. Danika Ellis, "All 850 Books Matt Krause Wants to Ban: An Analysis," *Book Riot*, Nov. 5, 2021, https://bookriot.com/texas-book-ban-list.

13. Simone Carter, "The 10 Most Absurd Titles on State Rep. Matt Krause's 'Banned Books' List," *Dallas Observer*, June 8, 2022, https://www.dallasobserver.com/news/matt-krause-banned-book-list-10-most-absurd-titles-library-texas-legislature-republicans-14167741; Christopher Tackett (@cjtackett), "Today in Granbury ISD, at the High School library, they came with a hand cart and carried away multiple boxes of books tagged with 'Krause's List,'" Twitter, Jan. 27, 2022, 11:50 a.m., https://twitter.com/cjtackett/status/1486788612511383553/photo/1.

14. Mike Hixenbaugh and Jeremy Schwartz, "Texas Superintendent Tells Librarians to Pull Books on Sexuality, Transgender People," NBC News and Texas Tribune–ProPublica Investigative Unit, Mar. 23, 2022, https://www.nbcnews.com/news/us-news/texas-superintendent-librarians-books-sexuality-transgender-rcna20992.

15. "School Boards, School Books and the Freedom to Learn," *Yale Law Journal* 59, no. 5 (Apr. 1950): 928–54, https://www.jstor.org/stable/793219.

16. "Ban on The Nation in Schools Upheld," *New York Times*, July 8, 1950, 15, https://www.nytimes.com/1950/07/08/archives/ban-on-the-nation-in-schools-upheld-state-sees-no-new-issues-since.html.

17. Kara Yorio, "Censorship Attempts Will Have a Long-Lasting Impact on School Library Collections, SLJ Survey Shows," *School Library Journal*, Sept. 8, 2022, https://www.slj.com/story/censorship-attempts-will-have-a-long-lasting-impact-on-school-library-collections-slj-survey-shows.

18. Kathy Lester (president of the American Association of School Librarians, 2022–2023), author interview, via telephone, Nov. 10, 2022.

19. Mary Lou White, "Censorship Threat over Children's Books," *Elementary School Journal* 75, no. 1 (Oct. 1975): 2–10, https://www.jstor.org/stable/1000464; William Steig, *Sylvester and the Magic Pebble* (New York: Windmill Books/Simon & Schuster, 1969). It was awarded the Caldecott Medal in 1970.

20. Henry Raymont, "Fig Leafs for Children Irk Librarians," *New York Times*, June 27, 1972, 34, https://www.nytimes.com/1972/06/27/archives/fig-leafs-for-children-irk-librarians.html.

21. The practice of school board members with no children in the schools seeking to ban materials they find objectionable, plus seeking taxpayer support for nonpublic schools, is again an issue.

22. Gene I. Maeroff, "Book Ban Splits a Queens School District," *New York Times*, May 9, 1971, https://www.nytimes.com/1971/05/09/archives/book-ban-splits-a-queens-school-district-ban-on-book-splits-a.html.

23. Leonard Buder, "School Ban Ends on Piri Thomas Book," *New York Times*, Dec. 27, 1975, 21, https://www.nytimes.com/1975/12/27/archives/school-ban-ends-on-piri-thomas-book.html.

24. John Darnton, "Ex-Junkie Author Brings Harlem Closer to Darien," *New York Times*, Apr. 16, 1969, 49, https://www.nytimes.com/1969/04/16/archives/exjunkie-author-brings-harlem-closer-to-darien.html.

25. Darnton, "Ex-Junkie Author Brings Harlem Closer to Darien," 49.

26. Darnton, "Ex-Junkie Author Brings Harlem Closer to Darien," 49.

27. Darnton, "Ex-Junkie Author Brings Harlem Closer to Darien," 49.

28. "Voucher System Advocated by Board of Regents Member," *Elmira Star-Gazette*, Sept. 21, 1975, 3.

29. Bob Buyer, "Parents Group Opposes Bussing, Human Relations, Sex Education," *Buffalo News*, Feb. 23, 1970, 8; "State Chairman of P.O.N.Y.-U, Inc. (Parents of New York United) Will Speak on Book Censorship in Our Schools," advertisement, *Ithaca Journal*, July 5, 1975, 3.

30. Alice Moore quoted in "Education Methods Destroy Children," *Charleston Daily Mail*, May 8, 1970, 17, cited in Adam Laats, *The Other School Reformers: Conservative Activism in American Education* (Cambridge, MA: Harvard University Press, 2015), 191.

31. Laats, *The Other School Reformers*, 196.

32. Laats, *The Other School Reformers*, 196, 197.

33. Rick Steelhammer, "2nd Boycott of Schools Advocated," *Charleston Gazette*, Oct. 7, 1974, 1, cited in Laats, *The Other School Reformers*, 209, 210.

34. "Two Found Guilty in Dynamiting Schools in Protest on Textbooks," *New York Times*, Apr. 19, 1975, 17, https://www.nytimes.com/1975/04/19/archives/2-found-guilty-in-dynamiting-schools-in-protest-on-textbooks.html.

35. Michelle Ingrassia, "Book Critic Tied to W. Va. Dispute," *Newsday* (Long Island, NY), Mar. 27, 1976, 7; Associated Press, "Vonnegut Joins Battle to Halt Book Banning," *Johnson City Press*, Jan. 5, 1977, 12.

36. George Vecsey, "Giving Books an 'F,'" *New York Times*, Mar. 28, 1976, 362, https://www.nytimes.com/1976/03/28/archives/long-island-weekly-giving-books-an-f-flunking-books.html; George Vecsey, "L.I. School Board Defends Removal of 11 Book Titles," *New York Times*, Mar. 20, 1976, https://www.nytimes.com/1976/03/20/archives/li-school-board-defends-removal-of-11-book-titles-island-trees.html.

37. Roy R. Silver, "L.I. School Board Bans Nine Books," *New York Times*, July 29, 1976, 37, https://www.nytimes.com/1976/07/29/archives/li-school-board-bans-nine-books-island-trees-panel-votes-on-11.html.

38. George Vecsey, "Island Trees: Rebuttal Time," *New York Times*, Apr. 4, 1976, 206, https://www.nytimes.com/1976/04/04/archives/long-island-weekly-island-trees-rebuttal-time.html.

39. Silver, "L.I. School Board Bans Nine Books," 37.

40. Piri Thomas, "The Right to Write and to Read," *New York Times*, Sept. 14, 1976, 39, https://www.nytimes.com/1976/09/14/archives/the-right-to-write-and-to-read.html.

41. Debra Lau Whelan, "NCAC Talks to the Man Behind Pico V. Board of Ed," *National Coalition Against Censorship* (blog), July 9, 2013, https://ncac.org/news/blog/ncac-talks-to-the-man-behind-pico-v-board-of-ed.

42. "L.I. Students File Suit to Overturn School Book Ban," *New York Times*, Jan. 5, 1977, 23, https://www.nytimes.com/1977/01/05/archives/li-students-file-suit-to-overturn-school-book-ban.html.

43. Linda Greenhouse, "High Court Limits Banning of Books," *New York Times*, June 26, 1982, 1, https://www.nytimes.com/1982/06/26/us/high-court-limits-banning-of-books.html.

44. Emily Donaldson and Talia Richman, "State Officials Investigating Whether North Texas District Has 'Sexually Explicit' Books in School," *Dallas Morning News*, Dec. 9, 2021, https://www.dallasnews.com/news/education/2021/12/09/state-officials-investigating-whether-a-north-texas-district-has-sexually-explicit-books-in-school.

45. For the text of HB 3979, "Relating to the social studies curriculum in public schools," see Texas House of Representatives, "Bill Text: TX HB3979 | 2021–2022 | 87th Legislature | Enrolled," https://legiscan.com/TX/text/HB3979/2021.

46. Audrey Wilson-Youngblood, author interview, via Zoom, June 9, 2022.

47. Wilson-Youngblood, author interview.

48. Abby Church, "Keller ISD Removes Book from Library After Parent Concerns About Graphic Sexual Imagery," *Fort Worth Star-Telegram*, Oct. 29, 2021, https://www.star-telegram.com/news/local/education/article255388551.html.

49. Kathy May (@BYECAHELLOTEXAS), "1. Welcome to Keller ISD. Yes, a Texas School. . . . ," Twitter, Oct. 26, 2021, 6:17 p.m., https://twitter.com/BYECAHELLOTEXAS/status/1453169035902951424?s=20; Kathy May, (@BYECAHELLOTEXAS), "2. We have a problem and need help. . . . ," Twitter, Oct. 26, 2021 6:20 p.m., https://twitter.com/BYECAHELLOTEXAS/status/1453169728344760323?s=20.

50. Jonathan Friedman and Nadine Farid Johnson, *Banned in the USA: The Growing Movement to Censor Books*, Pen America, Sept. 19, 2022, https://pen.org/report/banned-usa-growing-movement-to-censor-books-in-schools.

51. Maia Kobabe, "Schools Are Banning My Book. But Queer Kids Need Queer Stories," *Washington Post*, Oct. 29, 2021, https://www.washingtonpost.com/opinions/2021/10/29/schools-are-banning-my-book-queer-kids-need-queer-stories.

52. Maia Kobabe, *Gender Queer: A Memoir* (Portland, OR: Oni Press, 2019), 134.

53. Elizabeth A. Harris and Alexandra Alter, "Book Banning Efforts Surged in 2021. These Titles Were the Most Targeted," *New York Times*, Apr. 4, 2022, https://www.nytimes.com/2022/04/04/books/banned-books-libraries.html; Alexandra Alter, "How a Debut Graphic Memoir Became the Most Banned Book in the Country," *New York Times*, May 5, 2022, https://www.nytimes.com/2022/04/04/books/banned-books-libraries.html; Eesha Pendhakar, "Who's Behind the Escalating Push to Ban Books? A New Report Has Answers," *Education Week*, Sept. 19, 2022, https://www.edweek.org/leadership/whos-behind-the-escalating-push-to-ban-books-a-new-report-has-answers/2022/09.

54. Alter, "How a Debut Graphic Memoir Became the Most Banned Book in the Country."

55. Keller ISD, "Books Under Review," https://www.kellerisd.net/Page/7660, accessed Nov. 7, 2022.

56. Wilson-Youngblood, author interview.

57. Texas Education Agency, "Library Materials, Recommended Policies," https://tea.texas.gov/texas-schools/school-boards/recommended-policies, accessed Nov. 7, 2022; Brian Lopez, "Texas Education Agency's New School Library Standards Push for More Scrutiny and Parent Input," *Texas Tribune*, Apr. 11, 2022, https://www.texastribune.org/2022/04/11/texas-school-library-standards.

58. Texas Library Association, "Statement on Texas Education Agency's Model Policy Regarding School Library Content," https://txla.org/news/statement-on-texas-education-agencys-model-policy-regarding-school-library-content, accessed Nov. 9, 2022.

59. "Board Minutes, Special Meeting [of Keller ISD Board], Aug. 8, 2022, at 5:00 p.m.–Special Meeting Version 1, Executed Board Minutes 08-08-22," item 8C, BoardBook Premier (website), https://meetings.boardbook.org/Documents/CustomMinutesForMeeting/2320?meeting=542128; Keller ISD Board of Trustees, *Keller ISD Special Board Meeting, June 6, 2022*, YouTube video, https://www.youtube.com/watch?v=atnRzf6gDfI; Keller ISD Standing Strong, "Rating System for Movies, Television, Video Games. And Comics. Why Not Books?," Facebook post, Aug. 12, 2022, https://www.facebook.com/KellerISDStandingStrong, accessed Nov. 9, 2022.

60. Jennifer Price, email message, Aug. 16, 2022, copy sent to author.

61. ACLU of Texas (@ACLUtx), "ON NOTICE: We urge @KellerISD to return all removed books to classroom shelves. . . . ," Twitter, Aug. 18, 2022, 1:18 p.m., https://twitter.com/ACLUTx/status/1560363674241536000.

62. Keller ISD, *Keller ISD Board Meeting, August 22, 2022*, YouTube video, https://www.youtube.com/watch?v=iFD1nGS-GVY.

63. Sandi Walker, "Protecting Educators from the Woke Mob," Opinion, *Dallas Express*, Aug. 18, 2022, https://dallasexpress.com/opinion/opinion-protecting-educators-from-the-woke-mob; Keller ISD, *Keller ISD Board Meeting, August 22, 2022*.

64. Keller ISD, school library–related documents: "Feedback from: Library Book Purchases," online survey form, https://docs.google.com/forms/d/e/1FAIpQLSfJoMctmIX-tHN-WXFefew8rxEpao9q-Bejy_tzF2tRn_BG7A/viewform; "Instructional Resources, Library Materials," https://www.kellerisd.net/cms/lib/TX02215599/Centricity/Domain/2186/EFB_Local_220803.pdf; "Book Purchase Previews," https://www.kellerisd.net/Page/7710; "Library Content Guidelines," link at "August 22, 2022 at 5:00 PM—Regular Meeting," https://meetings.boardbook.org/Public/Agenda/2320?meeting=542053.

65. Tom Johanningmeier, "Keller Schools Add 'Gender Fluidity' to Topics That Are Off Limits in Library Books," *Fort Worth Star-Telegram*, Nov. 14, 2022, https://www.star-telegram.com/news/local/education/article268747597.html.

66. Keller ISD, *Keller ISD Board Meeting, October 24, 2022*, YouTube video, https://www.youtube.com/watch?v=B7ynIblxjeA.

67. Mike Hixenbaugh (@Mike_Hixenbaugh), "The conservative parent PAC in Keller is fundraising off of the book controversy . . . ," Twitter, Aug. 18, 2022, 6:11 p.m., https://twitter.com/Mike_Hixenbaugh/status/1560434133377097729.

CHAPTER 4: HOW WEAPONIZING CRT DISRUPTS LEARNING

1. Kyle Simcox, author interview, Johnson City, Tennessee, Oct. 18, 2022.

2. Summer Botts, author interview, via Zoom, Nov. 2, 2022.

3. Students' notes, viewed by author at Hawn's home in Kingsport, Tennessee, Oct. 19, 2022.

4. This quote is my recollection from an interview conducted with Beavers for a story on education equity issues for *CommonWealth* magazine in the early 1990s, just ahead of the education reform movement when funding equity cases were

making their way through the courts. The story focused on a student in Brockton, Massachusetts, and one in Weston, Massachusetts.

5. Kyle Simcox, author interview, Johnson City, Tennessee, Oct. 18, 2022; Michael D. Shear, "Trump Envisions a Parade Showing Off American Military Might," *New York Times*, Sept. 18, 2017, https://www.nytimes.com/2017/09/18/us /politics/trump-4th-of-july-military-parade.html.

6. US Census Bureau, "Quick Facts, Sullivan County, Tennessee," https:// www.census.gov/quickfacts/fact/table/sullivancountytennessee/PST045221, accessed Nov. 12, 2022; Sullivan County Election Commission, "Past Election Results," for Nov. 3, 2020, http://www.scelect.org/nov2020cumulativeresults.pdf.

7. Jonathan Mattise and Kimberlee Kruesi, "Tennessee Gov: Race Shouldn't Be Taught in 'Divisive' Way," Associated Press, May 7, 2021, https://apnews.com /article/tennessee-race-and-ethnicity-d85cc3957c7df9001e7243ad109036e6; for the text of SB 0623, see Tennessee General Assembly, "Bill Text: TN SB0623 | 2021–2022 | 112th General Assembly | Chaptered," https://legiscan.com/TN /text/SB0623/id/2409134; Kimberlee Kruesi, "Tennessee Bans Teaching Critical Race Theory in Schools," Associated Press, May 25, 2021, https://apnews.com /article/tennessee-racial-injustice-race-and-ethnicity-religion-education-9366 bceabf309557811eab645c8dad13.

8. David R. Cox, director of schools, *Sullivan County [Tennessee] BOE Monthly Meeting (6-8-21)*, YouTube video, https://www.youtube.com/watch?v=23ep9-bG5 Aw&t=23s, at 37:55; Bianca Marais, "Sullivan County School Board Approves Teacher Dismissal Charges, Supporters Outraged," WJLH, June 8, 2021, https:// www.wjhl.com/news/local/sullivan-county-teacher-facing-termination-at-school board-meeting-tuesday-supporters-to-gather.

9. N. Goldman, A. R. Pebley, K. Lee, T. Andrasfay, and B. Pratt, "Racial and Ethnic Differentials in COVID-19-Related Job Exposures by Occupational Standing in the US," *PLoS One* 16, no. 9 (Sept. 2021), doi: 10.1371/journal.pone.0256085; Centers for Disease Control and Prevention, "Risk for COVID-19 Infection, Hospitalization, and Death by Race/Ethnicity," updated Dec. 28, 2022, https://www.cdc .gov/coronavirus/2019-ncov/covid-data/investigations-discovery/hospitalization -death-by-race-ethnicity.html, accessed Mar. 1, 2023; Rashawn Ray, "Why Are Blacks Dying at Higher Rates from Covid-19?" Brookings Institution, Apr. 9, 2020, https://www.brookings.edu/blog/fixgov/2020/04/09/why-are-blacks-dying-at-higher -rates-from-covid-19.

10. Nikole Hannah-Jones, "The 1619 Project," *New York Times Magazine*, Aug. 14, 2019, https://www.nytimes.com/interactive/2019/08/14/magazine/1619-america -slavery.html.

11. Donald J. Trump, "Establishing the President's Advisory 1776 Commission," Executive Order 13598, Nov. 2, 2020, Federal Register, https://www.federal register.gov/documents/2020/11/05/2020–24793/establishing-the-presidents-advisory- 1776-commission; President's Advisory 1776 Commission, "The 1776 Report," Jan. 2021, https://trumpwhitehouse.archives.gov/wp-content/uploads/2021/01/The -Presidents-Advisory-1776-Commission-Final-Report.pdf; Michael Crowley and Jennifer Schuessler, "Trump's 1776 Commission Critiques Liberalism in Report Derided by Historians," *New York Times*, Jan. 18, 2021, https://www.nytimes.com /2021/01/18/us/politics/trump-1776-commission-report.html.

12. Phil Williams, "Revealed: Teachers Come from 'Dumbest Parts of Dumbest Colleges,' Tenn. Governor's Education Advisor Tells Him," NewsChannel5 Nashville, July 12, 2022, https://www.newschannel5.com/news/newschannel-5-investigates/revealed/revealed-teachers-come-from-dumbest-parts-of-dumbest-colleges-tenn-governors-education-advisor-tells-him.

13. Christopher F. Rufo, "Anarchy in Seattle," *City Journal*, June 10, 2020, https://www.city-journal.org/antifa-seattle-capitol-hill-autonomous-zone; Christopher F. Rufo, "CHAZ to CHOP: Seattle's Radical Experiment," *City Journal*, June 17, 2020, https://www.city-journal.org/seattle-chaz-chop-protests. For a list of Rufo's stories, see https://www.city-journal.org/contributor/christopher-f-rufo_1334.

14. Christopher F. Rufo, "Cult Programming in Seattle," *City Journal*, July 8, 2020, https://www.city-journal.org/seattle-interrupting-whiteness-training.

15. Christopher F. Rufo, "'White Fragility' Comes to Washington," *City Journal*, July 18, 2020.

16. Victor Garcia, report of Christopher Rufo interview by Tucker Carlson, Fox News video, Aug. 17, 2020, *Researcher Declares 'One Man War' on Critical Race Theory: "It's Racism Masquerading as Anti-Racism,"* https://www.foxnews.com/us/chris-rufo-one-man-war-race-theory.

17. Christopher F. Rufo (@realchrisrufo), "We're witnessing the collapse of public order in real time. . . . ," Twitter, July 28, 2020, https://twitter.com/realchrisrufo/status/1288133950632648704; Christopher F. Rufo (@realchrisrufo), "One senior employee told me the relentless bombardments of critical race theory content . . . ," Twitter, Aug. 20, 2020, https://twitter.com/realchrisrufo/status/1296477594058199041; Christopher F. Rufo (@realchrisrufo), "The Western Area Power Administration . . . ," Twitter, Aug. 24, 2020, https://twitter.com/realchrisrufo/status/1297965852470386689; Christopher F. Rufo (@realchrisrufo), "We have shut down critical race theory in the world's largest companies. Swords up!," Twitter, Sept. 29, 2020, https://twitter.com/realchrisrufo/status/1311063490753249280.

18. Christopher F. Rufo (@realchrisrufo), "SCOOP: The @FBI is now holding weekly "intersectionality workshops. . . . ," Twitter, Aug. 28, 2020, 9:11 a.m., https://twitter.com/realchrisrufo/status/1299379197253541888.

19. Sam Dorman, report of Christopher Rufo interview by Tucker Carlson, Fox News video, Sept. 2, 2020, *Chris Rufo Calls on Trump to End Critical Race Theory 'Cult Indoctrination' in Federal Government*, https://www.foxnews.com/politics/chris-rufo-race-theory-cult-federal-government.

20. Russell Vought, "Memorandum for the Heads of Executive Departments and Agencies," Executive Office of the President, Office of Management and Budget, Sept. 4, 2020, https://trumpwhitehouse.archives.gov/wp-content/uploads/2020/09/M-20-34.pdf.

21. Derrick Bell, *Silent Covenants: Brown v. Board of Education and the Unfilled Hopes for Racial Reform* (New York: Oxford University Press, 2004), 187.

22. Peggy McIntosh, author interview, Waltham, Massachusetts, Oct. 24, 2022.

23. Christopher F. Rufo (@realchrisrufo), "We have successfully frozen their brand—"critical race theory"—into the public conversation and are steadily driving up negative perceptions. . . . ," Twitter, Mar. 15, 2021, 12:14 p.m., https://twitter.com/realchrisrufo/status/1371540368714428416?lang=en; Christopher F.

Rufo(@realchrisrufo), "The goal is to have the public read something crazy in the newspaper and immediately think 'critical race theory' . . . ," Twitter, Mar. 15, 2021, 12:17 p.m., https://twitter.com/realchrisrufo/status/1371541044592996352.

24. Christopher Rufo, interviewed by Tucker Carlson, Fox News video, Aug. 17, 2020, *Researcher Declares 'One Man War' on Critical Race Theory: "It's Racism Masquerading as Anti-Racism,"* https://www.foxnews.com/us/chris-rufo-one-man -war-race-theory.

25. Robert Frank, email message to author, Nov. 15, 2022, with his analysis based on Mark Davies, NOW (Corpus) News on the Web, https://www.english -corpora.org/now.

26. Jed Legum, "New North Dakota Law Would Be Illegal to Discuss Under Terms of That Law," *Popular Information*, Nov. 15, 2021, https://popular.info/p/new -north-dakota-law-cant-be-discussed.

27. Michelle Griffith, "North Dakota Governor Signs Bill Banning Critical Race Theory in K–12 Schools," *InForum*, Nov. 12, 2021, https://www.inforum.com /news/north-dakota/north-dakota-governor-signs-bill-banning-critical-race-theory -in-k-12-schools.

28. Office of Governor Ron DeSantis, "Governor DeSantis Announces Legislative Proposal to Stop W.O.K.E. Activism and Critical Race Theory in Schools and Corporations," news release, Dec. 15, 2021, https://www.flgov.com/2021/12/15 /governor-desantis-announces-legislative-proposal-to-stop-w-o-k-e-activism-and -critical-race-theory-in-schools-and-corporations.

29. Office of Governor Ron DeSantis, "Governor Ron DeSantis Signs Legislation to Protect Floridians from Discrimination and Woke Indoctrination," news release, Apr. 22, 2022, https://www.flgov.com/2022/04/22/governor-ron-desantis -signs-legislation-to-protect-floridians-from-discrimination-and-woke-indoctrination.

30. Ana Ceballos and Jeffrey S. Solochek, "DeSantis Seeks Conservative Overhaul at Florida Liberal Arts College," *Tampa Bay Times*, Feb. 6, 2023, https:// www.tampabay.com/news/florida-politics/2023/01/06/desantis-conservative-hillsdale -rufo-college-liberal-sarasota.

31. James Call, "FSU Faculty Says It's 'Rubbish' As Christopher Rufo Targets FSU 'Radical' Diversity Programs," *Tallahassee Democrat*, Feb. 3, 2023, https://www. tallahassee.com/story/news/politics/2023/02/03/new-college-trustee-christopher -rufo-blasts-fsu-diversity-programs-florida-state-says-its-rubbish/69869875007; Christopher T. Rufo (@realchrisrufo), "SCOOP: Florida State University has adopted a radical DEI program . . . ," Twitter, Feb. 2, 2023, 1:45 p.m., https:// twitter.com/realchrisrufo/status/1621263614849204226; Christopher T. Rufo (@realchrisrufo), "Officially, Florida State administrators have claimed in a recent report . . . ," Twitter, Feb. 2, 2023, 1:47 p.m., https://twitter.com/realchrisrufo /status/1621264057486671873.

32. Jack Stripling, "Channeling Orwell, Judge Blasts Florida's 'Dystopian' Ban on 'Woke' Instruction," *Chronicle of Higher Education*, Nov. 17, 2022, https://www .chronicle.com/article/conjuring-orwell-florida-judge-blasts-dystopian-ban-on-woke -instruction?utm; Zach Weissmueller and Danielle Thompson, "The Problem with DeSantis' 'Stop Woke Act,'" *Reason*, Oct. 11, 2022, https://reason.com/video/2022 /10/11/the-problem-with-desantis-stop-woke-act.

33. Josh Moody, "The New Conservative Playbook on DEI," *Inside Higher Ed*, Feb. 7, 2023, https://www.insidehighered.com/news/2023/02/07/desantis-debuts -new-conservative-playbook-ending-dei.

34. Ryan Dailey, "Gov. DeSantis Requests Diversity and Equity Info from Florida Colleges and Universities," WFSU Public Media, Jan. 5, 2023, https:// news.wfsu.org/state-news/2023-01-05/gov-desantis-requests-diversity-and-equity -info-from-florida-colleges-and-universities; Sam Sachs, "'Toxic Political Ideology': Florida English Professor Fired over Racial Justice Unit Blames DeSantis," News Channel 8 Tampa, Mar. 16, 2023, https://www.wfla.com/news/politics/toxic -political-ideology-florida-professor-blames-desantis-fired-for-teaching-racial -justice-unit.

35. Jen Given, quoted in Laura Meckler and Hannah Natanson, "New Critical Race Theory Laws Have Teachers Scared, Confused and Self-Censoring," *Washington Post*, Feb. 14, 2022, https://www.washingtonpost.com/education/2022/02/14 /critical-race-theory-teachers-fear-laws.

36. J. Michael Butler, author interview, via Zoom, July 20, 2022.

37. Stephen A. Berry, "Obstacles to Freedom: Life in Jim Crow America," in *The Civil Rights Movement*, ed. Hasan Kwame Jeffries (Madison: University of Wisconsin Press, 2019), 62.

38. Hasan Kwame Jeffries, introduction to Jeffries, *The Civil Rights Movement*, 4–7.

39. J. Michael Butler, "'More Negotiations and Less Demonstrations': The NAACP, SCLC, and Racial Conflict in Pensacola, 1970–1978," *Florida Historical Quarterly* 86, no. 1 (Summer 2007): 71, https://www.jstor.org/stable/30150100.

40. J. Michael Butler, "Education Book—a Few Fact Check Questions," email to author, Feb. 6, 2023.

41. James Whitfield, author interview, Hurst, Texas, June 15, 2022.

42. Grapevine-Colleyville ISD, *GCISD's Board of Trustees Regular Meeting— July 26, 2021*, YouTube video, https://www.youtube.com/watch?v=xfnkBddvDQs, at 1:47:12.

43. Laura Leeman, #IStandWithDrWhitfield, petition, https://www.petitions .net/istandwithdrwhitfield.

44. Grapevine-Colleyville ISD, statement, Sept. 1, 2021, https://gcisd.ss18 .sharpschool.com/news/what_s_new/statement_from_gcisd; Grapevine-Colleyville ISD, *GCISD Special School Board Meeting—Sept. 20, 2021*, YouTube video, https:// www.youtube.com/watch?v=9LiJR9TQlhk; Karen Attiah, "A Win for White Power at School Board Meeting in Grapevine, Tex.," Opinion, *Washington Post*, Sept. 22, 2021, https://www.washingtonpost.com/opinions/2021/09/22/win-white-power -school-board-meeting-grapevine-tex; Katie Shepherd, "Families Beg for Black Principal to Be Reinstated After Critical Race Theory Dispute: 'Nothing Short of a Witch Hunt,'" *Washington Post*, Sept. 21, 2021, https://www.washingtonpost.com /nation/2021/09/21/james-whitfield-school-board-vote.

45. James Whitfield, Facebook post, July 31, 2021, https://www.facebook.com /photo.php?fbid=10161315196574535&set=pb.662019534.-2207520000; Christine Hauser, "Texas High School Principal Sees Racism in Call to Remove Intimate Photos," *New York Times*, Aug. 5, 2021, https://www.nytimes.com/2021/08/05/us /colleyville-hs-principal-beach-photos.html.

46. Katie Shepherd, "Families Beg for Black Principal to Be Reinstated After Critical Race Theory Dispute: 'Nothing Short of a Witch Hunt,'" *Washington Post*, Sept. 21, 2021.

47. Grapevine-Colleyville ISD, *GCISD Special Board Meeting, Sept. 20, 2021*.

48. Grapevine-Colleyville ISD, *GCISD Special Board Meeting, Sept. 20, 2021*.

49. Grapevine-Colleyville ISD, *GCISD Special Board Meeting, Nov. 8, 2021*, YouTube video, https://www.youtube.com/watch?v=riytfwHglwo; Christine Hauser, "Texas Principal in Spotlight over Race Issues Agrees to Resign with Paid Leave," *New York Times*, Nov. 10, 2021, https://www.nytimes.com/2021/11/10/us/texas-principal-critical-race-theory.html; Timothy Bella, "A Black Principal Was Accused of Embracing Critical Race Theory in the Classroom. He's Now Out of a Job," *Washington Post*, Nov. 10, 2021, https://www.washingtonpost.com/education/2021/11/10/texas-principal-critical-race-theory-whitfield.

50. Republican National Committee, "RNC–School Board Event," announcement, Cities Republican Women (website), https://www.parkcitiesrepublicanwomen.com/event-details/rnc-school-board-event, accessed Nov. 23, 2022.

51. Tammy Nakamura, seen in video posted on Colleyville Citizens for Accountability Facebook page, July 8, 2022, https://www.facebook.com/1066521359/videos/1308142273347774.

52. Katherine Schaeffer, "America's Public School Teachers Are Far Less Racially and Ethnically Diverse Than Their Students," *Pew Research Center Newsletter*, Dec. 10, 2021, https://www.pewresearch.org/fact-tank/2021/12/10/americas-public-school-teachers-are-far-less-racially-and-ethnically-diverse-than-their-students; Mildred J. Hudson and Barbara J. Holmes, "Missing Teachers, Impaired Communities: The Unanticipated Consequences of Brown v. Board of Education on the African American Teaching Force at the Precollegiate Level," *Journal of Negro Education* 63, no. 3 (Summer 1994): 388, https://doi.org/10.2307/2967189.

53. Hasan Kwame Jeffries, "History of U.S. Education: What's Race Got to Do with It?," lecture, Gilder Lehrman Center 24th Annual Conference, Teaching Race & Slavery in the American Classroom, Yale MacMillan Center, Gilder Lehrman Center for the Study of Slavery, Nov. 2022, https://glc.yale.edu/events/upcoming-events/2022-annual-conference (see embedded video); Daisha Brabham, "Key Takeaways from the Gilder Lehrman 24th Annual Conference: Teaching Race & Slavery in the American Classroom," *Yale MacMillan Center News*, Nov. 16, 2022, https://glc.yale.edu/news/key-takeaways-gilder-lehrman-center-24th-annual-conference-teaching-race-slavery-american. See also Valerie Strauss, "Brown v. Board of Education Is 63 Years Old. Was the Supreme Court's Desegregation Ruling a Failure?" *Washington Post*, May 16, 2017, https://www.washingtonpost.com/news/answer-sheet/wp/2017/05/16/the-supreme-courts-historic-brown-v-board-ruling-is-63-years-old-was-it-a-failure. Strauss quotes Marshall as saying that desegregation would take at most five years.

54. Paul Delaney, "Mondale Calls School Policy a 'Hoax,'" *New York Times*, Aug. 13, 1970, 20, https://www.nytimes.com/1970/08/13/archives/mondale-calls-school-policy-a-hoax.html.

55. Liam Adams, "Civics, Charters and Classical Ed: What to Know About Hillsdale College's K–12 Efforts in TN," *The Tennessean*, Feb. 2, 2022, https://www.tennessean.com/story/news/politics/2022/02/02/hillsdale-college-tennessee

-charter-schools-partnership-gov-bill-lee/9303810002; Phil Williams, "REVEALED: Hillsdale-Affiliated Charter Schools Withdraw Requests to Open in Tennessee," WTVF, Sept. 29, 2022, https://www.newschannel5.com/news/newschannel-5 -investigates/revealed/revealed-hillsdale-affiliated-charter-schools-withdraw-requests -to-open-in-tennessee; Melissa Brown, "Tennessee Charter Operator to Apply for Five Hillsdale-Operated Schools," *The Tennessean*, Dec. 5, 2022, https://www .tennessean.com/story/news/politics/2022/12/05/tennessee-charter-operator-america n-classical-education-to-apply-for-5-hillsdale-affiliated-schools/69703158007.

56. Bob Christie, "Huge Arizona School Voucher Plan in Effect After Foes Fail," Associated Press, Sept. 30, 2022, https://apnews.com/article/business -education-arizona-doug-ducey-7ebd4c9149508e9875f47e67bdc0ef69; Michael Foust, "Christian School Enrollment Booms: 79 Percent See Increase Post-Pandemic, Report Says," ChristianHeadlines.com, Sept. 20, 2022, https://www.christian headlines.com/contributors/michael-foust/christian-school-enrollment-booms -79-percent-see-increase-post-pandemic-report-says.html; Ruth Graham, "Christian Schools Boom in Revolt Against Curriculum and Pandemic Rules," *New York Times*, Oct. 19, 2021, https://www.nytimes.com/2021/10/19/us/christian-schools -growth.html; Melanie Hanson, "Average Cost of Private School," EducationData .org, Dec. 27, 2021, https://educationdata.org/average-cost-of-private-school.

57. Council of the Great City Schools, Amicus Curiae brief, p. 3–5, Students for Fair Admissions v. Harvard and Students for Fair Admission v. University of North Carolina, et al., July 29, 2022, Supreme Court of the United States (No. 20–1199 & 21–707), https://www.supremecourt.gov/DocketPDF/20/20–1199 /232217/20220729154446488_CGCS%20Amicus%20Brief.pdf.

58. US Government Accounting Office, *K–12 Education: Student Population Has Significantly Diversified, but Many Schools Remain Divided Along Racial, Ethnic, and Economic Lines*, report to the chairman, Committee on Education and Labor, House of Representatives, June 2022, https://www.gao.gov/assets/gao-22-104737.pdf.

59. US Census Bureau, "Quick Facts, Sullivan County, Tennessee," https:// www.census.gov/quickfacts/fact/table/sullivancountytennessee/PST045221, ac- cessed Dec. 1, 2022; DataUSA, "Sullivan County, TN," https://datausa.io/profile /geo/sullivan-county-tn#housing, accessed Dec. 1, 2022.

60. Sullivan Country School District, Raiders North High School, 1995 year- book, n.p., in Matthew Hawn's collection.

61. Becky Sullivan, "Kyle Rittenhouse Is Acquitted of All Charges in the Trial over Killing 2 in Kenosha," NPR, Nov. 19, 2021, https://www.npr.org/2021/11/19 /1057288807/kyle-rittenhouse-acquitted-all-charges-verdict; Julie Bosman, "What to Know About the Trial of Kyle Rittenhouse," *New York Times*, Nov. 19, 2021, https://www.nytimes.com/article/kyle-rittenhouse-trial.html; Brian Niemietz, "Kenosha Gunman Kyle Rittenhouse Launches YouTube Channel About Fire- arms," *New York Daily News*, Oct. 17, 2022, https://www.nydailynews.com/news /national/ny-kyle-rittenhouse-guns-youtube-20221017-ctbc4pz6wresxh7vx2eezqsq5y -story.html; Kyle Rittenhouse, *The Independent*, video, Oct. 18, 2022, available at YouTube, https://www.youtube.com/watch?v=JprepCbk1aA.

62. "Tenure Hearing Before Officer Dale Conder Jr. Pursuant to T.C.A. Sec- tion 49-5-512 in the Matter of Sullivan County Board of Education v. Matthew Hawn, Tenured Teacher Claimant, Findings of Fact and Conclusions of Law,"

Oct. 22, 2021, 10895–95143, https://bloximages.newyork1.vip.townnews.com
/timesnews.net/content/tncms/assets/v3/editorial/e/87/e87a6ba8-3376-11ec-9600
-bf43486855b3/61731fe98fc76.file.pdf, 6.

63. Chad Conner, Facebook post and comments, Oct. 2, 2020, https://www
.facebook.com/chadandamber/videos/10158951467543336, accessed Dec. 1, 2022.

64. Stan C. Edwards, speaking in Sullivan County Board of Education, *Sullivan County Tn Board of Education meeting (10-8-20)*, YouTube video, https://www
.youtube.com/watch?v=OSykUxb4jT8&t=3787s, at 1:01:26.

65. Ta-Nehisi Coates, "The First White President," *The Atlantic*, Oct. 2017,
https://www.theatlantic.com/magazine/archive/2017/10/the-first-white-president
-ta-nehisi-coates/537909.

66. Ingrid Deloach, assistant director of Sullivan County Public Schools, letter to Matthew Hawn, Feb. 3, 2021, exhibit 2, hearing documents, *Sullivan County Board of Education v. Matthew Hawn*, hearing documents, exhibit 2.

67. William Shakespeare, *Troilus and Cressida*, 2.3.1285–86, Folger Shakespeare Library.

68. Sullivan County Board of Education, *Sullivan County TN BOE Monthly Meeting (3-4-21)*, YouTube video, https://www.youtube.com/watch?v=-GH--x2zRhA;
Sullivan County Department of Education, "Mar. 4, 2021, 6:30 p.m., Board of Education Regular Meeting," https://meeting.boeconnect.net/Public/Agenda/561
?meeting=455180, "Show Everything" link.

69. Kyla Jenée Lacey, *White Privilege—Kyla Jenée Lacey*, YouTube video, https://
www.youtube.com/watch?v=HCY8qn1Rx1w; John Blake, "It's Time to Talk About Black Privilege," CNN.com, Mar. 31, 2016, https://www.cnn.com/2016/03/30/us
/black-privilege/index.html.

70. Matthew Hawn, "Sullivan County School District, in Re: Matthew Hawn, hearing, Aug. 16, 17, and 18, 2021," transcript (provided by Matthew Hawn).

71. Hawn, "Sullivan County School District, hearing," deposition of Ingrid Deloach, 257.

72. Sullivan County Board of Education, *Sullivan County BOE—Called Meeting, Dec. 14th, 2021*, YouTube video, https://www.youtube.com/watch?v
=R4x000V7Zdg; Sullivan County Board of Education, "December 14, 2021 at 4:30 PM, Board of Education Called Meeting," agenda and vote tally, https://
meeting.boeconnect.net/Public/Agenda/561?meeting=508533, "See Everything" link.

73. Gloria Oster, author interview, Bristol, Virginia, Oct. 19, 2022.

74. Jeff Keeling, "Fired Sullivan County Teacher Hawn Appeal Asks for Reinstatement, Back Pay," WJHL News Channel 11, Jan. 27, 2022, https://www.wjhl
.com/news/local/fired-sullivan-county-teacher-hawn-appeal-asks-for-reinstatement
-back-pay; Rick Wagner, "Updated with 38-Page Appeal; Watch Now: Hawn Appeals Firing as Sullivan Teacher to Chancery Court," Jan. 27, 2022, https://www
.timesnews.net/news/education/updated-with-38-page-appeal-watch-now-hawn
-appeals-firing-as-sullivan-teacher-to-chancery/article_3e838f00-7eec-11ec-bb4f
-93b68c695f54.html (with embedded videos).

75. Laura Hawn, author interview, Kingsport, Tennessee, Oct. 18, 2022.

76. "Tenure Hearing Before Hearing Officer Dale Conder Jr. Pursuant to
T.C.A. Section 49-5-512."

77. Peggy McIntosh, "White Privilege: Unpacking the Invisible Knapsack," *Peace and Freedom Magazine*, July–Aug. 1989, 10–12, available at National SEED Project, https://nationalseedproject.org/Key-SEED-Texts/white-privilege-unpacking -the-invisible-knapsack.

78. Peggy McIntosh, interviewed by Joshua Rothman, "The Origins of 'Privilege,'" *New Yorker*, May 12, 2014, https://www.newyorker.com/books/page-turner /the-origins-of-privilege.

79. McIntosh, "White Privilege: Unpacking the Invisible Knapsack."

80. Emmy Howe (SEED codirector), author interview, New Haven, Connecticut, Oct. 16, 2022.

81. Peggy McIntosh, author interview, Waltham, Massachusetts, Oct. 24, 2022.

82. Howe, author interview.

83. Gail Cruise-Roberson (SEED codirector), author interview, via telephone, Oct. 16, 2022.

84. Emmy Howe, email message to author, Oct. 26, 2022.

85. Chris Lindholm, quoted in Elizabeth Shockman, "Inside One Minnesota School District's Battle over an Equity Training Program," Minnesota Public Radio, June 30, 2021, https://www.mprnews.org/story/2021/06/30/inside-one-minnesota -school-districts-battle-over-an-equity-training-program, transcript.

86. On Parents of Pequot United, see Shockman, "Inside One Minnesota School District's Battle over an Equity Training Program"; Sean Bjerk, "Parents of Pequot Lakes HS Students Express Frustration with SEED Project, Transparency," R&J Broadcasting, June 2, 2021, https://rjbroadcasting.com/2021/06/02/parents -of-pequot-lakes-hs-students-express-frustration-with-seed-project-transparency /#page-content.

87. Shockman, "Inside One Minnesota School District's Battle over an Equity Training Program."

88. Cruise-Roberson, author interview.

89. Zachary Rogers, "Wisconsin Teacher on Leave for Lesson Involving Kids Acting as Slaves, Slave Owners," KATV, Dec. 20, 2021, https://katv.com/news /nation-world/wisconsin-teacher-on-leave-for-lesson-involving-kids-acting-as-slaves -slave-owners-slave-owners-wisconsin-madison-jefferson-middle-school-colonial -tea-party-revolutionary-war-black-white-kids-cynthia-ball-state-journal-meghan -walsh; Ashley Wong and Lola Fadulu, "Teacher Suspended for Asking Students to Pick Cotton in Slavery Lesson," *New York Times*, May 2, 2022, https://www .nytimes.com/2022/05/02/nyregion/rochester-teacher-cotton-slavery-suspension .html; Perry Stein and Joe Helm, "Students Asked Black Peers to Play Slaves During a Lesson. The School Said It Should not Have Happened," *Washington Post*, Dec. 30, 2019, https://www.washingtonpost.com/local/education/students -asked-black-peers-to-portray-slaves-during-a-lesson-the-school-said-it-shouldnt -have-happened/2019/12/30/f5a28f88-2660-11ea-b2ca-2e72667c1741_story.html; N'dea Yancey-Bragg, "Mock Slave Auctions, Racist Lessons: How US History Class Often Traumatizes, Dehumanizes Black Students," *USA Today*, Mar. 2, 2021, https://www.usatoday.com/story/news/education/2021/03/02/heres-why-racist -school-assignments-slavery-persist-u-s/4389945001; Tori Keafer, "WCS School Board Unanimously Approves Contract with Diversity Consultant," *Williamson Herald*, Feb. 15, 2021, https://www.williamsonherald.com/news/wcs-school-board

-unanimously-approves-contract-with-diversity-consultant/article_ee35a6f8-7011
-11eb-825f-b724f0d9f17c.html.

90. Texas State Legislature, "HB 3979—An Act Relating to the Social Studies
Curriculum on Public Schools," enrolled version, https://capitol.texas.gov/tlodocs
/87R/billtext/pdf/HB03979F.pdf#navpanes=0.

91. Sandra Sadek, "Carroll ISD Superintendent Issues Apology, Clarification
Regarding Holocaust Comment Administrator Made During Staff Training,"
Community Impact, Oct. 15, 2021, https://communityimpact.com/dallas-fort-worth
/grapevine-colleyville-southlake/education/2021/10/14/carroll-isd-superintendent
-issues-apology-clarification-regarding-holocaust-comment-administrator-made
-during-staff-training; Superintendent Lane Ledbetter, tweeting from Carroll ISD
(@carrollisd), "As the Superintendent, I express my sincere apology regarding the
online article and news story. . . . ," Twitter, Oct. 14, 2021, 8:22 p.m., https://twitter
.com/Carrollisd/status/1448851858391449600; Dr. Keven Ellis, chair, State Board of
Education, tweeting from Texas SBOE (@TXSBOE), official statement, Twitter, July
1, 2022, 1:06 p.m., https://twitter.com/TXSBOE/status/1542962848321748992.

92. Taifha Natalee Alexander, "Understanding the Map: Tracking the Reach
of the Assault on CRT," *CRT Forward* (blog), CRT Forward Tracking Project,
UCLA School of Law, originally published Mar. 23, 2022, updated Feb. 1, 2023,
https://crtforward.law.ucla.edu/understanding-the-map.

93. A RAND Corporation paper published in spring 2022 reported that the
2022 American Instructional Resources Survey found that about one-quarter of
teachers said restrictions placed on topics of race and gender had changed how
they addressed those issues or selected curricular materials. See Ashley Woo, Sabrina Lee, Andrea Prado Tuma, Julia H. Kaufman, Rebecca Ann Lawrence, and
Nastassia Reed, *Walking on Eggshells—Teachers' Responses to Classroom Limitations
on Race- or Gender-Related Topics: Findings from the 2022 American Instructional
Resources Survey* (Santa Monica, CA: RAND Corporation, 2023), https://www
.rand.org/pubs/research_reports/RRA134-16.html#:~:text=Key%20Findings&text
=Roughly%20one%2Dquarter%20of%20teachers,them%20as%20being%20in
%20place.

94. Ron DeSantis, "FL Gov Ron DeSantis Stands Up for Parental Rights,"
speech given at Moms for Liberty National Summit, Tampa, July 15, 2022, video,
https://www.momsforliberty.org/news/ron-desantis-parental-rights; Sara Schwartz,
"Map: Where Critical Race Theory Is Under Attack," *Education Week*, June 11,
2021, updated Sept. 28, 2022, https://www.edweek.org/policy-politics/map-where
-critical-race-theory-is-under-attack/2021/06.

95. Ileana Najarro, "Revamped Florida Civics Education Aims for 'Patriotism.'
Will It Catch on Elsewhere?," *Education Week*, July 12, 2022, https://www.edweek
.org/teaching-learning/revamped-florida-civics-education-aims-for-patriotism-will
-it-catch-on-elsewhere/2022/07.

96. Florida House of Representatives, "Enrolled—CS/HB 807—An act relating to civics education," https://www.flsenate.gov/Session/Bill/2019/807/BillText/er
/PDF; Steve Masy, "Florida's New Civics Standards Released for Public Comment," Apr. 14, 2021, Florida Joint Center for Citizenship, https://floridacitizens
.wordpress.com/2021/04/14/floridas-new-civics-standards-released-for-public
-comment (see "7th Grade Civics Benchmarks Comparison Chart," Florida Joint

Center for Citizenship, https://docs.google.com/document/d/1-l5D8lFQfLYmHgE9 KnToGeYIBTjEPj6YQmtB6n8iFr4/edit); CPALMS (official Florida education standards site), "Standards, Strand SS7CG, Civics and Government," https:// www.cpalms.org/public/search/Standard, accessed Nov. 29, 2022; Ana Ceballos and Sommer Brugal, "Conservative Hillsdale College Is Helping DeSantis Re-shape Florida Education," *Tampa Bay Times*, July 1, 2022, https://www.tampabay .com/news/florida-politics/2022/07/01/conservative-hillsdale-college-is-helping -desantis-reshape-florida-education.

97. Diane Rado, "The Legislature Inserted Groups Tied to Right-Wing Donors into Florida's New Law on Civics Education," *Florida Phoenix*, Aug. 22, 2019, https://floridaphoenix.com/2019/08/22/the-legislature-inserted-groups-tied-to-right -wing-donors-into-floridas-new-law-on-civics-education.

98. Diane Ravitch, "Florida: DeSantis Takes Control of Civics Curriculum," *Diane Ravitch's Blog*, Aug. 3, 2022, https://dianeravitch.net/2022/08/03/florida -desantis-takes-control-of-civics-curriculum.

99. Ana Ceballos and Sommer Brugal, "Some Teachers Alarmed by Florida Civics Training, Approach on Religion, Slavery," *Tampa Bay Times*, July 1, 2022, https://www.tampabay.com/news/florida-politics/2022/06/28/some-teachers-alarmed -by-florida-civics-training-approach-on-religion-slavery.

100. Christopher T. Rufo, "Radical Gender Theory Has Now Made Its Way into More Than 4,000 U.S. Schools," commentary for FoxNews.com, published on Manhattan Institute website, Aug. 24, 2022, https://www.manhattan-institute .org/radical-gender-theory-made-way-4000-us-schools.

CHAPTER 5: DECENCY AND DEFENDING LGBTQ+ STUDENTS

1. Office of Governor Ron DeSantis, "Governor Ron DeSantis Signs Historic Bill to Protect Parental Rights," news release, Mar. 28, 2022, https://flgov.com /2022/03/28/governor-ron-desantis-signs-historic-bill-to-protect-parental-rights -in-education.

2. Office of Governor Ron DeSantis, "Governor Ron DeSantis Signs Historic Bill to Protect Parental Rights"; Amber Phillips, "Florida's Law Limiting LGBTQ Discussion in Schools, Explained," *Washington Post*, Apr. 22, 2022, https://www .washingtonpost.com/politics/2022/04/01/what-is-florida-dont-say-gay-bill.

3. Anthony Zaguirre, "DeSantis to Expand 'Don't Say Gay' Law to All Grades," Associated Press, Mar. 21, 2022, https://apnews.com/article/dont-say-gay -desantis-florida-gender-d3a9c91f4b5383a5bf6df6f7d8ff65b6.

4. Oona Goodin-Smith, "Pennridge Tells Teachers to Remove LGBTQ Pride Flags, Crosses, and Other 'Advocacy Materials,' Per New Policy," *Philadelphia Inquirer*, Sept. 29, 2022, https://www.inquirer.com/news/pennridge-teacher -advocacy-policy-pride-flags-20220929.html?fbclid=IwAR3ZYnFmXo_EG8teqrg 2beqD9Yv9ijicBEyyQl7bNKGy4b_f-83Sr1OVG74.

5. Maddie Hanna, "Central Bucks Parents Protest Removal of Pride Flags and Other Actions They Say Are Hostile to LGBTQ Students," *Philadelphia Inquirer*, May 11, 2022, https://www.inquirer.com/news/central-bucks-lenape-middle-school -pride-flag-andrew-burgess-lgtbq-20220511.html; Jeff Werner, "Central Bucks Resi-dents Speak Out on Pride Flag, Library Book Policy," *The Patch* (Doylestown, PA), June 16, 2022, https://patch.com/pennsylvania/doylestown/central-bucks-residents

-speak-out-pride-flag-library-book-policy; Emily Rizzo, "Central Bucks West Tells Teachers Not to Use Students' Preferred Names and Pronouns Without Parent Approval," WHYY, Sept. 15, 2022, https://whyy.org/articles/central-bucks-west -students-pronouns-gender-policy; Federalist Society, "Paul Martino, General Partner, Bullpen Capital," https://fedsoc.org/contributors/paul-martino-2, accessed Oct. 5, 2022; Maddie Hanna and Julia Terruso, "A Buck's County Dad Angered by Covid-19 School Closures, Gave $500,000 to School Board Candidates. Critics Say It's Fueling 'Toxic' Politics," *Philadelphia Inquirer*, Oct. 15, 2022, https://www .inquirer.com/news/pennsylvania-school-board-races-campaigns-donors-paul -martino-20211015.html.

6. David Klein, author interview, Doylestown, Pennsylvania, Sept. 22, 2022.

7. Rizzo, "Central Bucks West Tells Teachers Not to Use Students' Preferred Names."

8. save_cbsd (Lenape Middle School), "The Lenape MS principal response to us giving out free pizza that was donated by @julesthincrust to support the cause along with other small businesses . . . ," Instagram, May 12, 2022, https://www .instagram.com/p/Cdd2aJoLdNP.

9. Emily Rizzo, "Student Protesters Threatened, While a New Policy to Censor Library Books Looms in Central Bucks School District," WHYY, https://whyy .org/articles/central-bucks-school-students-protest-teacher-placed-on-leave-new -book-censorship-looms; Chris Ullery, "'It Stops Now': Central Bucks' Lenape Principal Warns Students of Police Response over Protest Posts," *Bucks County Courier Times*, May 12, 2022, https://www.buckscountycouriertimes.com/story /news/education/2022/05/12/central-bucks-lenape-principal-threatens-students -protestors-with-police-on-video/65355198007; Sara Madonna, "CBSD Superintendent Speaks Out After Teacher Placed on Administrative Leave," 69News, May 10, 2022, https://www.wfmz.com/news/area/southeastern-pa/cbsd-superintendent -speaks-out-after-teacher-placed-on-administrative-leave/article_2fd0fade-d0c1 -11ec-a275-5f487b92fc06.html.

10. Madonna, "CBSD Superintendent Speaks Out After Teacher Placed on Administrative Leave."

11. Klein, author interview.

12. Alexandra Coffey, Rowan Hopwood, and Zandi Hall, author interviews, Doylestown, Pennsylvania, Sept. 23, 2022.

13. American Civil Liberties Union of Pennsylvania, "Discrimination Complaint," submitted simultaneously to the US Department of Justice and US Department of Education, Office of Civil Rights, Oct. 6, 2022, https://www.aclupa. org/sites /default/files/field_documents/cbsd_administrative_complaint_-_final_10-6-22 _redacted3.pdf.

14. Oona Goodin-Smith, "ACLU Has Filed a Federal Complaint Alleging Central Bucks Has Created a 'Hostile Environment' for LGBTQ Students," *Philadelphia Inquirer*, Oct. 6, 2022, https://www.inquirer.com/news/central-bucks -school-lgbt-bullying-harassment-aclu-complaint-department-of-justice-20221006 .html.

15. Maximilian Driks, "CB School Board Partners with PR Firm to Improve Community Relations," *Bucks County Herald*, Aug. 6, 2022, https://buckscounty

herald.com/stories/cb-central-bucks-school-board-partners-with-pr-devine-partners
-firm-to-improve-community-relations,18949.

16. Douglas Durham, Southern Lehigh Advocates for Full Education, private
Facebook group, "Hey morning call . . . correct the record . . . again. This sign
sparked the conversation way back in November and has been there for four
years!," screenshot with photos of sign, Mar. 15, 2022, at 9:49 p.m.

17. US Department of Education, "U.S. Department of Education Confirms
Title IX Protects Students from Discrimination Based on Sexual Orientation and
Gender Identity," press release, June 16, 2021, https://www.ed.gov/news/press-releases
/us-department-education-confirms-title-ix-protects-students-discrimination-based
-sexual-orientation-and-gender-identity.

18. Maria Ault, "Dear Fellow Community Members, Please take time to answer this question. What is a Girl? Thank You for your time!," screenshot, Southern Lehigh Moms, private Facebook group, Mar. 25, 2022, 7:53 p.m.; Douglas
Durham, "Guard your children from radical gender ideology. The radicals don't
care about your children. Their goal is to affirm their own twisted world view
while exploiting children. They are child abusers," Facebook post, July 17, 2022,
10:08 p.m., screenshot of Mar. 25, 2022, post.

19. Kristen Bruck, author interview, via Zoom, Sept. 6, 2022; Kristen Bruck,
author interview, Coopersburg, Pennsylvania, Sept. 24, 2022.

20. Lehigh Valley Charter High School for the Arts, "2021–2022 School Profile, as of 9/15/2021," https://www.charterarts.org/wp-content/uploads/2021/10
/Charter-Arts-School-Profile-2021-22-1.pdf.

21. Laura Pappano, "'Grit' and the New Character Education," *Harvard Education Letter* 29, no. 1 (Jan.–Feb. 2013), http://intellectualvirtues.org/wp-content
/uploads/2013/01/Harvard-Ed-Letter-on-the-New-Character-Ed.pdf; Geoffrey L.
Cohen, *Belonging: The Science of Creating Connection and Bridging Divides* (New
York: W. W. Norton, 2022).

22. Geoffrey Cohen, "The Psychology of Belonging, with Guest Geoffrey Cohen," episode 122, *School's In* (Stanford University Graduate School of Education
podcast), Sept. 8, 2021, https://ed.stanford.edu/news/psychology-belonging-0.

23. Research on "belonging" or "fitting in" has also been conducted at the
college level. Nicole Stephens at the Kellogg School of Management at Northwestern University has done interventions that show changing how low-income
first-generation students perceive their difference (creating a sense of belonging)
improves grades and well-being. An overview of her research is available at her
faculty page at Northwestern Kellogg, "Nicole Stephens," https://www.kellogg
.northwestern.edu/faculty/directory/stephens_nicole.aspx#research=page1. On
the challenge of the transition for low-income first-generation students following graduation from elite schools, see Laura Pappano, "Ivy Degree, Now What?
Low-Income Grades Struggle with Careers, Status," *Christian Science Monitor* and
Hechinger Report, Mar. 30, 2018, https://www.csmonitor.com/EqualEd/2018/0330
/Ivy-degree-now-what-Low-income-grads-struggle-with-careers-status.

24. Alexandra Cooperman, author interview, Coopersburg, Pennsylvania,
Sept. 23, 2022.

25. Cooperman, author interview.

26. Southern Lehigh School Board, *SLSD Board Meeting for 3/28*, YouTube video, https://www.youtube.com/watch?v=rr9-BXNHnbk, at 1:17.

27. Daniel Patrick Sheehan, "This Sign on a Classroom Wall Sparked Complaints. Now Some Want Lehigh Valley School District to Restrict What Teachers Can Post," *Morning Call*, Mar. 15, 2022, https://www.mcall.com/news /local/mc-nws-solehi-signs-policy-20220315-efysmrkhabcevdxvaegyrhvuca-story .html; Paul Muschick, "What School Boards Should Tell Parents Who Are Picking Ridiculous Fights," Opinion, *Morning Call*, Mar. 29, 2022, https://www.mcall.com /opinion/mc-opi-kutztown-schools-ukraine-southern-lehigh-sign-muschick-20220 329-bcoy5jpf3zd2ve6pl7vmnl5v6i-story.html; Jenny Roberts, "Bethlehem NAACP Calls on Southern Lehigh to Remove Avatars in Google Classrooms," *Morning Call*, Apr. 11, 2022, https://www.mcall.com/news/education/mc-nws-southern -lehigh-naacp-racist-avatars-20220411-gy5myphtubfbrm3cvqnpkykhdi-story.html.

28. Andrea Lycette, author interview, Coopersburg, Pennsylvania, Sept. 23, 2022.

29. YouBelongCampaign, https://www.youbelongcampaign.com/home, accessed Mar. 23, 2023.

30. Stella Rouse and Shibley Telhami, "Most Republicans Support Declaring the United States a Christian Nation," *Politico*, Sept. 21, 2022, https://www.politico .com/news/magazine/2022/09/21/most-republicans-support-declaring-the-united -states-a-christian-nation-00057736. "Understanding Christian Nationalism," Christians Against Christian Nationalism, https://www.christiansagainst christiannationalism.org/learn-more, accessed Sept. 26, 2022.

31. Joseph L. Conn, "Dominionism and Democracy," *Church & State* 64, no. 9 (Oct. 2011): 10. See also (citing Conn's article) Richard Tanksley and Marlin Schaich, "Marxist Parallels with the Seven Mountain Mandate," *Evangelical Review of Theology and Politics* 6 (2018): 7, http://www.evangelicalreview.net/tertp _vol_6_2018_single_edition-proof.pdf#page=23.

32. Keri Ladner, "The Quiet Rise of Christian Dominionism," *Christian Century*, Sept. 22, 2022, https://www.christiancentury.org/article/feature/quiet-rise -christian-dominionism; Tennessee Holler (@TheTNHoller), "Franklin Pastor: 'The agenda behind the charter school movement in TN is a theology called dominionism,'" Twitter, Sept. 26, 2022, 7:30 a.m., https://twitter.com/TheTNHoller /status/1574405954518585345?cxt=HBwWgsC4tfj3tNkrAAAA&cn=Zmxle GlibGVfcmVjcw%3D%3D&refsrc=email; Tanksley and Schaich, "Marxist Parallels with the Seven Mountain Mandate"; Betsy DeVos, "'End the Department of Education,' Betsy DeVos Sits Down with Moms for Liberty," speech given at Moms for Liberty National Summit, Tampa, July 16, 2022, video, https://www.moms forliberty.org/news/betsy-devos.

33. Sarah Posner, "The Christian Nationalist Boot Camp Pushing Anti-Trans Laws Across America," *The Insider*, Sept. 21, 2022, https://www.insider.com/christian -nationalist-trans-statesmen-academy-alabama-ohio-missouri-laws-2022-8.

34. Valeria Olivares and Talia Richman, "Grapevine-Colleyville Passes Limits on CRT, Books and Bathrooms," *Dallas Morning News*, Aug. 22, 2022, https:// www.dallasnews.com/news/education/2022/08/22/grapevine-colleyville-debates -limiting-lessons-on-race-gender-books-and-bathrooms; Talia Richman, "Grapevine Students Stage Walkout in Protest of 'Transphobic' Policies," *Dallas Morning*

News, Aug. 26, 2022, https://www.dallasnews.com/news/education/2022/08/26/grapevine-students-stage-walkout-in-protest-of-transphobic-policies.

35. National Center for Education Statistics, *State Comparisons of Education Statistics: 1969–1970 to 1996–1997*, report, NCES 98-018 (Washington, DC: US Department of Education, Nov. 1998), 45, https://nces.ed.gov/pubs98/98018.pdf; National Center for Education Statistics, *Racial/Ethnic Enrollment in Public Schools*, report (Washington, DC: US Department of Education, May 2022), https://nces.ed.gov/programs/coe/indicator/cge/racial-ethnic-enrollment#.

36. Office of Governor Ned Lamont, "Governor Lamont Announces Connecticut Becomes First State in Nation to Require High Schools Provide Courses on Black and Latino Studies," press release, Dec. 9, 2020, https://portal.ct.gov/Office-of-the-Governor/News/Press-Releases/2020/12-2020/Governor-Lamont-Announces-Connecticut-Becomes-First-To-Require-Courses-on-Black-and-Latino-Studies; Seamus McAvoy, "Connecticut to Be Among First States to Mandate Asian American and Pacific Islander History in Schools," *Hartford Courant*, May 5, 2022, https://www.courant.com/news/connecticut/hc-news-aapi-curriculum-requirement-20220505-ejs2j72y3ngrpa7s6lpzveg7pm-story.html.

37. Azeen Ghorayshi, "Report Reveals Sharp Rise in Transgender Young People in the U.S.," *New York Times*, June 10, 2022, https://www.nytimes.com/2022/06/10/science/transgender-teenagers-national-survey.html; Cara Murez, "Big Rise in U.S. Teens Identifying as Gay, Bisexual," *U.S. News & World Report*, June 15, 2021, https://www.usnews.com/news/health-news/articles/2021-06-15/big-rise-in-us-teens-identifying-as-gay-bisexual.

38. Goepferd quoted in Ghorayshi, "Report Reveals Sharp Rise in Transgender Young People in the U.S."

39. Members of the Student Anti-Racist Coalition and former Carroll High School students, author interview, Southlake, Texas, June 17, 2022.

40. Carroll ISD, "Draft Carroll ISD Cultural Competence Action Plan," July 9, 2020, https://www.southlakecarroll.edu/cms/lib/TX02219131/Centricity/Domain/97/Cultural%20Competence%20Action%20Plan%20DRAFT%20-%20July%209%202020.pdf.

41. Araceli Cruz, "A Latina Teen Organized a Black Lives Matter Protest in a Conservative Texas Town. Over 1,000 People Showed Up," *The Americano*, June 9, 2020, https://theamericanonews.com/2020/06/09/southlake-texas-protest; Elizabeth Campbell, "Southlake Mayor Says She Can't Guarantee Safety at Planned Student Protest, *Fort Worth Star-Telegram*, June 4, 2020, https://www.star-telegram.com/news/local/community/northeast-tarrant/article243263926.html; Progressive Activism Club (@activism_club), "Come join us for a Black Lives Matter & PRIDE Celebration on Saturday the 27th. Please wear masks. . . . ," Twitter, June 20, 2020, https://twitter.com/activism_club/status/1274476236581015558/photo/1; Mike Hixenbaugh and Antonia Hylton, "Just a Word," transcript, episode 2, *Southlake* (podcast), Jan. 13, 2022, NBC News, https://www.nbcnews.com/podcast/southlake/transcript-just-word-n1283145.

42. Southlake Anti-Racism Coalition, "Southlake Anti-Racism Coalition Demand Letter," https://www.documentcloud.org/documents/21092838-sarc-demand-letter, accessed Mar. 23, 2023.

43. Alex Cruz, "US Department of Education Investigating Two More Complaints Against Carroll ISD," WFAA, July 20, 2022, https://www.wfaa.com/article/news/local/us-department-education-investigating-discrimination-complaints-carroll-isd/287-e60abaf3-ce22-4d26-85e7-ee747133dcff.

44. Anya Kushwaha, author interview, via Zoom, June 23, 2022.

45. Mike Hixenbaugh, "Diversity Plan Opponents Win Control of School Board in Southlake, Texas," NBC News, Nov. 2, 2021, https://www.nbcnews.com/politics/elections/diversity-plan-opponents-win-control-school-board-southlake-texas-rcna4337; Sandra Sadek, "Carroll ISD Halts Work on Cultural Competence Action Plan Following Court's Temporary Restraining Order," *Community Impact Newspaper*, Dec. 3, 2020, https://www.wfaa.com/article/news/local/us-department-education-investigating-discrimination-complaints-carroll-isd/287-e60abaf3-ce22-4d26-85e7-ee747133dcff; Elizabeth Campbell, "Carroll School Board President, Vice President Indicted on Open Meetings Act Violations," *Fort Worth Star-Telegram*, Apr. 7, 2021, https://www.star-telegram.com/news/local/community/northeast-tarrant/article250465101.html; Elizabeth Campbell, "Southlake Carroll District's Diversity Plan Will Be Shelved as Part of Settlement," *Fort Worth Star-Telegram*, Jan. 6, 2022, https://www.star-telegram.com/news/local/community/northeast-tarrant/article257107687.html,

46. Meghan Mangrum, "Conservative Christian Patriot Mobile Donates 'In God We Trust' Signs to Southlake Schools," *Dallas Morning News*, Aug. 15, 2022, https://www.dallasnews.com/news/education/2022/08/15/conservative-christian-patriot-mobile-wants-to-donate-in-god-we-trust-signs-to-southlake; State of Texas Senate, "S.B. 797—AN ACT relating to the display of the national motto in public schools and institutions of higher learning," https://capitol.texas.gov/tlodocs/87R/billtext/html/SB00797F.htm.

47. Elizabeth Campbell, "Carroll Schools Reject 'In God We Trust' Signs Displaying Pride Flag," *Fort Worth Star-Telegram*, Aug. 30, 2022, https://www.star-telegram.com/news/local/education/article265061289.html.

48. Derek Lowe, "Florida Bill Would Allow Cameras in Classrooms, Microphones on Teachers," WPTV, Jan. 20, 2022, https://www.wptv.com/news/state/florida-bill-would-allow-cameras-in-classrooms-microphones-on-teachers.

49. Julia Manchester, "Youngkin Says Education Top Issue in Governor's Race: 'Parents Are Absolutely Angry,'" *The Hill*, Oct. 12, 2021, https://thehill.com/homenews/campaign/576323-youngkin-says-education-is-top-issue-in-virginia-governor-race-parents-are.

50. Virginia Department of Education, "2022 Model Policies on the Privacy, Dignity and Respect for All Students and Parents in Virginia's Public Schools," Sept. 2022, https://doe.virginia.gov/support/gender-diversity/2022-model-policies-on-the-privacy-dignity-and-respect-for-all-students-town-hall.pdf.

51. ACLU of Virginia, "Re: ACLU-VA Comment to Oppose the Proposed 2022 Model Policies on the Privacy, Dignity, and Respect for All Students in Virginia's Public Schools," comment sent to Virginia Department of Education, Sept. 29, 2022, https://acluva.org/sites/default/files/field_documents/acluva_comment_re_vdoe_anti-trans_model_policies_final42.pdf, accessed Oct. 1, 2022; Drew Wilder, "Virginia Students Planning Walkouts over Transgender Restrictions," News4

Washington, Sept. 27, 2022, https://www.nbcwashington.com/news/local/virginia
-students-planning-walkouts-over-youngkin-transgender-restrictions/3166751;
Ariana Coghill, "Thousands of Virginia Students Walk Out to Protest Youngkin's
New Anti-Trans Proposals," *Mother Jones*, Sept. 28, 2022, https://www.motherjones
.com/politics/2022/09/youngkin-virginia-transgender-policies-protests.

52. Mollie T. McQuillan, author interview, via Zoom, Sept. 30, 2022. On
gender-related health issues see K. R. Olson, L. Durwood, M. DeMeules, et al.,
"Mental Health of Transgender Children Who Are Supported in Their Iden-
tities," *Pediatrics* 137, no. 3 (Mar. 2016), e20153223; Mollie T. McQuillan, Lisa
M. Kuhns, Aaron A. Miller, Thomas McDade, and Robert Garofalo, "Gender
Minority Stress, Support, and Inflammation in Transgender and Gender-
Nonconforming Youth," *Transgender Health* (Apr. 2021), doi: 10.1089/trgh.2020
.0019; Amanda M. Pollitt, Salvatore Ioverno, Stephen T. Russell, and Arnold H.
Grossman, "Predictors and Mental Health Benefits of Chosen Name Use Among
Transgender Youth," *Youth & Society* 53, no. 2 (2021): 320–41, https://doi.org
/10.1177/0044118X19855898; Mollie T. McQuillan and Cris Mayo, "School Leaders
and Transphobia: Interrupting Direct, Facilitative Accommodative and Resistant
Forms of Gender-Based Bullying," pre-publication paper shared with Laura Pappano, https://orcid.org/0000-0002-2522-3871.

CHAPTER 6: THE NEW PARENT INVOLVEMENT
1. James Whitfield is the Black principal at Colleyville Heritage High School
who was pushed out of his job (see chapter 4).
2. Laura Leeman, text message to author, Oct. 5, 2022; Tracy Fisher, author interview, via Zoom, June 6, 2022; Timothy Bella, "A Black Principal Was Accused
of Embracing Critical Race Theory in the Classroom. He's Now Out of a Job,"
Washington Post, Nov. 10, 2021, https://www.washingtonpost.com/education/2021
/11/10/texas-principal-critical-race-theory-whitfield; Tracy Fisher (@antraasa),
"What can you do? Volunteer in your local schools. Vote in your local elections! . . . ," Twitter, Nov. 9, 2022, 7:38 a.m., https://twitter.com/antraasa/status
/1590368293423980544.
3. Laura Leeman, email message to author, Oct. 10, 2022.
4. Sari Kerr, "Equal Pay Day: How the Gender Wage Gap Changes over a
Woman's Career," *Women Change Worlds* (blog), Mar. 31, 2020, https://www.wcw
online.org/WCW-Blog-Women-Change-Worlds/Equal-pay-day-how-the-gender
-wage-gap-changes-over-a-woman-s-career.
5. Laura Leeman, author interview, Colleyville, Texas, June 15, 2022; Laura
Leeman, "November: A Time for Epilepsy & ACA Awareness," Little Lobbyists
Action Network, n.d., https://littlelobbyists.org/blog/2020/11/17/november-a-time
-for-epilepsy-amp-aca-awareness, accessed Oct. 11, 2022. Vic passed away in
July 2023 after an April hospitalization and several months of declining health.
Leeman shared on Facebook, https://www.facebook.com/l.p.leeman, posts July 24,
2023, and July 25, 2023.
6. "Diversity in the Classroom," *New York Times*, Apr. 15, 2021, interactive
data tool, https://www.nytimes.com/interactive/projects/immigration/enrollment
/texas/tarrant/grapevine-colleyville-isd; Grapevine-Colleyville Independent
School District, "GCISD Quick Facts," demographic data as of October 15, 2021,

https://gcisd.ss18.sharpschool.com/our_district/district_information/quick_facts
_about_gcisd.

7. Grapevine-Colleyville ISD, *GCISD's Board of Trustees Regular Meeting—July 26, 2021*, YouTube video, https://www.youtube.com/watch?v=xfnkBddvDQs, at 1:47:12.

8. James Whitfield, author interview, Hurst, Texas, June 15, 2022.

9. Laura Leeman, "#IStandWithDrWhitfield," petition, https://www.petitions.net/istandwithdrwhitfield, accessed Oct. 9, 2022.

10. RSMDesign, "City of Southlake," https://rsmdesign.com/work/city-of-southlake, accessed Mar. 23, 2023; "Twenty Most Affluent U.S. Neighborhoods," *Forbes*, Dec. 8, 2008, https://www.forbes.com/2008/12/08/america-affluent-neighborhoods-forbeslife-cx_ls_1209realestate.html?sh=39b109c45661.

11. Laura Durant, author interview, Southlake, Texas, June 17, 2022.

12. Durant, author interview; Brandi Addison, "Who Won Carroll ISD Races in May 7 Election," *Dallas Morning News*, May 10, 2022, https://www.dallasnews.com/news/elections/2022/05/10/who-won-carroll-isd-school-board-races-in-may-7-election.

13. Southlake Anti-Racism Coalition, "Southlake Anti-Racism Coalition Demand Letter"; for the signature count, see https://sites.google.com/view/southlakearc/our-demands/signatures?authuser=0, accessed Mar. 23, 2023.

14. "In Southlake Carroll ISD We Cannot Recommend a School Board Candidate," editorial, *Dallas Morning News*, Apr. 17, 2022, https://www.dallasnews.com/opinion/editorials/2022/04/16/in-carroll-isd-we-cannot-recommend-a-school-board-candidate. See also Stephanie Williams, CISD Board of Trustees, Place 7, Facebook, https://www.facebook.com/StephanieforCISD, accessed Oct. 20, 2022.

15. T. J. Callaway, email message to author, Oct. 18, 2022.

16. T. J. Callaway, author interview, via Zoom, June 20, 2022; Access Education RRISD (@AccessRRISD), "Thank you, Access RRISD candidates, volunteers, and community! You saved our schools," Twitter, Nov. 9, 2022, 1:54 p.m., https://twitter.com/AccessRRISD/status/1590462755592884225; Brian Lopez and Timia Cobb, "As Culture War Envelops Schools, North Texas Sees a Superintendent Exodus," *Texas Tribune*, Feb. 4, 2022, https://www.texastribune.org/2022/02/04/north-texas-superintendents-resign.

17. Rutgers University, Center for American Women and Politics, "Gender Differences in Voter Turnout," https://cawp.rutgers.edu/facts/voters/gender-differences-voter-turnout#NPGE, accessed Oct. 18, 2022; Jocelyn Noveck, "Women Crucial to Biden's Win Even as Gender Gap Held Steady," Associated Press, Nov. 16, 2020, https://apnews.com/article/election-2020-joe-biden-donald-trump-voting-rights-elections-84ef3db79532c0029894ff25a316370b; William H. Frey, *Biden's Victory Came from the Suburbs*, Brookings Metropolitan Policy Program (Washington, DC: Brookings Institution, Nov. 13, 2020), https://www.brookings.edu/research/bidens-victory-came-from-the-suburbs.

18. Jacob Jarvis, "Trump Keeps Trying to Win Over Suburban Housewives. They Keep Rejecting Him," *Newsweek*, Oct. 14, 2020, https://www.newsweek.com/suburban-housewives-rejecting-trump-win-over-1538930; Lisa Lerer, "'Please Like Me,' Trump Begged. For Many Women, It's Way Too Late," *New York Times*,

Oct. 17, 2020, https://www.nytimes.com/2020/10/17/us/politics/trump-women
-voters.html.

19. Katie Paris, author interview, via Zoom, Sept. 30, 2022; Ballotpedia, "Ohio
Elections, 2018," https://ballotpedia.org/Ohio_elections,_2018.

20. Julie Womack, author interview, via Zoom, Sept. 26, 2022.

21. Ohio Laws & Administrative Rules, Legislative Service Commission, Section 2919.195, "Performance of an Abortion After Detection of Fetal Heartbeat;
Penalty," effective date July 11, 2019, https://codes.ohio.gov/ohio-revised-code
/section-2919.195, accessed Oct. 21, 2022; Aaron Blake, "What an Ohio Law Says
About a 10-Year-Old Rape Victim," *Washington Post*, July 15, 2022, https://www
.washingtonpost.com/politics/2022/07/14/what-ohio-law-says-about-10-year-old
-rape-victim-abortion; Shari Rudavsky and Rachel Fradette, "Patients Head to
Indiana for Abortion Care as Other States Restrict Care," *Indianapolis Star*, July 1,
2022, https://www.indystar.com/story/news/health/2022/07/01/indiana-abortion
-law-roe-v-wade-overturned-travel/7779936001.

22. Jane Mayer, "State Legislatures Are Torching Democracy," *New Yorker*,
Aug. 6, 2022, https://www.newyorker.com/magazine/2022/08/15/state-legislatures
-are-torching-democracy; Mary Papenfuss, "Ohio House Bans Transgender
Students in Sports; Requires Genital Exams in Disputes," *Huffington Post*, June 3,
2022, https://www.huffpost.com/entry/genitalia-inspection-transgender-girls-barred
-from-high-school-college-sports_n_629982d3e4b016c4eef7afb4; Jeremy Pelzer,
"Ohio Gov. Mike DeWine Signs Law Allowing People to Carry Concealed Firearms Without Training or Permits," Cleveland.com, Mar. 25, 2022, https://www
.cleveland.com/news/2022/03/ohio-gov-mike-dewine-signs-into-law-bill-allowing
-people-to-carry-guns-without-training-or-permits.html; Bill Chappel, "Ohio Gov.
DeWine Signs Bill Arming Teachers After 24 Hours of Training," NPR, June 14,
2022, https://www.npr.org/2022/06/13/1104570419/ohio-dewine-guns-teachers.

23. Graeme Massey, "Donald Trump Claims Women Love Being Called
'Housewives' as He Begged for Their Support," *Independent*, Oct. 15, 2020, https://
www.independent.co.uk/news/world/americas/us-election-2020/trump
-election-2020-suburban-women-support-b1055522.html.

24. Red Wine & Blue, *The Parent Playbook: A Step-By-Step Guide for Mainstream Moms Who've Had Enough BS*, https://redwine.blue/guides (link to down-
load guide), accessed Oct. 20, 2022.

25. Red Wine & Blue, "Rally Your Squad with Amy Schumer!," email, Oct. 21,
2022.

26. Katie Paris/Red Wine & Blue, mass email, Nov. 9, 2022.

27. Blake Hounshell, "Smeared as a Groomer, a Michigan Democrat Goes on
Offense," *New York Times*, Apr. 25, 2022, https://www.nytimes.com/2022/04/25/us
/politics/mallory-mcmorrow-michigan.html.

28. Michigan State Senator Mallory McMorrow, quoted in Rebecca Tauber,
"'You Made Me Feel Like I Can Fight Again': Michigan Sen. Mallory McMorrow
on her Viral Speech," WGBH, May 18, 2022, https://www.wgbh.org/news
/politics/2022/05/18/you-made-me-feel-like-i-can-fight-again-michigan-sen-mallory
-mcmorrow-on-her-viral-speech; Adam Wren, "The Michigan Democrat Who
Could Solve Her Party's Identity Crisis," *Politico*, July 1, 2022, https://www.politico

.com/news/magazine/2022/07/01/mallory-mcmorrow-democratic-playboook
-00043340.

29. Red Wine & Blue, *National Troublemaker Training with Mallory McMorrow,* YouTube video, https://www.youtube.com/watch?v=7AY36ZWZFrQ.

30. Ballotpedia, "Mallory McMorrow," https://ballotpedia.org/Mallory _McMorrow.

31. Aaditi Lele, Simon Rosenbaum, and Jaylan Sims, "LGBTQ+ Policy Lab and Divinity School Host Michigan State Senator Mallory McMorrow," *Vanderbilt Hustler,* Oct. 6, 2022, https://vanderbilthustler.com/2022/10/06/lgbtq-policy -lab-and-divinity-school-host-michigan-state-senator-mallory-mcmorrow.

32. Gaylyn Welch, "Suffrage at the School House Door: The 1880 New York State School Suffrage Campaign," *New York History* 98, nos. 3–4 (Summer–Fall 2017): 329–42, https://muse.jhu.edu/article/712996; Edmund B. Thomas Jr., "School Suffrage and the Campaign for Women's Suffrage in Massachusetts, 1879–1920," *Historical Journal of Massachusetts* 1, no. 1 (Winter 1997): 25.

33. William J. Reese, "Between Home and School: Organized Parents, Clubwomen, and Urban Education in the Progressive Era," *School Review* 87, no. 1 (Nov. 1978): 3–28, https://www.jstor.org/stable/1084743.

34. Reese, "Between Home and School."

35. Marilyn Schultz Blackwell, "The Politics of Motherhood: Clarina Howard Nichols and School Suffrage," *New England Quarterly* 78, no. 4 (Dec. 2005): 570–98, https://www.jstor.org/stable/30045581.

36. Mrs. Frederick Schoff, "The National Congress of Mothers and Parent-Teacher Associations," in "New Possibilities in Education," special issue, *Annals of the American Academy of Political and Social Science* 67 (Sept. 1916): 139–47, https://www.jstor.org/stable/1013499; James R. Wetzel, "American Families: 75 Years of Change," *Monthly Labor Review* (Mar. 1990): 5, https://www.bls.gov/mlr /1990/03/art1full.pdf.

37. Mrs. John B. Cleaver, "The Blue Hen," *Child-Welfare Magazine* 16, no. 12 (Aug. 1922): 329–30.

38. Charl Ormand Williams, "The Democratic Awakening and Professional Organization," *Child-Welfare Magazine* 16, no. 12 (Aug. 1922): 320.

39. Floyd J. Calvin, "Atlanta Woman Named on White House Committee," *Pittsburgh Courier,* Jan. 18, 1930, 6; Personal Papers, Atlanta Community Chest, 1924–39, series I, box 1, folder 3, Selena Sloan Butler papers, aarl09-002, Auburn Avenue Research Library on African-American Culture and History.

40. National Trust for Historic Preservation, African American Cultural Heritage Action Fund, "Rosenwald Schools," https://savingplaces.org/places/rosenwald -schools#.Y1fuSOzMJAd, accessed Oct. 25, 2022.

41. "Negro P.T.A. Merges with White Group, Ending Five Years of Negotiations," *New York Times,* June 28, 1970, 41, https://www.nytimes.com/1970/06/28 /archives/negro-pta-merges-with-white-group-ending-5-years-of-negotiations .html.

42. Reese, "Between Home and School," 8.

43. Reese, "Between Home and School," 9 (citing *Annual Report of the Congress of Mothers,* 1904, 49).

44. Mary L. Langworthy, "The Social Side of the Convention," *Child-Welfare Magazine* 16, no. 12 (Aug. 1922): 315–17.

45. The Boston Parents' Council, 1930–1938, Collection Overview, Schlesinger Library, Radcliffe Institute for Advanced Study, Collection MC220, https:// hollisarchives.lib.harvard.edu/repositories/8/resources/5260.

46. Richard Mitton, president of Jordan Marsh, letter to Abigail Eliot, president of the Boston Parents' Council, Sept. 24, 1935, Records of the Boston Parents' Council, 1930–1938, Schlesinger Library, Radcliffe Institute for Advanced Study, MC 220, Box 3-35.

47. Paige Meltzer, "'The Pulse and Conscious of America': The General Federation and Women's Citizenship, 1945–1960," in "Women's Clubs at Home and in the World," special issue, *Frontiers: A Journal of Women Studies* 30, no. 3 (2009): 52–76, https://www.jstor.org/stable/40388747.

48. Pen America, "Banned in the USA: Rising School Book Bans Threaten Free Expression and Students' First Amendment Rights," Apr. 2022, https://pen .org/banned-in-the-usa, accessed Oct. 27, 2022; American Library Association, "Total Book Challenges in 2022 Set to Exceed 2021 Record," press release, Sept. 16, 2022, https://www.ala.org/news/press-releases/2022/09/ala-releases-preliminary -data-2022-book-bans.

49. Kate Nazemi, author interview, Doylestown, Pennsylvania, Sept. 21, 2022.

50. Laney Hawes, author interview, Keller, Texas, June 16, 2022; Laney Hawes (@Laneyhawes), tweets: "Thank you, Access RRISD candidates, volunteers, and community! You saved our schools," Nov. 16, 2021, 4:26 p.m., https://twitter.com /LaneyHawes/status/1460766357734273024; "I am at a school board meeting right now—and I'm here to tell you progressives—YOU NEED TO GET INVOLVED. . . . ," Nov. 15, 2021, 5:28 p.m., https://twitter.com/LaneyHawes/status/146042196899 8637571; "I Served on a book challenge committee for my school district today. Someone tried to get the graphic novel adaptation of The Diary of Anne Frank pulled from shelves. . . . ," Apr. 13, 2022, 9:21 p.m., https://twitter.com/LaneyHawes /status/1514458785477181442; "I'm at my local @KellerISD school board meeting. Im once again telling progressives YOU must get involved. . . . ," Mar. 28, 2022, 5:36 p.m., https://twitter.com/LaneyHawes/status/1508603982813573122.

EPILOGUE: HOW TO FIGHT FOR SCHOOL COMMUNITIES

1. Tom Moore, author interview, June 29, 2022, Croydon, New Hampshire.

2. Ian Underwood, in *Free State Live #26: "Cutting the Budget," Feat[uring] Ian Underwood*, Apr. 26, 2022, YouTube video, https://www.youtube.com/watch?v =MXpZuwZmkOc.

3. Dan Barry, "One Small Step for Democracy in a 'Live Free or Die' Town," *New York Times*, July 10, 2022, https://www.nytimes.com/2022/07/10/us/croydon -free-state-politics.html.

4. Ian Underwood, "Budget or Ransom?," Granite Grok, Mar. 11, 2022, https:// granitegrok.com/blog/2022/03/budget-or-ransom?

5. Ian Underwood, "Budget or Ransom? Croydon School District Meeting, Mar. 12, 2022," pamphlet, in author's collection; Dan Barry, "What Croydon, a 'Live Free or Die' Town, Learned About Democracy," *New York Times*, July 10, 2022, https://www.nytimes.com/2022/07/10/us/croydon-free-state-politics.html.

6. Amanda Leslie, author interview, June 29, 2022, Croydon, New Hampshire.

7. Kathy Ivey, author interview, June 29, 2022, Croydon, New Hampshire.

8. Chris Prost, author interview, June 29, 2022, Croydon, New Hampshire.

9. Zandra Rice Hawkins (executive director, Granite State Progress), author interview, via Zoom, June 21, 2022.

10. Zandra Rice Hawkins, email to author, "Book follow-up Croydon DEADLINE questions," Jan. 9, 2023.

11. Darren Marcy, "Croydon Residents Petition for Chance to Overturn Cuts to School Budget," *Valley News*, Mar. 25, 2022, https://www.vnews.com/Croydon -voters-may-have-long-shot-to-overturn-slashed-budget-45643215.

12. Angi Beaulieu, author interview, June 29, 2022, Croydon, New Hampshire.

13. Patrick Adrian, "'Jeopardized': Croydon Residents Voice Opposition to School Budget Cut," *Eagle Times*, Mar. 15, 2022, https://www.eagletimes.com /jeopardized-croydon-residents-voice-opposition-to-school-budget-cut/article _9902f69d-1b17-52a8-815f-089a6ecf7cb8.html.

14. Croydon School Board, *Croydon School Board Meeting Entire Meeting 2022-3-14*, YouTube video, accessed March 24, 2023, https://www.youtube.com /watch?v=yQsTvkxDfBI&list=WL&index=4&t=5s.

15. Darren Marcy, "Croydon School Funding Battle Turns to Turnout as Voting Official Quits," *Valley News*, Apr. 15, 2022, https://www.vnews.com/croydon -nh-official-resigns-45964720; Leslie, Ivey, and Prost author interviews.

16. Prost, author interview.

17. "Croydon Man Who Tried to Cut School Budget in Half Steps Down from Selectboard," *Valley News*, Sept. 10, 2022, https://www.vnews.com/Ian-Underwood -has-left-Croydon-Selectboard-47962447.

18. *Valley News*, "Croydon Voters Oust Underwood from School Board," New Hampshire Public Radio, Mar. 15, 2023, https://www.nhpr.org/nh-news/2023-03-15 /croydon-nh-voters-oust-underwood-from-school-board.

19. New Futures, ACLU of New Hampshire, and Others, "SUPPORT HB 61 Public Hearing; Repealing Banned Concepts," meeting announcement, Facebook, reposted by Hope Damon, Hope For NH, "This is a very important bill . . . ," Jan. 7, 2023, 1:28 p.m., https://www.facebook.com/events/466177169049902/?ref =newsfeed.

20. Edward Spiker, "There will be a selectboard budget working meeting this evening @ 7 p.m. for anyone inte[re]sted in attending. Hope to see you there!," post at We Stand Up for Croydon Facebook page, Jan. 3, 2023, https://www .facebook.com/groups/3101969696798666.

21. Hope Damon, email to author ("Congrats!!"), Dec. 14, 2022.

22. Edward Spiker, author interview, June 29, 2022, Croydon, New Hampshire.

23. *Valley News*, "Croydon Voters Oust Underwood from School Board," New Hampshire Public Radio, Mar. 15, 2023.

24. Edward Spiker, messages to author, via Facebook Messenger, Jan. 11 and 30, 2023.

25. Alex Hanson, "Croydon Meeting Passes School Budget with Help of Large Turnout," *Valley News*, Mar. 19, 2023, https://www.vnews.com/Croydon-Town -Meeting-results-50231102?fbclid=IwAR2ndWxLCBoGIXenoER5MHcv350Q6O xXOAMA8QFbl_5_jb5tL52YoT_Fq4Y.

26. Matthew Weimann, author interview, Sept. 23, 2022, Macungie, Pennsylvania.

27. Matthew Weimann, "Controversy Can Be Classy," https://thecaptain ofclass.com/controversy-can-be-classy, accessed Mar. 24, 2023.

28. Mark Sirota, author interview, Conshohocken, Pennsylvania, Sept. 24, 2022.

INDEX